MW00773335

THE LIFE

OF

ROGER SHERMAN

BY

LEWIS HENRY BOUTELL

CHICAGO

A. C. McCLURG AND COMPANY

1896

TO

HON. GEORGE FRISBIE HOAR,

IN ACKNOWLEDGMENT OF THE RESEARCHES WHICH HAVE
MADE THIS MEMOIR POSSIBLE, AND IN TOKEN
OF THE HIGHEST REGARD FOR HIS PUBLIC
SERVICES AND PRIVATE CHARACTER,

This Life of his Grandfather

IS, WITH AFFECTIONATE ESTEEM, RESPECTFULLY
DEDICATED.

PREFACE.

IN 1823, a brief memoir of Roger Sherman was published in Sanderson's Lives of the Signers of the Declaration of Independence. Gov. Roger S. Baldwin, a grandson of Roger Sherman, in a letter dated May 2, 1855, says of this memoir: "It was prepared in part by Robert Waln, Jr., of Philadelphia, with whom I was in correspondence, and in part by the late Jeremiah Evarts, Esq., of Boston (father of William M. Evarts, Esq., of New York), who married a daughter of Mr. Sherman, and gives, I think, a just view of his life and character and public services." Robert Waln, Jr., was, when this memoir was prepared, the editor of Sanderson's Lives. This memoir was necessarily brief, to conform to the plan of Sanderson's book. The materials for a complete biography of Mr. Sherman were not then accessible, especially Madison's report of the Debates in the Constitutional Convention of 1787.

Mr. Sherman left, at his death, a large mass of papers. They were supposed to be in the possession of his son Oliver, a merchant in Boston, who died unmarried, in Havana, in 1820; but as very

few of them have been found, it is supposed the
rest were lost or destroyed.   A part of them are
in the collections of the Massachusetts Historical
Society.   Some years ago, Hon. George F. Hoar,
a grandson of Roger Sherman, began making a
collection of letters and documents relating to his
grandfather, from all known sources.   By the summer of 1895, he expected to begin the preparation
of a new and more complete biography of Roger
Sherman ; but he found his public duties so engrossing that he was obliged to abandon his long
cherished plan.   In September of 1895, he proposed to me to take the material he had gathered,
and write the biography, to which he found he
could not give the necessary time.

Having read before the American Historical
Association, in the summer of 1893, a paper on
Roger Sherman's services in the Constitutional
Convention of 1787, I felt the more inclined to
accept Mr. Hoar's generous offer, because it seemed
to me there had been no adequate recognition of
Mr. Sherman's great services in that Convention,
or of the masterly ability displayed by him in support of the tariff measures of 1789, and of Alexander Hamilton's plan for the support of the public
credit.

I thought, moreover, it was worth while to describe, with as much fulness as existing materials
would allow, the career of a man whose public
life covered the entire period of that most important part of our political history, extending from
the beginning of the French and Indian war to the
close of the first administration of Washington,

and who was one of the most conspicuous figures in that formative period of our national life.

It seemed desirable also to give some explanation of the influence which Mr. Sherman exerted over the men of his generation. How did it happen that a man, who was no orator, won the highest admiration from the greatest orators of his time, from such men as Patrick Henry, Richard Henry Lee, and Fisher Ames? How came this reserved, bashful, unemotional man to be the intimate friend of the ardent and impulsive John Adams? How did it happen that this man of no academic training not only occupied for many years the highest legislative and judicial positions in his own State, but, in the Continental Congress, was at once recognized as one of its foremost men, and placed on its most important committees, notably on the committee of five to prepare the Declaration of Independence? What were the qualities that fitted him to be the leader in the compromise measures of the Convention that framed our national Constitution, and that enabled him, in his seventieth year, on the floor of the House of Representatives, to be the foremost advocate of the great measures for the support of the public credit? The story of such a life is certainly well worth telling. Such a character is deserving of most careful study.

As the claim has been made on behalf of John Dickinson, William Samuel Johnson, and George Mason, respectively, that each of them was the author of the compromise by which representation according to population was secured in the House of Representatives, and equal representation of the States in the Senate, I have done what has never been done before, given a detailed statement of the various steps in that compromise, as related in Madison's Debates. From that statement it will be seen that, while others, and especially Oliver Ellsworth, Dr. Johnson, and Mr. Dickinson, supported with great ability this compromise measure, Roger Sherman introduced it, and throughout the debate was its foremost champion. I have also called attention to the fact, which has been generally overlooked, that, eleven years before this debate, Mr. Sherman proposed substantially the same plan in the Continental Congress, in discussing the Articles of Confederation.

I have also endeavored to describe Mr. Sherman's religious character and opinions; and to point out that, while he was a Puritan of the Puritans, he brought to the discussion of theological questions the same clear insight and strong sense that distinguished his legal and his political career, and that saved him from the harsh and extravagant views which disfigured the creed of some eminent divines of his day.

Mr. Hoar has so thoroughly explored the field, that I have been able to add very little to the mass of letters and documents relating to Mr. Sherman which he had collected. I have vainly endeavored to learn who were the persons, and what were the books, that influenced the early years of this self-educated man. Unfortunately there is very little of a personal character in his correspondence. Apparently he was not accustomed to think or write much about himself. His life was devoted to the public service. He was content to do his duty, and unmindful to preserve a record of what he had done.

In a volume of Sir Walter Raleigh's History of the World, belonging to Mr. Sherman, were found some leaves of Peter Heylin's "Microcosmos," containing a poem by Edward Heylin, addressed "To my brother, the Author," in which occurs a line fittingly descriptive of the controlling principle of Roger Sherman's life, —

"The guerdon of well doing is the doing."

From some newspaper articles by Ellis Ames, and from Huntoon's History of Canton, I have gathered a few facts about Mr. Sherman's early home; and from Orcutt's History of New Milford, I have derived assistance in describing Mr. Sherman's life in that town. The Life of Roger Sherman in Sanderson's biographies has furnished important facts and documents. Some of the statements in that Life I have been able to correct, or make more full and exact, by means of the Connecticut Records published since that life was written.

CONTENTS.

APPENDIX.

The frontispiece is from the Hartford Statue,
by C. B. Ives.

THE LIFE

OF

ROGER SHERMAN.

———•———

CHAPTER I.

ANCESTRY.

THE branch of the Sherman family to which
Roger Sherman belonged came from Dedham,
Essex county, England, and settled in Watertown,
Massachusetts, about 1634. Dedham is situated
on the river Stour, in a beautiful rural district on
the highway from London to Ipswich. It was
formerly a prosperous town, the seat of large
woollen manufactures. The only evidence remaining of its old importance is its fine large church,
with a pinnacled tower 131 feet high, and a beautiful Galilee porch.

The Shermans, and the families with which they
married, were, as they were then called, clothiers,
what we should now call woollen manufacturers,
and seem to have been of a good deal of importance. There were several members of Parliament
in the line of Mr. Sherman's ancestry. The first
of them to which his pedigree can be directly

traced is Henry Sherman, of Dedham, who was born about 1520, and died in 1589. His wife, who died in 1580, was Agnes, whose surname is supposed to have been Butler. He is described as a clothier, and at various times as of Dedham and Colchester.

Edmond Sherman, of Dedham, clothier, son of Henry, was the founder of the English School in Dedham, still surviving there, and occupying Edmond Sherman's house, known as " Sherman Hall." Several of his sons were benefactors of this school. Edmond Sherman married, as his second wife, Anne Cleave. She was grand-daughter of John Cleave, of Colchester, a clothier, alderman, and member of Parliament. His son Nicholas Cleave, of Colchester, by his first wife Jane, was a clothier, alderman, and member of Parliament. He married Anne, widow of Thomas Haselwood.

Samuel Sherman, a son of Edmond Sherman and Anne Cleave, married Hester Burgess, and had a son named Bezaleel, who became a prosperous merchant in London. Elizabeth, the daughter of Bezaleel, married Sir Henry Vincent, Bt. They had a son, Sir Francis, whose daughter, Mary, married Neil, third Earl of Roseberry, the grandfather of the present (fifth) Earl of Roseberry.

In a memorandum prepared by Hon. William M. Evarts, he says, " I had made the acquaintance of this young Earl during his several visits to this country, before he entered public life, and I veri- fied this relationship by a correspondence through my and Lord Roseberry's friend Samuel Ward, after Lord Roseberry's last return to England."

Edmond 2d, son of Edmond Sherman and Anne Cleave, was born in Dedham, June 23, 1595, came to New England in 1634, and died in New Haven, Conn., about 1641. By his second wife, Judith, daughter of William Angier of Dedham, he had a son John, who was born in Dedham, came to New England about 1634, and settled in Watertown, Mass. He was a clergyman of great ability and eloquence, and was the ablest mathematician in the colony.

Another son of Edmond 2d and Judith Angier was Samuel, who came to New England with his brother John, and settled in Weathersfield, Conn., and afterwards in Stratford, Conn., where he died in 1700. He was the ancestor of Gen. William T. Sherman, and of U. S. Senator John Sherman.

John Sherman, of Dedham, clothier, a son of Edmond Sherman and Anne Cleave, is supposed to have married a Sparhawk. He was the father of Captain John Sherman, or Shearman, as he spelt his name, who was born in 1613, and came to New England about 1634, and settled in Watertown, Mass. He was captain, surveyor, representative in the General Court, and town clerk. He was steward of Harvard College in 1660, and probably for years thereafter. He was with Governor Winthrop when the northern boundary of Massachusetts was surveyed, and when the corner was established at Wier's Landing, Lake Winnepesaukee. His active and useful life ended Jan. 25, 1690. His wife, Martha Palmer, daughter of Roger and Grace Palmer, of Long Sutton, County of South Hampton, died Feb. 7, 1701. His land in Watertown adjoined that owned by the ancestors of President Garfield, afterwards known as the " Governor Gore Place."

The last descendant from the first Edmond of the Sherman name in England, was his great-grandson, Edmond Sherman of Dedham, who died, *sine prole*, in 1741, leaving a large estate to Thomas and John Haywood, sons of his sister Martha. His beautiful tomb is still seen near the tower of the church in Dedham. At his death, the male line of his family became extinct in England.

Joseph Sherman, son of Captain John, was born in Watertown, May 14, 1650. He married Elizabeth Winship, daughter of Lieutenant Edward Winship of Cambridge. He was a representative in the General Court in 1702-3-4-5, and often selectman and assessor. He was a blacksmith by trade. He seems to have been foremost on the side of the old town of Watertown in the Town Church controversy, in which Captain Benjamin Garfield was the foremost representative on the other side, which led to the separation of Waltham from Watertown. He had eleven children, of whom the ninth child and seventh son, William, born June 23, 1692, was the father of Roger Sherman.

William Sherman is described in the deeds of the land which he purchased in Stoughton as a cordwainer. He appears to have been a farmer as well as a shoemaker. His first wife was Rebecca Cutler, of Watertown, by whom he had one son, William, who died in infancy. He married for his second wife, Sept. 3, 1715, Mehetabel Wellington, of Watertown, daughter of Benjamin, son of Roger

Wellington, who came from England. In the record of this marriage he is said to be of Watertown. He moved to Newton shortly thereafter. His children by this second marriage were William, Mehetabel, Roger, Elizabeth, Nathaniel, Josiah, and Rebecca.

2

CHAPTER II.

LIFE IN STOUGHTON.

ROGER SHERMAN was born in Newton, Mass., April 19, 1721, O. S. In Smith's History of Newton it is stated that he was born near the Skinner place, on Waverly Avenue; the precise location is not known. In 1723, his father, William Sherman, moved to that part of Stoughton, Mass., which has since become Canton. Stoughton was incorporated in 1726.[1]

In 1725, William Sherman and John Wentworth, by permission of the General Court, purchased of the Indian proprietors two hundred and seventy acres of the Punkapoag Plantation, in the northeastern part of Stoughton. Owing to a delay in the Legislature to fix the value of this land, the deed of it was not executed till 1734; but the purchasers seem to have resided on it from 1725. In the division of this property between the purchasers, William Sherman took in part seventy-three acres lying west of Pleasant Street, formerly Stoughton Road, which became his homestead.

Here Roger Sherman lived till he was twenty-two years of age. From his father he learned the

---

[1] At the time William Sherman moved there, it formed part of the town of Dorchester. Canton was set off from Stoughton in 1797.

trade of a shoemaker, and he worked beside him in the shop and on the farm. So far as is known, he had no other assistance in his education than that which the common country schools of that time afforded. But he must have been more or less influenced by the Rev. Samuel Dunbar, the pastor of the church which his family attended.

Mr. Dunbar, born in Boston in 1704, studied at the Boston Latin School, graduated at Harvard in 1723, and immediately afterward accepted the position of usher in the Latin School, at the same time pursuing his theological studies under the direction of Cotton Mather. In 1727, he was ordained pastor of the church in Stoughton, and he remained in that position until his death in 1783. He was a fine scholar, possessing a critical knowledge of Latin, Greek and Hebrew. He had a vigorous constitution, and a fearless spirit. After the fashion of the day, he sought to persuade men rather by " the terror of the Lord " than by his goodness. He was frequently called on councils by neighboring churches, and by his tact and good sense was skillful in restoring harmony in the case of church troubles.

He was a man of great public spirit, and during the Revolutionary War he relinquished half his salary. While the third meeting-house was building, a period of sixteen years, he relinquished one-tenth of his salary. In 1745, he asked for leave of absence from his pulpit to become chaplain in a regiment about to be sent with his Majesty's army to Louisburg. But the request was not granted. Ten years later he served as chaplain to a Con-

necticut regiment in the expedition to Crown
Point. It was said of him, in the sermon preached
at his funeral by Rev. Jason Haven of Dedham,
" He was honored with long life and usefulness,
and was perhaps an unparalleled instance of carrying on ministerial labors without being interrupted
by any bodily infirmity, for the space of fifty-three
years from the time of his settlement." His last
public service was a prayer of thanksgiving on the
return of peace, at a celebration in Stoughton in
honor of that event on the 2d of June, 1783. One
of his sermons, written in the forty-ninth year
of his ministry, is numbered 8,059, which shows
that he must have composed, on an average, no
less than one hundred and sixty-four sermons a
year, or a little more than three a week.

In an appendix to a sermon preached at the
ordination of Rev. William Richey, at Canton, July
1, 1807, by Rev. Elijah Dunbar, Jr., a grandson of
Samuel, the pulpit services of Samuel Dunbar are
thus described: " His plain and pungent preaching, unadorned with the graces of composition, was
enforced by a peculiar zeal and pathos, and a very
commanding eloquence. He spoke as one having
authority. In prayer he was much admired; he
was pertinent, copious, and fervent."

We do not know that Mr. Dunbar assisted
Roger Sherman in his work of self-education, but
he could hardly have witnessed the industry, and
the thirst for knowledge, of his young parishioner,
without feeling a deep interest in him, and a desire
to help him. He must at least have offered him
the use of his library, and given him the benefit of

his counsel, even if he did not act as his teacher. However this may have been, young Sherman acquired at this time those habits of study which enabled him eventually to become proficient in logic, geography, history and mathematics, in the general principles of philosophy and theology, and especially in law and politics, which were his favorite studies, and in which he particularly excelled. It is recorded of him that he was accustomed to sit at his work with an open book before him, devoting to study every moment that his eyes could be spared from the occupation in which he was engaged.

If he acquired any knowledge of Latin or Greek, it was probably very slight. He doubtless learned the meaning of the Latin words and phrases of common occurrence in law books. His love of Bible study must have made him desirous of reading the New Testament in Greek. But the most that we certainly know on this point is that he knew how to write the Greek characters. In a quotation in one of his memorandum books in his handwriting is the word " prototokos," in Greek letters.

On March 20, 1741, William Sherman died, in the 49th year of his age. He was not a member of the church. As the oldest son William had moved to New Milford, Conn., the care of settling the estate devolved upon Roger. The widow was appointed administratrix. It appearing that the real estate could not be divided without damage, the Probate Court, Nov. 26, 1742, assigned the same to the son Roger Sherman, and ordered that he should pay to the other children their share, and that the widow should have her dower therein. Immediately thereafter, Roger Sherman conveyed the land to Stephen Badlam for £157 10s. In the deed Roger Sherman is described as a cordwainer.

On the 14th of March, 1742, Roger Sherman united with Mr. Dunbar's church. The circumstances which led to this act are not known. It occurred during that period of religious interest, known as the "Great Awakening," which began with the preaching of Jonathan Edwards at Northampton in 1734, and gradually spread over the country, being intensified by the preaching of George Whitefield from 1739 to 1741. The records of Mr. Dunbar's church do not indicate that Stoughton shared in this interest. Nor does it appear whether Roger Sherman was influenced in this act by the preaching of Mr. Dunbar, or by reading the sermons of Jonathan Edwards, or by other causes. One thing however is certain, that in this matter he never took a backward step. It is probable that in uniting with the church he exercised the same thoughtfulness and calm deliberation that he exhibited in all the other acts of his life. The consociation of churches in Connecticut, in 1741, passed resolves disapproving of certain irregularities connected with the Great Revival. A copy of these resolves made by Mr. Sherman in 1746 is still in existence.

Little as we know of Roger Sherman's life at Stoughton, it must have been full of pleasant memories. He often revisited the home of his childhood and youth, and renewed the friendships of early days. Six years after leaving it, he returned to claim as his bride Elizabeth, the eldest daughter of Deacon Joseph Hartwell. An ancient record contains this entry, June 21, 1767, " Esquire Sherman, with his wife and two boys, here to meeting." He was accompanied by his brother, the Rev. Nathaniel Sherman, who was born in Stoughton, and who, on this occasion, "preached in the afternoon."

There is a tradition in Canton that Elizabeth Hartwell had another suitor besides Roger Sherman, a young lawyer; and that, while the father favored Sherman, the mother favored the lawyer, because she thought he might become a judge.

CHAPTER III.

NEW MILFORD PERIOD.   1743–1761.

In June, 1743, the family moved to New Milford, where William, the oldest son, had gone three years before. It is said that Roger performed the journey on foot, carrying the tools of his trade with him. At first they took up their abode with William, who lived on a farm in that part of the town called New Dilloway. It is probable that, until he got established in other business, Roger worked at his trade. It is said that the object of his going to New Milford was to engage in the business of a surveyor.

At the October session of the General Assembly, 1745, Roger Sherman was appointed "Surveyor of Lands for the County of New Haven," the town of New Milford being at that time included in New Haven County. This was his first official position, and he continued in it till Litchfield County was organized in 1752, in which New Milford was included, and then he was appointed to the same office in that county, which position he held until he resigned it in 1758.

The office of surveyor was more than ordinarily remunerative in those days. Mr. Sherman was often employed in that capacity by the colony, to lay out portions of the ungranted lands of the colony to individuals. One commission which he executed for the colony as surveyor, in 1751, brought him £83 14s.; and this was only one of a number of orders he fulfilled for the colony within a few years. For ten years his employment by private individuals to resurvey tracts of land which had been laid out by estimation at first, in New Milford, must have taken a large amount of his time, and brought him a remuneration that but few people obtained at that date.

This occupation naturally led him to make investments in land, and he became one of the largest buyers and sellers of land in the town, as his numerous transfers in the land records testify. September 10, 1746, he bought of his brother William land to the amount of £60 in the north part of the town. In the deed of this land, William is described as a yeoman, and Roger as a cordwainer. In all subsequent deeds to and from Roger Sherman, his name is given without prefix or suffix, except in a deed from Edward Allen to him of March 9, 1749/50, in which he is described as *Mr.* Roger Sherman. In 1748, he purchased of Gamaliel Baldwin a house and lot in Park Lane for £1,500 and made his residence there; but afterwards he removed to the village, and came into possession of his brother William's home, near the site of the present Town Hall, where he resided until his removal to New Haven. He was the owner of several hundred acres of land, and a dwelling house, before he had been in New Milford seven years, for which he paid in old tenor money £2,000.

After the purchase of the property in Park Lane,

in 1748, he began to take an active part in town
affairs, and filled all sorts of town offices. He was
in different years grand juryman, list-taker, leather
sealer, fence viewer, selectman, gauger, treasurer
to receive money raised for a new meeting-house,
clerk pro tem, whenever the town clerk was absent, agent to represent the town in various matters before the General Assembly, and before the
County Court. The proprietors of the town lands
appointed him on a committee, with others, to lay
out divisions of land, and highways, examine the
boundary line of the town, run a boundary line,
apply to the General Assembly relating to boundaries, etc. Donation lands were then given for the
support of a minister, and Mr. Sherman was appointed to lay out and sell these by the proprietors
of the common and undivided lands. His name
occurs very frequently in the land records as acting
in that capacity, and these records show that his
land work for the town, together with similar work
for the colony, kept him extremely busy during
those years.

Two months after leaving Stoughton (August
28, 1743), he was dismissed from the church there,
and recommended to the church in New Milford.
December 21, 1753, he was chosen clerk of the
Ecclesiastical Society, and annually re-elected to
that office till he removed to New Haven. He was
treasurer while the third meeting-house was building, for which he received £30. He was on the
School Committee, and on various other committees to manage the affairs of the Society, one of
which was to confer with the " Rev. Mr. Nathaniel

Taylor on account of his encumbering himself with other affairs, whereby he is too much diverted from his studies and ministerial work." On the report of this committee, the Society were " well satisfied." It appears from the church records that Mr. Sherman was chosen to the office of deacon, on trial, March 12, 1755; and at a church meeting March 17, 1757, he was " established deacon " of the church.

His great business ability led to his being appointed on various committees for churches and adjoining towns, and entrusted with all sorts of commissions which needed care and energy. As a citizen he engaged in every useful and improving enterprise. When the bridge over the Housatonic was carried away by a flood, he rallied a few of the leading men of the town to venture with himself in rebuilding it, and making it a toll bridge. Just before leaving town, he with a few others introduced inoculation for the small-pox.

The first store-building in the village of New Milford was erected by William Sherman, near the site of the present Town Hall, in 1750. Here he carried on the business of a general country merchant, in connection with his brother Roger, until his death in 1756, at the age of forty. Roger Sherman became the owner of the property at that time, and continued the business till 1760, when he sold the property to Abel Hine.

While engaged in this business, Roger Sherman became so impressed with the evils of a currency consisting of depreciated and depreciating bills of credit of the colonies, that he published a pam-

phlet on the subject in 1752.[1] The title-page reads
as follows : —

" A Caveat against Injustice, or an enquiry into
the evil consequences of a fluctuating medium of
exchange.   Wherein is considered whether the
Bills of Credit on the Neighboring Governments
are a legal tender in payments of money in the
Colony of Connecticut for debts due by Book and
otherwise, where the contract mentions only Old
Tenor Money.   By Phileunomos.   New York,
Printed by Henry De Forest in King Street : 1752."

The author begins by stating the injurious effects
of allowing the bills of credit of the neighboring
colonies to circulate as a medium of exchange in
Connecticut, as they were constantly depreciating
from the neglect of those colonies to provide for
their redemption.   This resulted directly in a loss
to those receiving the bills, and indirectly in a depreciation of the bills of Connecticut itself.   Those
in favor of the circulation of these foreign bills
insisted that the custom of receiving them in the
payment of debts had continued so long that it
must be considered a part of the common law.
The greater part of the pamphlet is taken up with
an argument in reply to this claim.

The author insists that, as Connecticut has never
authorized the circulation of these foreign bills as
currency, the reception of them in payment was
a purely voluntary act, and that, in the case of a
credit, there could be no implied contract to receive in payment bills which were of less value

[1] The only copy of this curious pamphlet known to be in existence is in the possession of Senator George F. Hoar.

when the credit expired than when it was given;
that whatever value the claim might have as to a
currency possessing intrinsic value, it could have
none as to a currency which had no intrinsic value;
and that, even in the case of coin, the creditor
would not be expected to take in payment coin
which had been lessened in value by clipping or
otherwise.

At the close, to the objection that, if it were not
for these foreign bills of credit, Connecticut would
have no money to trade with, the author replies as
follows: — "If that were indeed the case, one had
better die in a good cause than live in a bad one.
But I apprehend that the case in fact is quite the
reverse, for we in this colony are seated on a very
fruitful soil, the product whereof with our labor
and industry, and the divine blessing thereon,
would sufficiently furnish us with and procure us
all the necessaries of life, and as good a medium
of exchange as any people in the world have or
can desire. But so long as we part with our most
valuable commodities for such bills of credit as are
no profit, but rather a cheat, vexation, and snare
to us, and become a medium whereby we are continually cheating and wronging one another in our
dealings in commerce; and so long as we import
so much more foreign goods than are necessary,
and keep so many merchants and traders employed
to procure and deal them out to us, great part of
which we might as well make among ourselves, and
another great part of which we had much better be
without, especially the spirituous liquors, of which
vast quantities are consumed in the colony every

year unnecessarily, to the great destruction of the
estates, morals, health, and even the lives of many
of the inhabitants: — I say so long as these things
are so, we shall spend a great part of our labor and
substance for that which will not profit us. Whereas
if these things were reformed, the provisions and
other commodities which we might have to export
yearly, and which other governments are dependent on us for, would procure us gold and silver
abundantly sufficient for a medium of trade, and
we might be as independent, flourishing, and happy
a colony as any in the British Dominions.

"And with submission, I would hereby beg
leave to propose it to the wise consideration of
the Honorable General Assembly of this colony
whether it would not be conducive to the welfare
of the colony to pass some act to prevent the bills
last emitted by Rhode Island Colony from obtaining a currency among us; and to appoint some
reasonable time (not exceeding the term that our
bills of credit are allowed to pass) after the expiration of which none of the bills of credit on
New Hampshire or Rhode Island shall be allowed
to pass in this colony, that so people, having previous notice thereof, may order their affairs so as
to get rid of such bills to the best advantage that
they can before the expiration of said term; and
whether it would not be very much for the public
good to lay a large excise upon all rum imported
into this colony, or distilled herein, thereby effectually to restrain the excessive use thereof, which is
such a growing evil among us, and is leading to almost all other vices. And I doubt not but that if

those two great evils that have been mentioned were restrained, we should soon see better times."

A few years after his removal to New Milford, Mr. Sherman employed his mathematical knowledge in preparing a series of Almanacs which bore his name, and which were published simultaneously in New York and in some place in New England, either New London, New Haven, or Boston. The introduction to the first of these Almanacs, prepared for 1750, is as follows: —

TO THE READER, — I have for several years past for my own amusement spent some of my leisure hours in the study of the mathematics. Not with any intent to appear in public, but at the desire of many of my friends and acquaintances, I have been induced to calculate and publish the following almanack for the year 1750.[1]   I have put in everything that I thought would be useful that could be contained in such contracted limits.   I have taken much care to perform the calculations truly, not having the help of any Ephemeris.   And I would desire the reader not to condemn it, if it should in some things differ from other authors, until observations have determined which is in the wrong.   I need say nothing by way of explanation of the following pages, they being placed in the same order that has been for many years practiced

[1] The original is in the possession of the American Antiquarian Society.

See Joseph Sabin's Dictionary of Books relating to America, Vol. 19, pp. 458 to 460, nos. 80,395 to 80,403, for a list of Roger Sherman's Almanacs from 1750 to 1761. There are no numbers given for 1757, 1758, 1759.

by the ingenious and celebrated Dr. Ames, with which you are well acquainted. If this shall find acceptance, perhaps it may encourage me to serve my country this way for time to come.

R. SHERMAN.

NEW-MILFORD, August 1, 1749.

It would appear from the following letter to Nathaniel Ames that Mr. Sherman made astronomical calculations for the Ames Almanac.

NEW-MILFORD, July 14, 1753.

SR: — I received your letter this day and return you thanks for the papers you sent inclosed. I find that there was a considerable mistake in the calculation of the two lunar eclipses which I sent to you in my last letter which was occasioned by my mistake in taking out the mean motion of the sun for the radical year and I have now sent inclosed (them) with the rest of the eclipses as I have since calculated them for the meridian of New London, which I reckon 4 hours and 52 min. west from London — I have also sent one of my Almanacks. I expect to go to New Haven in August next and I will enquire of Mr Clap about the comet you mentioned and will write to you what intelligence I can get from him about it the first opportunity — I am Sr your very

humble servt,

ROGER SHERMAN.

The Roger Sherman Almanacs contain the astronomical calculations as to eclipses, etc., usually

found in almanacs. In the monthly calendars are
given the stated festivals and fasts of the Church
of England, "judgments of the weather," and
, moral reflections. The last two pages of the
Almanac for 1753 are taken up with a statement of
the loss and damage sustained by Connecticut on
account of the depreciation of the bills of credit of
Rhode Island and New Hampshire. The moral
evils of such a depreciated currency are thus
described : —

"It is evident that such an uncertain medium of
exchange puts an advantage into the hands of people' to wrong one another many ways without
danger of being called to an account or punished
by the civil authority; and 't is to be feared that it
has been a means of insensibly rooting principles
of justice out of the minds of many people, occasioning them to think that what they gain of their
neighbor, by keeping him out of his just due, and
then taking advantage of the depreciation of the
bills of credit to pay their debts with less than
was the real value of them at the time of contract,
is just and honest gain. And others by receiving
their debts in such depreciated bills are necessitated
either to be great sufferers in their estates, or else
to make reprisals, taking advantage of the uncer-
tainty of the medium of exchange to get an exorbitant price for the wares and merchandises which
they sell for the future, to countervail their former
loss. But is suffering wrong a sufficient excuse
for doing wrong? "

At the head of each monthly page are a few lines
of poetry usually selected from one of the following

poets, viz.: Denham, Prior, Dryden, Milton, Young, and Pope.   These are interesting, as showing with what poets Mr. Sherman was familiar.   Some of these lines appear to be original.   If they are not very poetical, they are at least very loyal.   The lines for July, 1753, are: —

> " Brittania's free born sons ! how happy they !
> Under a George's mild and gentle sway.
> A king whose Godlike mind is big with joy
> To guard his subjects and their foes destroy.
> Heaven bless him with a long and happy reign,
> Subdue his foes, and make their counsels vain."

The lines for the next month are as follows: —

> " As English subjects, freeborn, brave,
> Our rights and liberties we have,
> Secured by good and righteous laws,
> Which ought, in judging every cause,
> To be a standing rule; whereby
> Each one may have his property."

Similar sentiments were expressed in the Almanac for 1760.

In the Almanac for 1754, under date of May 13, is the following entry: "The tyrany of old Tenor, that mystery of iniquity, source of injustice, and disturber of the peace, is now expiring, to the joy of all honest men."

In the same Almanac there is the following prediction for December 2d: "freezing cold weather, after which comes storm of snow, but how long after I don't say."

In respect to these weather predictions, a lady who remembered Mr. Sherman used to relate the following anecdote which was current in his day. He had been holding court in the forenoon of a very fair day. When the court adjourned for dinner, some of the young lawyers reminded him that his Almanac predicted a heavy rain for that day. He said nothing, but came into court after dinner with his cloak. Before the adjournment at night a severe storm came up, in which all the company at the Court-House were drenched, except Mr. Sherman, who was protected by his cloak.

In Sanderson's Lives, the following account is given of the circumstances which led Mr. Sherman to devote himself to the study of the law : —

" A neighbor or acquaintance, in transacting some affairs relative to the family of a deceased person, required the assistance of legal counsel. As Mr. Sherman, then a young man, was going to the county town, he was commissioned to obtain it from an eminent lawyer. To prevent embarrassment, and secure the accurate representation of the case, he committed it to paper, as well as he could, before he left home.

" In stating the case, the gentleman with whom he was consulting observed that Mr. Sherman frequently recurred to a manuscript which he held in his hand. As it was necessary to make an application, by way of petition, to the proper tribunal, he desired the paper to be left in his hands, provided it contained a statement of the case from which the petition might be framed. Mr. Sherman consented with reluctance, telling him that it was merely a memorandum drawn up by himself for his own convenience. The lawyer, after reading it, remarked, with an expression of surprise, that, with a few alterations in form, it was equal to any petition which he could have prepared himself, and that no other was requisite. Having then made some inquiries relative to Mr. Sherman's situation and prospects in life, he advised him to devote his attention to the study of the law."

Whatever were the circumstances which first directed his attention to the study of the law, his mind was so constituted that he was instinctively drawn to it. He made such progress in the mastery of its principles, and obtained such reputation as a counsellor, that, by the advice of his friends, he applied for admission to the bar, and was admitted to practice by the County Court held at Litchfield in February, 1754.

In May, 1755, he was appointed by the General Assembly a justice of the peace for Litchfield County; and in May, 1759, he was appointed a justice of the quorum for the same county. By virtue of this latter office, he became a member of the County Court, sometimes called the Court of Common Pleas, which was composed of a judge and three or more justices of the quorum. This court heard many small actions, also applications for new highways, or the alteration of old ones. It appears from the records of this court that he took part in its proceedings for nearly a year after he removed to New Haven.

On the first day of February, 1758, a complaint was made by the grand-jurymen of New Milford before Roger Sherman, as a justice of the peace, " that Samuel Peet of sd New Milford, on ye

Lords Day, the 29th day of January last, did not
attend the publick worship of God in any congregation allowed by law in sd New Milford or elsewhere, neither hath he attended the publick worship of God in any lawful congregation at any
time on ye Lord's day for one month next before
sd 29th of January, but did willingly and obstinately, without any lawful or reasonable cause or
excuse forbaire and neglect to do the same, contrary to the statute of this colony in such case
provided."

The record, at the foot of this complaint, in
Roger Sherman's handwriting, is as follows : —

" Feb'y 9th 1758, Sam'l Peet appeared to Def'd
adjudged guilty, fined 3 /, paid it down."

During Mr. Sherman's residence in New Milford,
seats in the meeting-house were assigned by vote
in town meeting. The chief fact taken into consideration in assigning these seats was the amount
of taxes paid, but age and station had something
to do with it. At a town meeting held June 7,
1748, it was "voted that Mr. Roger Sherman's
place shall be in the fore seat in the front gallery."

In May, 1755, he was chosen to represent the
town of New Milford in the General Assembly, and
was re-elected to that office at each semi-annual
election thereafter, except for the years 1756 and
1757, until he removed to New Haven in 1761.
This was the beginning of his political career, which
continued with but slight interruptions till his death.

When Roger Sherman first entered the legislature, he was thirty-four years of age. It was at
the commencement of the French and Indian

war, and the experience which he acquired in the
Connecticut Legislature, at this time, fitted him for
the active and important part which he took in the
Continental Congress during the Revolutionary
War.

In 1754, the year before the war with France,
and in anticipation of it, at the request of the home
government, a convention of delegates from the
different colonies was held at Albany for the purpose of forming a union of the colonies for general
defence, etc. A plan for a confederate government
was submitted by Franklin; but it was rejected by
the colonies as giving too much power to the central government, and by the English authorities as
likely to give too much force to any movements
that might be formed in opposition to the mother
country. Connecticut was especially opposed to
its provisions that all nominations of commissioned
officers, by land and sea, should be made by this
central government. Although nothing came of
this attempt to form a confederate government,
thoughtful men, like Roger Sherman, were led to
consider the necessity of union among the colonies,
and the form of government best calculated to
secure and preserve it.

The Colonial Records of Connecticut show that
Mr. Sherman was as active and laborious in the
legislature as he had been in town and county
affairs. His reputation as an advocate of sound
currency led to his being placed, just after his entry into public life, in August, 1755, on a committee
" to consider how the treasury should be supplied
with money or bills of credit to pay the charges of

this government for the expedition to Crown
Point." In May, 1761, he was placed on a committee "to make provision for sinking the outstanding bills of credit of March, 1758."

In May, 1756, he was on a committee "to view
Indian lands and examine and report on matters of
Indian complaint." In May, 1759, he was appointed
" Commissary to reside at Albany to receive, secure, and forward the supplies for the Connecticut
troops, and take into custody guns and other
stores that shall be returned from the army, and
ship them to the Commissaries in the colony."

On the 14th of February, 1760, Mr. Sherman
entered into a written agreement with about forty
other persons to settle a Township of about twelve
miles square, lying eastward of Fort Edward upon
Wood Creek, in the province of New York, with
one hundred and sixty families within three years
from the expiration of the war then existing between Great Britain and France, provided a patent
for the same could be obtained. One family was
to be settled on each five hundred acres subscribed
for; and two rights of five hundred acres each
were to be set apart, one for the ministry, and one
for a school.

For some reason, perhaps because a patent
could not be obtained, nothing came of this agreement. Whether Mr. Sherman entered into it as a
land speculation, or to aid a relative, or with the
intent of becoming one of the settlers himself, is
not known. The desire of educating his children
would probably have prevented him from moving
his family into the wilderness.

On the 17th of November, 1749, at Stoughton, the Rev. Samuel Dunbar united in marriage Roger Sherman and Elizabeth Hartwell, the eldest daughter of Deacon Joseph Hartwell of Stoughton. Seven children were the fruit of this marriage, namely, John, William, Isaac, Chloe 1st, Oliver, Chloe 2d, and Elizabeth. Two of these children, Chloe 1st and Oliver, died early. The three oldest sons were officers in the Revolutionary Army, John a Lieutenant and Paymaster, William a Lieutenant and Paymaster, Isaac a Lieutenant Colonel Commandant. Two of these sons, William and Isaac, were educated at Yale, both graduating in 1770. The first wife of Roger Sherman died at New Milford, October 19, 1760, aged thirty-four.

The eighteen years spent by Roger Sherman in New Milford were busy and prosperous. He gradually rose from the humblest position to the highest offices in the gift of his town and county. He was public-spirited, and ever ready to lend his aid to every useful enterprise. Conscious of the defects in his own education, he generously aided his brothers Nathaniel and Josiah in their course through college, and in preparation for the ministry. A mature man, in comfortable circumstances, skilled in affairs, and with a widening reputation, he was prepared, at forty years of age, to enter the broader field and improve the larger opportunities which opened before him in New Haven.

CHAPTER IV.

NEW HAVEN PERIOD.

MR. SHERMAN removed to New Haven June 30, 1761. Instead of resuming the practice of the law, he engaged in mercantile pursuits. In a letter to Theophilact Bache, August 15, 1764, he states that he no longer practices as an attorney. In President Stiles's Diary there is this entry with regard to Mr. Sherman, July 23, 1793 : " He removed to New Haven in 1761, and went into trade, in which he was very successful. . . . After several years of successful business in trade, which he well understood, he consigned it over to his sons, and devoted himself to civil affairs and public life, in which he was fully employed." His accounts show that, besides carrying on the ordinary business of a country merchant, he was accustomed to import books such as would be needed by the professors and students in the college. From advertisements in the Connecticut Gazette, it appears that in July, 1760, nearly a year before he removed his residence to New Haven, Mr. Sherman opened a store in that town, and also in Wallingford, Connecticut. Advertisements in the Connecticut Journal indicate that Roger Sherman retired from business, and was succeeded by his son William, in December, 1772.

It is interesting to note that, in his first year in New Haven, Mr. Sherman was a contributor to a fund for building a college chapel. In President Clap's Annals of Yale College, in a list of donations in 1761 for building the chapel, there is set opposite the name of Roger Sherman £7 and 10s. This was one of the larger donations. Mr. Sherman was the treasurer of Yale College from 1765 to 1776. In 1768 he received from the college the honorary degree of Master of Arts.

On the 4th of October, 1761, Mr. Sherman was admitted to the White Haven Church in New Haven by letter from the church in New Milford. He at once took an active part in all matters relating to the church and society, and was appointed on all sorts of committees. Mr. Bird, the pastor, resigned on account of ill health, in 1767, and the Rev. Jonathan Edwards, the younger, was chosen to succeed him in 1769, and continued pastor of the church till 1795.

The city of New Haven was incorporated in 1784. By the act of incorporation, it was provided that " the Mayor having been chosen by the city assembled in legal meeting, should hold his office during the pleasure of the General Assembly." Roger Sherman was elected the first mayor, and the General Assembly having never intimated that it was their pleasure that he should be removed from the office, he continued mayor as long as he lived.

The motives which influenced the legislature in making this singular provision can be inferred from the following extract from a letter to Mr. Sherman, written just after his election as mayor, by his pastor, Rev. Jonathan Edwards : —

"Last Tuesday came on our election of city officers, when the Hon. Roger Sherman, Esq., was chosen Mayor. Some of your friends have been fearful that you would not accept of the place. But I hope and entreat that you will not refuse it, and this, I presume is the earnest desire of all your friends. · If you should refuse it, Mr. Howell would certainly be chosen. I cannot bear that the first Mayor of this infant city should be a tory. If therefore there were no other motive to induce you to accept it but this, to keep out a tory, I conceive it would be a sufficient ground of procedure. The disgrace which would be brought on the city, the mortification to every real whig, the triumph of the tories, all come into view on this occasion. Besides it will be at best as well for the city, if you retain the place, even when you are absent, as it would be if you were to decline it ; because the city court will, during your absence, consist of the very same members. Mr. Howell is now first Alderman, and if you should refuse, would be the Mayor. I hope the Place will produce some little profit to you. It will be entirely in your way to attend the business when you are at home, and the fees will be something. All things considered, I hope, Sir, you will not decline the appointment."

In October, 1764, Mr. Sherman was elected a deputy from New Haven to the legislature, and was re-elected to that office in May and October, 1765, and in May, 1766. He was elected an assistant, or member of the upper house of the legis-

lature in May, 1766, and was annually re-elected to
that office for nineteen years, and until an act was
passed making the office of assistant incompatible   .
with that of Judge of the Superior Court, which last
office he preferred to retain.

He was appointed a Justice of the Peace, for
New Haven County, in May, 1765, and a Justice
of the Quorum, for that county, in October, 1765.
In May, 1766, he was appointed a Judge of the
Superior Court, and was annually reappointed to
that office for twenty-three years, until he resigned
it to take a seat in the Congress of the United
States.

One of the most curious documents that have
been preserved connected with Mr. Sherman's proceedings as a Justice of the Peace, is a complaint
made before him by two grand jurors of the riot-
ous conduct of Benedict Arnold and ten others, on
January 29, 1766, in breaking into a dwelling house
and seizing one Peter Boles, and stripping him of
his clothing, and fastening him to a whipping-post,
and beating him in a shocking, cruel, and dangerous manner; on which complaint Mr. Sherman
issued a warrant for the arrest of the offenders,
who were brought before him, and bound over for
trial.

Roger Sherman married for his second wife,
May 12, 1763, Rebecca Prescott of Danvers, Massachusetts, daughter of Benjamin Prescott, a magistrate there, and granddaughter of Rev. Benjamin
Prescott, for many years settled over the parish
known as the second precinct of Salem, Mass.   The
second precinct of Salem was afterwards incorpor-

ated as Danvers, and a portion of it incorporated
with the town of Peabody, where the old church
stood in which Mr. Prescott so long preached and
where is now standing the old house in which he
lived. This house contains a curious little closet,
known as the minister's study, not more than eight
feet square. One of its sides is taken up principally by a window; another by a door; the third
by a place for a desk or table; and the fourth by
a fire-place. It is to be hoped that the fire-place
did not have an undue influence on the sermons.
In the adjoining parlor Rebecca Prescott was married to Roger Sherman by her grandfather.

Eight children were the fruit of this marriage,
five daughters and three sons, all but one of whom,
a daughter, Mehetabel 1st, grew up to maturity.
They were Rebecca, Elizabeth, Roger, Mehetabel
1st, Mehetabel 2d, Oliver, Martha, and Sarah.
As Mr. Sherman's public duties took him away
from home a great deal of the time, the care of the
family, including the children of the former marriage, was largely borne by this young wife. She
was a woman of great personal beauty, and cheer-
ful wit, and shrewd common sense, which qualities
all her daughters seem to have inherited.[1] She
was descended from John Prescott, the founder of
Lancaster, and first settler of Worcester County,
Mass., who was the ancestor of Colonel William
Prescott, of Bunker Hill, and of Judge William
Prescott, and of William H. Prescott, the historian.

---

[1] A genealogical table, showing her descent through Francis
Higginson from a sister of Geoffrey Chaucer, is in the possession
of Hon. George F. Hoar.

Her first meeting with her husband is not without a tinge of romance. Mr. Sherman made a horseback journey from New Haven to visit his brother Josiah, then settled over the church in Woburn, Mass. He had stayed about three weeks, when it seemed to him that the time had come to end his visit. He was urged to prolong his stay, but he thought he had stayed long enough. Accordingly he mounted his horse, and started for New Haven. His brother accompanied him some little distance, when they stopped to say a few parting words. As they were bidding each other good-bye, there rode up on horseback a beautiful young girl of eighteen. It was Rebecca Prescott, who was riding over from Salem to visit her aunt, Mrs. Josiah Sherman, at Woburn. Mr. Sherman was presented to her, and they remained conversing together for a little while. It was an instantaneous and fatal shot. Mr. Sherman told his brother that on the whole perhaps it was not absolutely necessary that he should go home at once, and he would accept his kind invitation to remain a little longer. What would have been the fate of a numerous body of descendants, if Rebecca Prescott had been five minutes longer on the road, is a question like that which Lord Brougham raises in the beginning of his memoir as to what sort of a person he would perhaps have been if his father had married somebody else than his mother, as was at one time expected.

Unfortunately little of the correspondence of Roger Sherman and his wife has been preserved. There is this fragment of a letter to her, dated May 30, 1770: —

"This is your birth day. Mine was the 30th of last month. May we so number our days as to apply our Hearts to wisdom: that is, true Religion. Psalm 90: 12.

"I remain affectionately yours,

"ROGER SHERMAN.

"REBECCA SHERMAN."

At the time of Rebecca Prescott's marriage to Mr. Sherman, she was not a member of the church; but a few years after her marriage, she united with the White Haven Church, as appears from the following record. "Dec. 13, 1767, Rebeccah, wife of Roger Sherman received into church in full communion on profession of faith."

Mr. George Sherman, a son of Roger Sherman, Jr., writes April 6, 1894, — "Grandmother, who was a Prescott, took interest in everybody and in everything, was very clear and quick in calculating, much more so than grandfather. I wish more of her character and work had been appreciated and handed down to us. Her influence and good counsel were felt wherever she was known."

The Honorable William M. Evarts was an inmate of the family of Judge Baldwin, soon after his entering Yale College, in 1833. That was about twenty years after the death of Mrs. Sherman, and when Judge Baldwin, President Day, Dr. Skinner, Roger Sherman, the younger, and his wife, and Mrs. Baldwin, daughter of Roger Sherman, were living, and many of the contemporaries of Roger Sherman and his wife. He heard the following anecdote in the family, which is undoubtedly authentic.

Mrs. Sherman was visiting her husband at the seat of government, and was invited by General Washington to a dinner-party, and was conducted into dinner by the General and had the seat of honor on his right. Madam Hancock was one of the guests. She thought that that distinction was due to her, and complained of the slight a day or two after to General Washington's secretary, who repeated her grievance to General Washington. He replied that it was his privilege to give his arm to the handsomest woman in the room. Whether the explanation was conveyed to Madam Hancock, and if so, whether it tended to lessen her annoyance, does not appear.

CHAPTER V.

STAMP ACT.

MR. SHERMAN took his seat in the General Assembly of Connecticut, as a deputy from New Haven, at the October session of 1764. It was in the midst of the excitement caused by the announcement of the British ministry that they proposed to collect a revenue from the American Colonies by means of a Stamp tax. Notice of this intended action was sent to the Connecticut Assembly, at its May session, 1764, by Richard Jackson, its agent in London. The Assembly thereupon appointed Ebenezer Silliman, George Wyllys, and Jared Ingersoll a committee to set forth the objections to this proposed tax.

This committee made its report to the Assembly, at its October session, 1764, setting forth the "Reasons why the British Colonies in America should not be charged with internal taxes." This report was adopted, and ordered to be forwarded to the agent of the colony in London, to be presented, with an address from the Governor, to the Parliament. As Jared Ingersoll was about to sail for England, he was ordered to assist Mr. Jackson, the agent of Connecticut.

The remonstrances of the colonies were of no effect, and on the 22d of March, 1765, the Stamp Act received the royal assent. Instantly a storm

4

of indignation swept over the country. Taxation without representation was everywhere denounced as a badge of slavery which the colonies would not endure. On the 7th of October, 1765, the delegates from nine colonies met in the City Hall at New York, and adopted a declaration of rights and grievances, an address to the King, a memorial to the House of Lords, and a petition to the House of Commons. The Connecticut delegates were not authorized to sign these papers, but on their return home, the Assembly authorized the delegates to sign them, and ordered that they be forwarded to Great Britain.

These various remonstrances were alike in expressions of loyalty to the King, and affection for the mother country, of uncompromising hostility to any tax laws made by a legislature in which the colonies were not represented, and of their willingness to submit to any reasonable regulations ot trade. The Connecticut remonstrance was one ot the ablest of these firm but temperate papers. Besides these manifestoes of public bodies, a private publication, which attracted general attention in this country and in England, was "The rights of the British Colonies asserted and proved," published by James Otis in 1764. This pamphlet was thought by some, and among them Roger Sherman, to concede to Parliament too great power over the colonies.

In the meantime, the people had formed themselves into organizations called the "Sons of Liberty," who were determined by threats and violence to prevent the Stamp Act from being enforced. It is a little singular that Jared Ingersoll, who was employed to prevent the passage of the Stamp Act, should have been so impressed, while in England, with the uselessness of a contest with Great Britain, that he accepted the office of Stamp Commissioner. He was not prepared for the storm of popular wrath which he encountered on his return home. As he rode on his white horse from New Haven to Hartford, he was followed by a cavalcade of a thousand armed men, who insisted that he should resign his office, which he wisely concluded to do, as he thought that "the cause was not worth dying for." He said afterward that he realized at last what the book of Revelation meant by "Death on the pale horse, and hell following him."

The following paragraph from the Connecticut Gazette shows what instructions Mr. Sherman received from his constituents on his re-election to the legislature in the fall of 1765:—

"NEW HAVEN Sept. 20, 1765.

"On the 17th inst the Freemen of this town met here. After choosing Roger Sherman Esq. and Mr. Samuel Bishop to represent them in the General Assembly to be holden next month, they unanimously desired those Representatives to use their utmost endeavors (at the assembly now sitting at Hartford and also at the ensuing session here) to obtain a Repeal of the Stamp Act. The Stamp Master General of this Colony was at the said meeting when these words were read aloud, *Likewise voted that the Freemen present earnestly desire Mr.*

Ingersoll to resign his Stamp Office immediately.
Numerous were the signs of consent to this vote,
when a gentleman condemned it as needless and
inconsistent after their former proceedings. The
officer then arose and declared in the strongest
terms that he would not resign till he discovered
how the General Assembly were in this respect.
'T is said he has gone to Hartford in order to make
that important discovery, and that he has wrote to
New York requesting that the Stamp papers be retained there till they are wanted here."

The excesses committed by many of the " Sons
of Liberty " led the more sober and thoughtful
persons in the community to fear that the cause of
the colonies would be discredited by these unlawful
acts. It was this which drew out the following
letter from Roger Sherman to Matthew Griswold:

SIR, — I hope you will excuse the freedom
which I take of mentioning, for your consideration,
some things which appear to me a little extraordinary, and which I fear (if persisted in) may be
prejudicial to the interests of the Colony — more
especially the late practice of great numbers of
people Assembling and assuming a kind of legislative authority passing and publishing resolves &c
— will not the frequent assembling such large
bodies of people, without any laws to regulate or
govern their proceedings, tend to weaken the
authority of the government, and naturally possess
the minds of the people with such lax notions of
civil authority as may lead to such disorders and
confusions as will not be easily suppressed or re-

formed? especially in such a popular government
as ours, for the well ordering of which good rules,
and a wise steady administration are necessary. —
I esteem our present form of government to be one
of the happiest and best in the world. It secures
the civil and religious rights and privileges of the
people, and by a due administration has the best
tendency to preserve and promote publick virtue,
which is absolutely necessary to publick happiness.
. . . There are doubtless some who envy us the
enjoyment of these . . . privileges, and would be
glad of any plausible excuse to deprive . . . therefore behooves . . . to conduct with prudence and
caution at this critical juncture, when arbitrary
principles and measures, with regard to the colonies, are so much in vogue; and is it not of great
importance that peace and harmony be preserved
and promoted among ourselves; and that everything which may tend to weaken publick government, or to give the enemies of our happy constitution any advantage against us, be carefully
avoided? I have no doubt of the upright intentions of those gentlemen who have promoted the
late meetings in several parts of the Colony, which
I suppose were principally intended to concert
measures to prevent the introduction of the Stamp
papers, and not in the least to oppose the laws or
authority of the government; but is there not
danger of proceeding too far in such measures, so
as to involve the people in divisions and animosi-
ties among themselves, and . . . endanger our charter privileges? May not . . . being informed of
these things, view them in such light . . . our pre-

sent democratical state of government will not be sufficient to secure the people from falling into a state of anarchy, and therefore determine a change necessary for that end, especially if they should have a previous disposition for such a change? Perhaps the continuing such assemblies will now be thought needless, as Mr. Ingersoll has this week declared under oath that he will not execute the office of distributor of Stamps in this Colony, which declaration is published in the New Haven Gazette. I hope we shall now have his influence and assistance in endeavoring to get rid of the Stamp duties. . . .

I hear one piece of news from the east which a little surprises me, that is, the publication of some exceptionable passages extracted from Mr. Ingersoll's letters, after all the pains taken by the Sons of Liberty to prevent their being sent home to England. I was glad when those letters were recalled, and that Mr. Ingersoll was free to retrench all those passages which were thought likely to be of disservice to the government, and to agree for the future, during the present critical situation of affairs, not to write home anything but what should be inspected and approved by persons that the people of the government would confide in; but by means of the publication of those passages in the newspapers, they will likely arrive in England near as soon as if the original letters had been sent, and perhaps will not appear in a more favourable point of light.

Sir, I hint these things for your consideration, being sensible that, from your situation, known abilities and interest in the affections and esteem of the people, you will be under the best advantage to advise and influence them to such conduct as shall be most likely to conduce to the public good of the colony. I am, Sir, with great esteem, your obedient, humble serv't

ROGER SHERMAN.

NEW HAVEN, Jan. 11, 1766.

In July, 1765, the Grenville Ministry was defeated, and the Whigs, under Lord Rockingham, came into power. In the session of Parliament which followed, Pitt and Burke put forth their utmost efforts to procure the repeal of the Stamp Act. Macaulay, speaking of this brilliant display, says, "The House of Commons heard Pitt for the last time, and Burke for the first time, and was in doubt to which of them the palm of eloquence should be assigned. It was indeed a splendid sunset and a splendid dawn."

On the 18th of March, 1766, the King signed the bill for the repeal of the Stamp Act. The news of the repeal filled the colonies with transports of joy. It was everywhere greeted with the ringing of bells, with salvos of artillery, with bonfires and illuminations. The loyalty and gratitude which it evoked are well expressed in the following resolution by the Connecticut Assembly at its May session, 1766: —

"This Assembly desires his Honor the Governor to consider of and prepare an humble, dutiful and loyal address to his Majesty, expressive of the filial duty, gratitude and satisfaction of the Governor and Company of this Colony, on the happy

occasion of the beneficial repeal of the late American Stamp Act; . . . and his Honor the Deputy
governor, Hezikiah Huntington, Matthew Griswold,
Eliphalet Dyer, William Pitkin, Jr., Roger Sherman, Robert Walker, William Samuel Johnson,
George Wyllys, Zebulon West, John Ledyard,
Alexander Wolcott, Jedediah Elderkin, and William
Williams, Esqrs. are hereby appointed a Committee,
fully authorised and directed, to assist and advise
His Honor the Governor in preparing and completing such address, and any other address, as they
shall judge expedient and proper on this joyful and
happy event: . . . and also desire His Honor the
Governor to return the most ardent and grateful
thanks of this Assembly to all those who have distinguished themselves as the friends and advocates
of the British Colonies in America, on this important occasion, whether as members of the British
Parliament or otherwise."

On the 30th of July, 1766, the administration of
Lord Rockingham came to an end; and with it
came to an end the just and liberal treatment of
the American Colonies of which Edmund Burke
had been so brilliant an advocate. The Earl of
Chatham was nominally at the head of the ministry which succeeded; but he had frequent attacks
of illness, when men with a very different policy
from his own took the lead. In one of these intervals, Charles Townshend introduced and carried
through, June 29, 1767, a bill for raising a revenue
from the colonies by a tax on glass, paper, paint-
er's colors, and tea. This rekindled the flames of
discontent in the colonies. From every quarter

came petitions and remonstrances against the Act. The relation of the colonies to the mother country was discussed in the newspapers with great fulness and force. The ablest statement of the whole question was contained in a series of letters entitled " Letters from a Farmer in Pennsylvania," published in the Pennsylvania Chronicle and Universal Advocate, by John Dickinson, from December, 1767, to February, 1768. They were copied into other journals, and widely circulated. They were also printed in a pamphlet form in America and London. Among the letters of thanks received by the author, that from a public meeting of the citizens of Boston was most noteworthy.

This new tax was opposed, not by acts of violence, but by a non-importation agreement, which, although not strictly observed, sufficiently alarmed the British merchants to lead them to procure a repeal of the Townshend tax on all articles except tea. This the King insisted should be retained for the sake of preserving the principle of the right of Parliament to tax the colonies. After this repeal, the New York merchants insisted that the non-importation agreement should apply only to tea, and though this was violently opposed in the other colonies, it resulted in the destruction of the agreement. This was followed by a period of inaction among the colonies. During the existence of this non-importation agreement, Mr. Sherman acted as a member of a committee of New Haven merchants to secure its enforcement.

The following letter signed by this committee is

given, though from its style it was apparently not written by Mr. Sherman.

NEW HAVEN, July 26th, 1770.

GENT. — The time is now come for us to determine whether we will be freemen or slaves, or in other words — whether we will tamely coalesce with the measures of our backsliding brethren of New York who by resolving on importation at this juncture have meanly prostituted the common cause to the present sordid prospect of a little pelf; or by a virtuous and manly effort endeavor to heal this breach in the common Union by adhering more firmly than ever to our first agreement. There is no time to lose — and can we hesitate a moment in choosing whether we will continue our connection with those degenerate impostors, and with the prospect of a little temporary wealth bequeath infamy, poverty and slavery to our posterity; or by discarding them entirely until they shall return to their agreement evince to future ages, God and ourselves that we are still uncontaminated and free? Let not our present connection with any of them deter us: it is the cause of our country, it is the cause of liberty, it is the cause of all; and our country betrayed, our liberty sold, and ourselves enslaved, what have we left? With what can New York supply us that can't be had on equal advantage and perhaps on a more generous footing from our natural friends and neighbors of Boston, whose manly fortitude and persevering measures justly claim our preference.

It is with peculiar satisfaction we have the pleasure to inform you of the determinate resolutions and spirited behavior of all ranks and denominations among us who with one voice determine upon the expediency of abiding by the general non-importation agreements and breaking off all connection with any of our neighbors who have or shall infringe the same as you 'll see by the copies of the inclosed letters and resolves passed in a fuller meeting than has ever been known on the like occasion. We have free confidence that our brethren among you will now manifest their sense of the defection of the majority of the merchants of New York in a manner proper and consistent with ourselves, for which purpose we have transmitted the same intelligence to our brethren throughout the Colony not doubting they have even gone before us on these our virtuous endeavors — and are, with esteem and regard Gent, your most obedt. humble Servts.

ROGER SHERMAN
THO. HOWELL
JESSE LEAVENWORTH
JOSEPH MUNSON
DAVID AUSTIN
ADAM BABCOCK

Committee

To the merchants at Weatherfield and Hartford.

It was at this period of depression that the following correspondence took place between Thomas Cushing, one of the leaders of the Boston patriots, and Roger Sherman. In a letter dated " Boston, January 21st, 1772," after referring to certain matters of private business, Mr. Cushing writes: —

" I heartily wish, with you, that some measures

might be come into to revive the union of the Colonies; to place any great dependence upon the
virtue of the people in general, as to their refrain-
ing from the use of any of the dutiable articles,
will be in vain — The only thing we can at present
depend upon is the conduct of the several assemblies thro' the continent; and however the people
in general may be induced, for peace sake or from a
sense of their inability, to submit at present in some
instances to the exercise of, what they apprehend,
the usurped authority of Parliament, the assemblies
ought to keep a watchful eye upon their liberties
and from time to time to assert their rights in
solemn resolves and continually to keep their
agents instructed upon this important subject and
to renew their memorials to the King for the redress of their grievances and the restoring their
privileges.   It might be well also for each assembly to be considering what shall be their conduct
as soon as a war commences.   It is highly probable it will not be long before the nation is involved
in a bloody war with some of the European Nations, perhaps next spring, upon the commencement of which we may depend upon their applying
to the several colonies for assistance by furnishing
them with men and money.   It is of great importance, therefore, that the Colonies at such a juncture
should act one and the same part.   Is it not therefore high time that each assembly should be medi-
tating what answers they should give and what
conduct they should pursue in consequence of any
such requisitions?   Then certainly will be the time
to settle matters upon a secure and permanent

footing especially if we can all agree upon one and ye same plan of conduct: Would it not then be expedient to consult one another upon this subject as soon as possible. You are sensible this province by being foremost in such measures has brought the whole resentment of Great Britain upon them, we suffer at this day more than all ye colonies together — would it not therefore be reasonable that your Colony or some other should take the lead in this matter, pray consider of it and let me know your sentiments upon this subject. I write in confidence as to a friend and therefore shall depend upon your not mentioning this proposal as coming from me, for many reasons which I shall communicate to you when I have the pleasure of seeing you at Boston. In ye mean remain with respect,

" Your most humble serv't

" THOMAS CUSHING."

To this letter, Mr. Sherman sent the following reply, dated " New Haven, April 30, 1772." After disposing of certain business matters, he writes : —

" The observations you make relative to the measures proper to be taken to preserve the rights of the Colonies I esteem just, but in order to do anything effectual it will be needful for the people of the several Colonies to be agreed in sentiment as to the extent of their rights. . . . It is a fundamental principal in the British Constitution and I think must be in every free State, that no laws bind the people but such as they consent to be governed by, therefore so far as the people of the Colonies are bound by laws made without their consent, they must be in a state of slavery or absolute subjection to the will of others: if this right belongs to the people of the Colonies, why should they not claim it and enjoy it? If it does not belong to them as well as to their fellow subjects in Great Britain, how came they to be deprived of it? Are Great Britain and the Colonies at all connected in their legislative power? (Have not each Colony distinct and complete powers of legislation for all the purposes of public government, and are they in any proper sense subordinate to the Legislature of Great Britain tho' subject to the same King?) And tho' some general regulations of trade &c. may be necessary for the general interest of the nation, is there any constitutional way to establish such regulations so as to be legally binding upon the people of the several distinct Dominions which compose the British Empire, but by consent of the Legislature of each Government?

"These are points which appear to me important to be agreed in and settled right, and any concessions made by any of the assemblies, disclaiming any privileges essential to civil liberty which the Colonies are justly entitled to, must greatly disserve the common cause. If they think it not prudent, at present to assert every right in the most explicit manner, yet all concessions which may be construed as a disclaimer, ought to be carefully avoided.

"I am Sir, your humble servant

"ROGER SHERMAN.

"Hon. THOMAS CUSHING Esqr."

In this letter, Mr. Sherman went a step beyond that taken by most of the advocates of American rights up to this time. In the report adopted by the Connecticut Assembly in 1764, in the argument of Stephen Hopkins of Rhode Island, in the papers prepared by James Otis and by Samuel Adams, and finally in the "Farmer's Letters," by John Dickinson, the right of Parliament to bind the colonies by regulations of trade and commerce was conceded in the fullest manner. For over a hundred years Parliament had passed acts regulating the trade of the colonies, and its right to do so had never been questioned. The binding force of such acts was conceded as late as the Congresses of 1774 and 1775. In a paper sent by Thomas Jefferson to the Williamsburg convention, in the summer of 1774, there is a similar assertion that, while the colonies owed allegiance to the King, they were independent of Parliament; but the convention refused to adopt it. In the draft of the Declaration of Independence, as originally prepared by Jefferson, there was a similar claim of the independence of the colonies of Parliament, but it was stricken out by the Congress of 1776. Mr. Jefferson states, in his autobiography, that he had always been of that opinion, but that the only person who agreed with him was his old law teacher, Mr. Wythe.

The opinion expressed by Mr. Sherman in his letter to Mr. Cushing was repeated by him two years afterward. John Adams, on his way to Philadelphia, stopped at New Haven, and makes this record in his Diary, August 17, 1774: —

"This morning Roger Sherman, Esq. of the delegates from Conn. came to see us at the tavern, Isaac Bears's. He is between fifty and sixty, a solid, sensible man. He said he read Mr. Otis's Rights &c. in 1764, and thought that he had conceded away the rights of America. He thought the reverse of the declaratory act was true, namely, that the Parliament of Great Britain had authority to make laws for America in no case whatever. He would have been very willing that Massachusetts should have rescinded that part of their Circular Letter where they allow Parliament to be the supreme legislative over the Colonies in any case." [1]

Mr. Adams, in his Diary, September 8, 1774, gives the following speech by Mr. Sherman in Congress : —

" MR. SHERMAN. The ministry contend that the Colonies are only like corporations in England, and therefore subordinate to the legislature of the Kingdom. The Colonies not bound to the King or Crown by the act of settlement, but by their consent to it. There is no other legislative over the Colonies but their respective assemblies. The Colonies adopt the common law, not as the common law, but as the highest reason." [2]

In the midst of the controversy with the mother country about taxation, alarm was excited by the efforts on the part of the Episcopalians in this country to secure the appointment of a bishop for America. The opposition to this movement did not result from any hostility to the Episcopal

----

[1] Adams's Works, v. ii. 343.   [2] Ibid., 371.

Church, but from the fear that there would be claimed for such bishop all the power annexed to that office by the common law of England, unless this should be prohibited by act of Parliament. The following letter, found among the papers of Roger Sherman, and in his handwriting, is supposed to have been addressed to William Samuel Johnson, in 1768, on that subject, Mr. Johnson being at that time in England, acting in behalf of the colony of Connecticut in reference to the title of the colony to certain Indian lands.

SIR, — We understand sundry petitions have been sent home by some of the Episcopal clergy in these Colonies in order to obtain the appointment of a Bishop here, and that it is a determined point on your side of the water to embrace the first opportunity for that purpose. Their affairs, we must confess, give us much anxiety, not that we are of intolerant principles; nor do we envy the Episcopal church the privileges of a Bishop for the purposes of ordination, confirmation and inspecting the morals of their clergy, provided they have no kind of superiority over, nor power any way to affect the civil or religious interest of other denominations, or derive any support from them. Let this be settled by an act of Parliament, and such Bishop divested of the power annexed to that office by the common law of England and then we shall be more easy about this. The introduction of a Diocesan into the Colonies would throw us into the utmost confusion and distraction. For though it is alleged that no other than the above

5

moderate Episcopacy is desired or designed, yet if it shall not be fixed by Parliamentary authority, we have no security that matters will be carried no further. Yea, from the restless spirit which some have discovered, we have reason to apprehend there is more in view. Our fathers and even some of ourselves have seen and heard the tyranny of Bishops' Courts. Many of the first inhabitants of these Colonies were obliged to seek an asylum among savages in this wilderness in order to escape the tyranny of Archbishop Laud and others of his stamp. Such tyranny, if now exercised in America, would drive us to seek new habitations among the heathen where England could never claim any jurisdiction, or excite riots, rebellions, and wild disorders. We dread the consequences as oft as we think of this danger. Gentlemen acquainted with the law inform us that the Bishop is a public minister of the State known in the common law of England and invested with power of erecting courts to take cognisance of all affairs testamentary and matrimonial, and to inquire into and punish for all matters of scandal; might he not plead as well as any man that the common law of England is his birth right and that the laws in force in England before the settling of the Colonies were brought hither and took place with the first settlers? What is to hinder him from claiming all the power exercised by Archbishop Laud and his Ecclesiastical Courts? All acts made in England since that time to lessen the power of Bishops and their courts can be of no service to us for it is not mentioned in any of them that they are extended to the Colonies; and the reason is plain no such exorbitant powers were claimed or exercised among us. Now can anything less than the most grievous convulsion in the Colonies be expected from such a revolution? Will it at all go down with us to have the whole course of business turned into a new channel? Would it be yielded that the register office, the care of orphans, &c should be transferred from the present officers to such as a Bishop might appoint? Would not the Colonies suffer the last extremities before they would submit to have the legality of marriages and matters relating to divorce tried in an Episcopal court? 'T is not easy to conceive what endless prosecutions under the notion of scandal may be multiplied. A covetous, tyrannical, and domineering prelate or his chancellor would always have it in their power to harrass our country and make our lives bitter by fines, imprisonments, and lawless severity. Will the numerous Colonies who came here for the sake of freedom from ecclesiastical oppression, and by whose toil a great increase of dominion and commerce hath arisen to the mother country bear to find themselves divested of the equality and liberty they have so long enjoyed and brought under the power of a particular denomination and see them monopolize all important places of trust in order to secure that power?

That the Episcopal churches should enjoy all the privileges of their own discipline and government is a matter we have nothing against, but let the Bishop be by law confined to the care of the people and clergy of their own church and stript

of all their formidable power over other denominations, and let us be secured against bearing the
burden of their support.   But without this we shall
look upon ourselves reduced to a most miserable
state, enslaved to the power of those whose interests or ambition may lead them to oppress us,
without the advantage of being near the throne to
beg relief, while they would be supported by all
the power and influence of the Bishops at home.
We have no more to object to a Bishop over the
Episcopal churches in America, than among the
Canadians, and provided they shall have no more
to do with us, we only desire the interest of our
friends that if a Bishop must be sent which we fear
will be attended with bad consequences, they may
be under such restraints as are consistant with our
present happy state of peace and liberty, and beg
their influence to prevent these evils which will inevitably disturb the peace of our Colonies without
doing any real service to religion, or the Episcopal
churches.

Do us the justice to assert that we love our most
gracious King and the English Constitution, that
we upon principle are loyal as well as profitable
subjects and that our importance to Great Britain
will every day become more evident and take
proper opportunities to lay these dangers before
our friends with you which will oblige thousands in
America and in particular,

Yours &c.

The colonists had always submitted to the
commercial regulations imposed upon them by

Parliament; but the method of enforcing them
was becoming vexatious and oppressive. The
commander of an armed schooner, the Gaspee,
employed in the revenue service, had rendered
himself specially obnoxious by his harshness and
insolence and illegal acts. In June, 1772, the
Gaspee ran aground in Narragansett Bay, while
chasing an American vessel. That night she was
boarded by a party of men, who put the crew
ashore, and burned the vessel to the water's edge.
By a royal order in council, the offenders were to
be arrested and sent to England for trial. But as
the offenders were not caught, the excitement
caused by the threat to take them out of the country soon subsided.

In 1773, the British government made a final
attempt to collect the tax on tea. A drawback of
the duty paid on importing tea into England from
China was allowed to the East India Company
on exporting it to America. It was supposed the
Americans would thus be induced to pay the three
pence in the pound, as the tea, even after the payment of that duty, would be cheaper in America
than in England. But this action simply made
the colonists determine that no tea should be
landed. At Charleston, Philadelphia, and New
York, the consignees were intimidated into resigning their commissions. In Boston, the Governor
refused the request of the citizens to permit the tea
ships to pass out of the harbor, and consequently,
on the evening of the 16th of December, 1773, a
party of men, disguised as Indians, boarded the
ships, and threw the tea overboard.

CHAPTER VI.

WYOMING.

IN January, 1774, Mr. Sherman was appointed by the Connecticut Assembly on a committee to consider the claims of the settlers near the Susquehannah River. He thereupon prepared the following statement of the Susquehannah controversy. This statement was found among Mr. Sherman's papers, but it does not appear what use he made of it.

"As the late disturbances among the people inhabiting the lands on the Susquehannah River, in controversy between the proprietors of Pennsylvania and the colony of Connecticut, have drawn the attention of the public, it may not be amiss to give a short and impartial state of the facts relative to that affair, to prevent misapprehension and unjust censure of any of the persons concerned on either side.

"There is a real claim of title and jurisdiction by both parties over a tract of territory about seventy miles wide north and south, and about two hundred and fifty miles long east and west, bounded east by the river Delaware, and south by forty-one degrees north latitude.

"The colony of Connecticut claim by a charter granted by King Charles II., dated the 23rd day of April, 1662.

"The proprietors of Pennsylvania claim by a charter granted by the same King, dated March 4th, 1681. Said proprietors acknowledge that the land in controversy is contained in the charter to Connecticut, as appears by their late Petition to the King in Council, and there is no dispute but that it is also cont ned in the charter to said proprietors of Pen· ιvania.

"A numbe. of the inhabitants of Connecticut, in the year 1754, purchased the native right to that part of said land which is now inhabited, on the east and west branches of Susquehannah River, of the sachems of the six nations of Indians in a grand congress at Albany — which purchase was approved by an Act of the General Assembly of the Colony of Connecticut, in May, 1755, and said purchasers began a settlement thereon about the year 1762, but it being represented to the Secretary of State that continuing said settlement would likely bring on an Indian war, a requisition was made by the King to the Governor of Connecticut, to recall the letters until proper measures should be taken to prevent any fresh troubles with the Indians, upon which said settlers removed off from said lands, and in 1768, a line was settled by the King's order between the English and Indian lands, upon which the proprietors of Pennsylvania made a purchase of part of the same lands of the Indians which had before been purchased by the people of Connecticut. This settlement of the line was in the fall of the year 1768, and in February, 1769, the Connecticut people returned to their former possessions on said lands, since which time great part of said lands have been by the proprietors of Pennsylvania granted and surveyed to particular persons in Pennsylvania and the Assembly of that province has annexed the same to the counties of Northampton and Northumberland.

" The Colony of Connecticut also incorporated a Town called *Westmoreland*, including all the inhabited part of said lands and annexed it to the County of Lichfield, which is since made a distinct County, called the County of *Westmoreland*.

" The settlers under the claim of Connecticut are on the lands near the east branch of Susquehannah River, and the settlers under the Pennsylvania Proprietors, on or near the west branch of said river."

The incorporation of these settlers into a town clothed with the same privileges that the other towns in the colony enjoyed created quite a tumult in Connecticut, as many persons believed the claim of the colony to these lands to be unfounded. Public meetings were called to protest against the action of the Assembly, and the papers teemed with angry and sarcastic essays denouncing the legislative proceedings. But the legislature persevered in its measures, and the representatives of Westmoreland were admitted to a seat in the Assembly. Mr. Sherman, thereupon, published in the Connecticut Journal, April 8, 1774, the following clear and forcible argument: —

" There has been much altercation of late concerning the doings of the honorable general assembly, relative to the western lands contained in our charter, and many false insinuations have been industriously circulated by some men, to prejudice

the minds of the people against the assembly; from
what motives I shall not undertake to determine.
It is h'ard to suppose that the good of the colony
has been the motive, when the measures taken
have the most direct tendency to its destruction;
for every *kingdom divided against itself is brought
to desolation.* I am sensible that the good people
of the towns concerned in the late Middletown
convention, have been greatly deceived and misled; but I can't but wonder at their credulity in
giving credit to an anonymous writer in a newspaper, whose character they knew nothing of, who,
in an audacious, as well as false manner, has undertaken to impeach the integrity of the general
assembly of the colony. But, as Luther once said,
when he was condemned by the pope, he would
appeal from the pope uninformed, to the pope
rightly informed, so I would take leave to inform
the people of some facts which I know to be true,
as to the doings of the general assembly relative
to the matters in question, and then appeal to the
people, whether the assembly hath not acted a
wise and prudent part therein.

"In May, 1770, in consequence of a memorial
preferred by more than four thousand of the freemen of the colony, (none of them interested in the
Susquehannah purchase,) praying the assembly to
assert and support the claim of this colony to the
lands contained in our charter, lying west of Delaware River, as they esteemed it to be a valuable
interest which the governor and company held in
trust for the freemen of the colony; the assembly,
after mature deliberation, ordered a true and full
statement *of the case* to be laid before counsel

learned in the law in England; accordingly the case was stated, and laid before four of the principal lawyers in the kingdom, who unanimously gave their opinion in favor of the title of the colony.[1] And this measure was not taken by influence of the Susquehannah Company, for the principal proprietors thought it a needless precaution, they having no doubt about the validity of the colony's claim.

" After the opinion of counsel was obtained, the assembly in October last, by a very full vote, resolved to assert, and in some proper way, support the colony's claims to said lands; and then appoint a committee to consider of proper measures to be taken for that end, who reported, for substance, all the resolutions since come into by the assembly, (the exercising of jurisdiction over the people settled there, not excepted,) which report was accepted in full assembly. A great clamor has been made about the assembly's suffering the members interested in the Susquehannah purchase to sit and vote in those matters; but that complaint, I conceive, is without any just foundation. I was in the lower house in the year 1755, when the assembly acted on the memorial of the Susquehannah company, and then all that were of the company, were excluded; and I understand that the same method has been taken by the house, at all times since, when any matter has been debated, or vote taken, that concerned the peculiar interest of the company. But I don't remember any vote, taken by the assembly in October or January last, wherein they were particularly interested.

[1] This ⬛⬛⬛⬛ given by Thurlow, Wedderburn, Jackson, and Du⬛

"The acts then passed, relative to the western lands, were such as concerned the colony in general; and they could not, by any rule or principle of law or equity, have been excluded.

"The assembly considered the governor and company to be vested with the legal title to all the lands contained in our charter, lying between the rivers Delaware and Mississippi, except what the Indians are possessed of; and no persons can acquire a title to any part of them by purchase from the Indians, without a grant of the assembly; and the Susquehannah purchasers don't pretend that they have any legal title to any part of said lands. But, if the government avail themselves of their purchase of the native right, the purchasers will expect to be quieted in such a part of the land as will be an equitable compensation for their expense therein; which must be determined by the assembly; in which determination none of the company will be allowed to vote. If the idea here suggested is just, it will obviate the present difficulty suggested in the petition, drawn up and published by the convention at Middletown.

"They seem to make some further difficulty about exercising jurisdiction over the people of the town of Westmoreland, because, they say, the colony's title to those lands is contested. In answer to which, I would say, that it is not contested, but acknowledged, by the proprietors of Pennsylvania, that the lands are contained within the original boundaries of our charter, as may appear by a petition presented by them to the king in council, a few years ago. If it once belonged

to the colony, and we have never yielded it up,
nor have been divested of it by any judicial determination, what can be the mighty danger of exercising government over the people who claim the
privilege of being under the jurisdiction of the
colony?   I should think the greatest danger
would be on the other hand; if the colony claim a
title to the lands as being within their charter, I
don't see how they could excuse themselves in
neglecting to govern the people settled on the
lands, for their right of soil and of jurisdiction, by
the charter, are commensurate.   But it is further
said, that the doings of the assembly will tempt
great numbers of the people to settle on those
lands, and if they should be evicted, they will be
reduced to poverty, &c.   But this is a groundless
surmise; for the assembly have caused a proclamation to be issued, expressly forbidding any more
persons settling on said lands without leave first
obtained from the assembly.   As to their fears of
what bloody tragedies may ensue from clashing
jurisdictions, &c — exercising jurisdiction was
judged by the assembly the most likely measure
to prevent all mischiefs of that kind, and to preserve peace and good order among the people.

"As to what the convention say concerning the
title of the colony to the lands in question, that it
is a matter of which they are not so competent
judges, nor furnished with facts and documents by
which a judgment might be made, and so are willing
and desirous that the right of the colony to them,
and the prudence and policy of asserting that
right, should be judged of, and determined, by a

disinterested assembly; — if this had gone to the
whole of their proceedings, they would have done
justice to the cause, and they would have merited the
applause of their constituents. It is a little extraordinary, when the colony has a cause to be tried,
which all parties seem to think best should be
tried, that those who profess to be so very zealous
for the public good, should use every method in
their power to defeat its success. Much has been
said to alarm the people about the expense of
a trial before the king and council. Governor
Penn, in his late conference with our commissioners, says that an adversary suit can't occasion
much delay or expense. I presume it would not
cost more than one farthing on the pound in the
list of this colony, to decide the question whether
this colony joins to Pennsylvania or not; and, if
that is determined against us, there would be an
end of the controversy; but, if in our favor, a
further expense would be incurred in fixing our
south boundary, which could not amount to any
great sum. Great part of the expense in the
Mason cause, was occasioned by the delay, because
Mason was not able to carry it on. But the final
decision of that cause in our favor, furnishes us
with an evidence of the safety of confiding in the
integrity of that high court, when acting as a court
of law. Mr. Ingersoll, in a piece lately published
in the newspapers, says, ' a defeat will be very detrimental; but a victory must be absolute ruin; at
least I think so.' But he gives no reason for his
opinion; and can his bare assertion make the people of this colony, who are a company of farmers,

believe that to be quieted in their claim to a large
tract of valuable land would ruin them? I know
some gentlemen, who love to monopolize wealth
and power, think it best for lands to be in a few
hands, and that the common people should be
their tenants but it will not be easy to persuade the
people of this colony, who know the value of freedom, and of enjoying fee-simple estates, that it
would be best for them to give up the lands acquired for them by their ancestors, for the privilege
of enjoying the same lands as tenants under the
proprietaries of Pennsylvania.

"The lands in question are situated about the
centre, as to latitude, of the English territories in
North America, in a healthy climate; and the soil
is said to be generally very good; and there is
enough purchased of the Indians to supply the
inhabitants of this colony, that may want land to
settle on, perhaps for half a century to come.

"They will be connected with us, and by sharing
in our civil and religious privileges, will be under
the best advantages to be virtuous and happy;
and those who continue in this part of the colony,
may be greatly benefited by monies that may be
raised by the sale of those lands; and yet the purchasers have them on better terms than they can
procure lands elsewhere; and if, in time to come,
that part of the colony should be so populous as
to render it inconvenient to be connected with this
part of the colony in government, the crown would
doubtless be ready, upon application, to constitute
them a distinct colony.

"Thus I have given you a short account of the

doings of the assembly, and endeavored to obviate the difficulties and misapprehensions which some people have labored under, relative to the affair, and also to mention some of the advantages which may accrue to the colony by supporting their claim to the lands. And, as I have no interest in the affair but in common with every freeman in the colony, nor any party views to serve, I am quite willing the freemen should show their minds, and determine it as they shall think best. About half the freemen have already manifested their desire to have the colony's claim supported; viz., the four thousand memorialists afore-mentioned, and the Susquehannah and Delaware companies, which, I suppose, will amount to about one thousand more; — and I hope the other freemen will not relinquish the colony's claim, without full information and mature deliberation, least they injure themselves, their brethren and posterity. I think no more need be done than to choose gentlemen of known virtue, integrity, and prudence, to be members of the next general assembly, who have approved themselves firm friends to our civil and religious liberties, and not embarrass them with petitions or instructions: they will be under a solemn oath to act as, in their consciences, they shall judge most for the good of the colony, and that must be the only rule of their conduct.

"But I must conclude, and can, with sincerity, subscribe myself a cordial well wisher to the peace and welfare of the colony.

" R. SHERMAN."

Such a paper, from a man of Mr. Sherman's character and standing, was effectual in tranquilizing the public mind. But the contest in Wyoming went on with ever increasing violence, until it ended in bloodshed. Various attempts were made to settle the difficulty, but they were all in vain. At last the contestants were summoned before a court of commissioners under the provisions of the ninth article of the Act of Confederation, and after a hearing in the city of Trenton from the 18th of November to the 30th of December, 1782, judgment was pronounced in favor of Pennsylvania.

Although Connecticut was thus defeated in her claim to this particular territory, yet the assertion of her title was productive of large and lasting advantages, as it enabled her, on ceding to the United States, in 1786, her claim to lands in the northwestern territory, held by the same tenure as the Wyoming lands, to obtain a recognition of her title to that portion of those lands, about three and a half millions of acres, which she reserved to her own use, situated in the present limits of Ohio, and known as the Connecticut Reserve, and from the sale of which she has obtained the school fund of over two millions of dollars, which her citizens now enjoy.

·

CHAPTER VII.

THE CONTINENTAL CONGRESS.

TEN years of controversy passed before the colonies could be brought to present a united front to the aggressions of Great Britain. A few clear-headed and far-sighted statesmen may have, at a very early day, despaired of maintaining the rights of the colonies if the connection with Great Britain were preserved. But nothing could show more clearly the loyalty of the great body of the people, and their unwillingness to sever the tie which bound them to the mother country, than the eagerness with which they welcomed every appearance of concession to their claims. The outburst of indignation which the Stamp Act provoked was followed by an outburst, no less passionate, of loyalty and gratitude on its repeal. The excitement produced by the Charles Townshend act was largely allayed by the partial repeal of that act. The alarm excited by the threat to remove to England for trial the destroyers of the Gaspee subsided as soon as that plan was abandoned. The hostility to the Tea Act, which culminated in the destruction of the tea in Boston harbor, was soon followed by a period of lethargy. So late as April 9, 1774, John Adams wrote to James Warren, "I am of the same opinion that I have been for years, that

6

there is not spirit enough on either side to bring
the question to a complete decision. . . . Our children may see revolutions, and be concerned and
active in effecting them, of which we can form no
conception."

But the revolution was nearer than John Adams
thought. The British ministry were determined to
make an example of Massachusetts, for the destruction of the tea. By the Boston Port Bill, its
commerce was destroyed. By the Regulating Act,
its charter was so altered as to deprive that colony
of some of its most important rights. An act relating to the administration of justice provided for
the transportation of offenders and witnesses to
other colonies or to England for trial. To enforce
these acts the harbor of Boston was inclosed with
a cordon of war vessels, and General Gage, who
was made the new Governor of Massachusetts,
landed a body of troops in the doomed city.

The limit of endurance was at last reached. The
other colonies made the cause of Massachusetts
their own. Resolutions of sympathy poured in
from every quarter, and at the same time supplies
were generously forwarded to relieve the wants of
the suffering. The necessity for united action was
at length apparent to all, and Massachusetts was
requested to name the time and place for a Congress of all the colonies.

On the 5th of September, 1774, the delegates
from twelve colonies assembled in Philadelphia,
and formed the first Continental Congress. Connecticut elected as its delegates Eliphalet Dyer,
William S. Johnson, Erastus Wolcott, Silas Deane,

and Richard Law. Of these Johnson, Wolcott, and Law declined to serve on account of other engagements, or ill health, and in their place Roger Sherman and Joseph Trumbull were elected. Those who attended the Congress were Dyer, Sherman, and Deane.

The object of this Congress, as set forth in the commissions of the delegates, was to procure a redress of grievances, and to restore harmony between Great Britain and America. It was therefore determined to limit the action of Congress to the following objects, — a declaration of rights and an account of their violation, a petition to the King, a memorial to the inhabitants of the colonies, a memorial to the people of Great Britain, a memorial to the non-represented colonies, and a non-importation, non-exportation, and non-consumption agreement.

The first question that came before the Congress was as to the manner of voting, the smaller colonies insisting that each colony should have one vote, and the larger that representation should be in proportion to population or property. This question, which created so much discussion in the debates on the Confederation, and afterwards on the Constitution, was for the present deferred; and it was decided that each colony should have one vote, assigning as a reason, to prevent this action from being considered as a precedent, that the Congress was not possessed of, or at present able to procure, proper materials for ascertaining the importance of each colony.

The Committee on the Declaration of Rights

consisted of two from each colony. The members from Connecticut were Eliphalet Dyer and Roger Sherman. The article in the Declaration of Rights which excited most debate was that in reference to laws of trade and commerce. Five of the colonies were in favor of conceding to Parliament the right of regulating trade, five were opposed to it, and two — Massachusetts and Rhode Island — were divided. Finally, John Adams, by request, drew up a statement which was adopted. It forms the last part of the fourth resolution, and is as follows : — " But from the necessity of the case, and a regard to the mutual interest of both countries, we cheerfully consent to the operation of such acts of the British Parliament as are bona fide restrained to the regulation of our external commerce, for the purpose of securing the commercial advantages of the whole empire to the mother country, and the commercial benefits of its respective members; excluding every idea of taxation, internal or external, for raising a revenue on the subjects in America without their consent."

We have already seen that Mr. Sherman was unwilling to concede to Parliament the right to legislate for the colonies in any case whatever, and have given from Mr. Adams's diary the remarks which he made in Congress on this subject.

The non-importation agreement, which was signed by the delegates, and which provided for a committee of vigilance in every town and county to enforce its provisions, constituted a new bond of union, which kept alive the national spirit during the recess of Congress. John Adams called it

" The memorable league of the continent in 1774, which first expressed the sovereign will of a free nation in America." The second article of this agreement was a provision against the slave trade. This agreement is known as the Association of 1774.

Congress was dissolved the 26th of October, after having provided for another Congress on the 10th of May, 1775, unless meantime there should be a redress of grievances, and invited all the colonies in North America to send deputies to it. Eliphalet Dyer, Roger Sherman, and Silas Deane were again chosen to represent Connecticut in Congress.

When the Congress of 1775 assembled, the conflict at Lexington and Concord had taken place, and the royal troops had been shut up in Boston by the New England militia which had gathered to aid the Massachusetts patriots. A handful of troops from Vermont had captured Ticonderoga and Crown Point. Notwithstanding this state of hostilities, and the rejection of the petition of the former Congress, it was resolved to make one more attempt at conciliation by presenting another petition to the King. At the same time it was resolved that the colonies be immediately put in a state of defence. The force besieging Boston was adopted by Congress, and a code of rules was prepared for the government of the army of the United Colonies.

The important matter of the selection of a commander-in-chief now came up for decision. John Adams at once declared himself in favor of Washington, but some were in doubt whether a southern man would be acceptable to the New England troops. Mr. Adams, in his diary, says : " The subject came under debate, and several gentlemen declared themselves against the appointment of Mr. Washington, not on account of any personal objection against him, but because the army were all from New England, had a general of their own, appeared to be satisfied with him, and had proved themselves able to imprison the British army in Boston, which was all they expected or desired at that time. Mr. Pendleton of Virginia, Mr. Sherman of Connecticut, were very explicit in declaring this opinion."[1]   But when, on June 15th, the matter came to a vote, which was by ballot, the election of Washington was unanimous.

Mr. Sherman was disappointed in not being able to secure for Major General David Wooster, in command of the Connecticut forces near New York, the same rank in the Continental army that he held in the Connecticut army, as will appear from the following correspondence.

PHILADELPHIA, June 23, 1775.

DEAR SIR, — The Congress having determined it necessary to keep up an army for the defence of America at the charge of the united colonies, have appointed the following general officers. George Washington Esq., Commander-in-Chief, Major Generals Ward, Lee, Schuyler, and Putnam, Brigadier Generals Pomroy, Montgomery, yourself, Heath, Spencer, Thomas, Major Sullivan of New Hampshire, and one Green of Rhode Island.   I am

[1] Adams's Works, v. ii. 417.

sensible that according to your former rank, you
were entitled to the place of a Major General;
and as one was to be appointed in Connecticut I
heartily recommended you to the Congress. I informed them of the arrangement made by our
Assembly, which I thought would be satisfactory,
to have them continue in the same order: but as
General Putnam's fame was spread abroad and especially his successful enterprise at Noddle's
Island, the account of which had just arrived, it
gave him a preference in the opinion of the Delegates in general so that his appointment was unanimous among the colonies. But from your known
abilities and firm attachment to the American
cause we were very desirous of your continuance
in the army, and hope you will accept of the appointment made by the Congress. I think the pay
of a Brigadier is about one hundred and twenty-
five dollars per month. I suppose a commission
is sent to you by General Washington. We received intelligence yesterday of an engagement at
Charlestown, but have not had the particulars.
All the Connecticut troops are now taken into the
Continental army. I hope proper care will be
taken to secure the Colony against any sudden invasion, which must be at their own expense. I
have nothing further that I am at liberty to acquaint you with of the doings of the Congress but
what have been made public. I would not have
anything published in the papers that I write, lest
something may inadvertently escape one which
ought not to be published. I should be glad if
you would write to me every convenient opportu-

nity and inform me of such occurrences and other matters as you may think proper and useful for me to be acquainted with. I am with great esteem, your humble servant,

ROGER SHERMAN.

P. S. The General officers were elected in the Congress, not by nomination but by ballot.

DAVID WOOSTER, Esq.

CAMP NEAR NEW YORK, July 7th, 1775.

DEAR SIR, — Your favor of the 23rd ult I re-'ceived, in which you inform me that you recommended me, but without effect to the Congress for the berth of Major General. Your friendship I never doubted, and this fresh instance I shall ever gratefully remember.

I enclose with this the commission delivered to me by General Washington. You will see that somehow by mistake it was never dated. You will be good enough to deliver it to Mr Hancock with my best compliments, and desire him not to return it to me. I have already a commission from the assembly of Connecticut. No man feels more sensibly for his distressed country, nor would more readily exert his utmost for its defence, than myself. My life has been ever devoted to the service of my country from my youth up; though never before in a cause like this, a cause which I could most cheerfully risk, nay lay down my life to defend.

Thirty years I have served as a soldier; my character was never impeached nor called in question before. The Congress have seen fit, for what

reason I know not, to point me out as the only officer among all that have been commissioned in
the different colonies, who is unfit for the post
assigned him.   The subject is a delicate one.   For
further particulars, as well as for an account of the
stores taken at Turtle Bay, I must refer you to my
letter of this date to Col. Dyer.   I am, Sir, in haste
your sincere friend and humble servant

DAVID WOOSTER.

To the Hon. ROGER SHERMAN.

During the year 1775, a portion of the committees on which Mr. Sherman was chosen ·to
serve were the following, viz.: to devise ways and
means to put the militia of America into a proper
state of defence; to consider the Susquehannah
case; to consider the instructions to New Hampshire on the formation of a local government; to
consider the treaty with the Indians by the commissioners of the northern department; to inquire
into frauds in army contracts; to inquire into the
needs of the inhabitants of Nantucket for fuel and
provisions.

The second petition to the King was answered
by a proclamation denouncing as rebels all those
who opposed the measures of government, and
threatening them with condign punishment.   The·
vessel that brought this proclamation brought also
the news that ten thousand Hanoverians were about
to join the British forces in America.

This proclamation put an end to all hope of reconciliation with the mother country.   Congress no
longer hesitated to advise the colonies to call a full

and free representation of the people, and establish in each such a form of government as would best promote their well being.   This was substantial independence, though it took six months before all the colonies were ready for its formal declaration.   But from this time on, the leading patriots bent all their energies to devising means for the successful prosecution of the war with Great Britain. " I am sick," said John Adams, " of the words mother country."

At the outbreak of hostilities, Mr. Sherman's son Isaac, then in his twenty-second year, was in Massachusetts, looking for an opening in business.   He at once entered the Massachusetts army with the rank of captain.   He remained in the military service of his country to the close of the war.   On March 26, 1776, he was promoted to the rank of major, and on October 28, 1776, on the recommendation of General Washington, he was given command of the Eighth Connecticut Regiment, with the title of lieutenant colonel commandant.   His record was among the most honorable in the Connecticut Line, and he received favorable notice from Washington.   He fought bravely at New Rochelle, Trenton, Princeton, where he led the advanced guard, Monmouth, and Stony Point.   In 1785, he was appointed by Congress assistant surveyor of western territory.   His later years were spent in Connecticut and New Jersey.   He died unmarried in Hunterdon County, New Jersey, February 16, 1819.   While with the army besieging Boston, in the fall of 1775, he wrote the following letter to his father : —

BROOKLINE FORT AT SEWALLS POINT Sept. 8, 1775.

HONORED SIR, — I received your letter dated August 21st, which is the only one received since that favored by Col. Folsom. It gives me great pleasure to hear that my friends are in a good state of health. Mr Dagget's stay was so very short, that I could not possibly have wrote, he told me you would set out for Philadelphia before his return. I was appointed by the Mass. Province. Business of almost every kind was entirely stagnated in this Province by reason of the public difficulties which rendered it almost impossible to obtain any employment sufficient to procure a maintenance, was an inducement for me to enter the army: but far from being the only one. The goodness of the cause, a desire of being an useful member of society and of serving my country, a thirst for glory, real glory, were the grand incentives. I hope by the assistance of the Deity I shall be enabled to serve every useful end, never to reflect dishonor upon the family or myself. The distance being so great, the necessity of being expeditious in recruiting rendered it almost impossible to have consulted with you on the affair. I am so far from thinking the advice of the experienced disadvantageous to youth, that I apprehend it to be the incumbent duty of young men to consult and advise with those who are acquainted with the various manœuvres of mankind, and especially with a kind indulgent parent, who always consults the good of his children. The questions you proposed I shall answer with pleasure. I am situated at

Brookline Fort at Sewalls Point situated between Cambridge and Roxbury on Charles River. We have no great prospect of a battle at present. They will never presume without a very considerable reinforcement to attempt to force our lines which are very strong: Nor we theirs. The army is very healthy, in fine spirits, resolute in the cause. We have no certain news from the British troops. A few deserters now and then, but their relations are to be but little depended on. The people in Boston have been and are still in a very disagreeable situation. They have liberty to come out but they come out very slow, for a few boats pass a day and those over Winipinet Ferry only. The Generals are well. We have various accounts from England but no intelligence to be depended on. Nothing remarkable has happened here of late. Judges nor justices are appointed. But the assembly in their next session I understand are a going to appoint them. The Council at present are settling the militia of the Province. I should esteem it a great favor to be informed as soon as possible of the plan preferred by the Continental Congress for raising troops for the ensuing campaign. Whether I could obtain the command of a regiment if I could raise one. There are a number of things I stand in great need of, which cannot easily be procured here but at a very extravagant price, should be glad if you would furnish me with a genteel hanger, a yard and an half of superfine scarlet broadcloth, with suitable trimmings, for a coat of uniform, and a piece of Holland. I am in good health, very much pleased with a military life, tho' attended with many inconveniences. I shall for the future take every opportunity of writing, and when anything of importance occurs, shall endeavor to give the earliest intelligence. I am Sir,

Your most dutiful son, `

ISAAC SHERMAN.

N. B. I should be glad to know what number of men a regiment will consist of in the ensuing campaign. Mr Seevar the bearer of this will tarry some days in Philadelphia, he is after goods. You may, if agreeable, have an opportunity of sending the things I wrote for with his, and they will be conveyed with safety to me. Mr Seevar will purchase the quantity of goods he proposes at New York, these things may be obtained there and sent with his, if equally agreeable to you.

To the Honorable ROGER SHERMAN Esq. at Philadelphia.
favored by Mr Seevar.

In the beginning of the year 1776, news was received at Philadelphia of a conflict between the Connecticut settlers and the Pennsylvanians at Wyoming. Mr. Sherman immediately wrote the following letter to Zebulum Butler, of Wyoming, for the purpose of preventing further disturbances.

PHILADELPHIA Jan. 19, 1776.

SIR, — The enclosed paper contains several resolutions of the Congress and an Act of the Assembly of Connecticut. Col. Dyer informs me that he sent copies of the resolves of Congress immediately after they were passed to you and to the

magistrates in the county of Northumberland. We
have had an account of an attack on our people by
some of the Pennsylvanians who were repulsed with
the loss of two men killed, but heard nothing from
the Connecticut people relative to that action,
or whether they sustained any loss. There is a
report here that your people have given some disturbance to the settlers under Pennsylvania. I
should be glad of a particular account from you of
the situation of affairs relative to that unhappy controversy which tends to weaken the union of the
Colonies at the present alarming crisis. I hope
you will do all in your power to prevent any disturbances being given to the settlers under Pennsylvania by our people and that the resolutions of
Congress be duly observed. You will observe that
the Assembly of Connecticut have shortened the
western limit of Westmoreland. I would advise
that no jurisdiction be exercised over the settlers
under Pennsylvania within the limits of the said
town, if any be contrary to their mind. Col. Dyer
and Mr Dean have left Congress, the time they
were appointed for being expired, and Oliver Wolcott and Samuel Huntington Esqrs. are now attending in their stead. You will observe that the
Congress have recommended that all the effects
taken and detained from any persons in the con-
troverted lands be restored. It will be proper to
apply to the magistrates who took cognizance of
that matter for restitution or to the sheriff who
had the goods in custody, and if they are not restored that the case may be represented to the
Congress and if anything hath been taken from the

people of Pennsylvania by the Connecticut people
that the same be restored. I am Sir, with due
regards,   Your humble servant
                          ROGER SHERMAN.
ZEBULUM BUTLER Esqr.

The confidence reposed in the abilities and integrity of Mr. Sherman is shown in the great number of important committees on which he was
appointed. May 6, 1776, he was appointed on a
committee to devise ways and means to raise ten
million dollars. May 25, 1776, he was appointed
on a committee to concert plans, with General
Washington, General Gates, and General Mifflin,
for the ensuing campaign. On the 11th of June,
1776, a committee of five to draft a Declaration of
Independence was appointed, consisting of Thomas
Jefferson, John Adams, Benjamin Franklin, Roger
Sherman, and Robert Livingston. On the 12th of
June, 1776, Mr. Sherman was placed on a committee of one from each colony to prepare Articles
of Confederation. On the 13th of June, 1776, the
Board of War and Ordnance was created, consisting
of John Adams, Roger Sherman, Benjamin Harri-
son, James Wilson, and Edward Rutledge. June
24, 1776, he was placed on a committee to inquire
into the cause of the miscarriage in Canada. September 20, 1776, he was placed on a committee
of three to visit headquarters, and inquire into the
state of the army, and the best means of supplying
its wants.

To perform the duties required by these various
and important appointments would seem to have
tasked *a giant's strength*. John Adams thus

speaks of his own labors on the Board of War:
"The duties of this board kept me in continual
employment, not to say drudgery, from the 12th of
June 1776, till the 11th of November 1777, when I
left Congress forever.   Not only my mornings and
evenings were filled up with the crowd of business
before this board, but a great part of my time in
Congress was engaged in making, explaining, and
justifying our reports and proceedings."

The Articles of Confederation were reported by
John Dickinson, and were debated from time to
time.   August 1, 1776, the 17th Article, with re-
ference to the method of voting, was discussed.
The delegates from the larger States, John Adams,
Franklin, and others, insisted that the representa-
tion should be according to population or wealth.
The opinions of Mr. Sherman are thus recorded in
John Adams's diary: — [1]

"Sherman thinks we ought not to vote according to numbers.   We are representatives of States,
not individuals.   States of Holland.   The consent
of every one is necessary.   Three colonies would
govern the whole, but would not have a majority of
strength to carry the votes into execution.   The vote
should be taken two ways; Call the colonies and
call the individuals, and have a majority of both."

Mr. Sherman, in this proposition, anticipated
the compromise plan which, eleven years later, he
suggested and carried through the Constitutional
Convention of 1787.

In October of this year Rev. Samuel Hopkins
sent to Mr. Sherman a pamphlet, entitled "A dia-
logue concerning the Slavery of the Africans; and

1 Works, vol. ii. 499.

an address to Slaveholders,"and with it the following letter, which is interesting as showing that in
this early anti-slavery movement, it was proposed
to send missionaries to the Africans in the Southern
States.

STOCKBRIDGE, 8th Oct. 1776.

MUCH HONORED SIR, — As a good opportunity presents, I take leave to send you a pamphlet,
which I find is dedicated to the most honorable
Congress, not knowing that any of them have yet
reached Philadelphia. I also enclose to you several copies of a piece relating to a proposed
African Mission, desiring you to make the use of
them you shall think best. I also take leave to
ask your judgment and advice whether it will be
thought proper, and will answer any good purpose
or tend to promote this design if Dr Stiles and
myself shall particularly apply to Congress for
their patronage and encouragement in any way
which they shall think most proper.

And as no way now opens to send these proposed
Missionaries to Guinea, it has been proposed by
several gentlemen if no way shall open for their going to Africa in the Spring, to send them into the
Southern States to teach the negroes there, many
thousands of whom are almost, if not quite as much
in a heathen state, as are the natives of Africa. It
is thought that if they can be recommended by the
Synod in these states and obtain the approbation
of Congress, in making their attempt there will be
encouragement sufficient for them to undertake it.
The approbation of the Synod may doubtless be
obtained. But there is a doubt whether the honor-

7

able members of Congress would be inclined or think proper to do anything in such an affair, should they be applied to. I therefore presume to use the freedom to ask you to give me your judgment and advice on this head also, when you have consulted with any of the honorable members, and taken measures to learn their sentiments respecting it as you shall think best.

I am now here on a visit to my family and hope to return to Newport in a few weeks. If you will be so good as to write me an answer to the above, you will doubtless have opportunity to send to Newport by the same conveyance by which Mr. Ellery sends to his family, if no other opportunity presents.

Wishing your precious life may be spared and that you may be made a very great blessing in your present most honorable and important station, I am most honorable Sir with great respect and esteem your sincere friend

and humble servant

SAMUEL HOPKINS.

The currency problems now began to create great anxiety in Congress. In a letter to Governor Trumbull, of March 4, 1777, Mr. Sherman says: "The evil occasioned by the fluctuating and exorbitant prices of things is very sensibly felt here. . . . The best way to preserve the credit of the currency, and render the prices of articles stable, is to raise the supplies for carrying on the war by taxes, as far as possible, and the rest by loans. It seems to be the present opinion of Congress that there be no further emission of Bills than what is already ordered, if it can possibly be avoided, and that the most effectual measures be taken to support the credit of those already emitted. Accordingly a tax is recommended to the several States, and as the rule to determine the quotas is not yet established by the legislatures of the several States, (which is to be done by the Confederation,) each state is called upon to raise as large a sum as circumstances will admit, with an engagement to allow interest at six per cent for what any state may raise more than its just quota of the whole sum that shall be raised."

At the close of the letter he refers to an attempt to raise money by a lottery. " Doctor Jackson, one of the managers of the Lottery of the United States, by whom I expect to send this, is on a journey through New England to dispose of the lottery tickets. He requested me to recommend to him suitable persons in Connecticut to receive a number of them for sale." He then states that he named several persons in the western counties, and that he referred him to the Governor for others in the eastern.

At the October session, 1781, of the Connecticut Assembly, a resolution, in the handwriting of Roger Sherman, was passed repealing an act of the previous Assembly authorizing a lottery at Hartford, the proceeds to be used for sinking $6,000,000 of the old Continental bills.

The severe and incessant labors performed by Mr. Sherman began at last to tell upon even his vigorous constitution. In a letter written by him to Governor Trumbull, April 30. 1777, he says, —

" I must leave Congress soon whether they (his associates) come or not, for my constitution will not admit of so close an application to business much longer, as I have been confined to for four months past."

The following letter contains some interesting statements as to the work of the American cruisers.

PHILADELPHIA, April 17th, 1777.

SIR, — . . . Our last letter from Dr Franklin and Mr Dean was dated the 6th of February. No treaty had been then concluded. Some probability that France and Spain would make war with Great Britain, but nothing certainly determined on. Both French and Spaniards favor our cause — Accounts from England are that the King's subjects have lost 1,800,000 pounds by the American cruisers. That insurance is at 28 per cent. That the Ministry intend to bend their force against New England to extirpate them and enslave the inhabitants of the Southern States. There has been talk that the enemy designs to come to this city but I don't think they will attempt it before they are reinforced. I wish some of the other delegates of Connecticut would attend Congress. The Confederation will be entered on next Monday and finished as soon as possible. I write in haste as the Hon Mr Collens of Rhode Island by whom I send this waits. I am with great regard

Your Honor's obedient humble Servant,

ROGER SHERMAN.

GOVERNOR TRUMBULL.

The following letter condemns the practice of trying by court martial citizens not connected with the army. It also refers to the battle in which Gen. Wooster lost his life.

PHILADELPHIA, May 21, 1777.

SIR, —The enclosed letters came to hand yesterday by the Post. I was in doubt whether it was best to send them back, or keep them until you return here. I hope it will not be long before a delegation arrives, that I may have leave of absence. I understand that an inhabitant of Connecticut has been lately executed by a sentence of a General Court Martial. I think it dangerous to admit citizens not connected with the army to be tried by a Court Martial. The resolution of Congress concerning spies does not warrant it. That respects such only as are not subjects of any of the States. It is easy to accuse any person with being a spy and so put his life into the power of a Court Martial. I have no doubt but that the person executed was an atrocious offender and deserved death, but if he was an inhabitant of the State he ought to have been tried before the Supreme Court.

We have nothing new here since my last. General Arnold is here. Congress has ordered the Quarter Master General to procure and present to him a horse properly caparisoned for his bravery in attacking the enemy who   to Danbury, in which action he had one horse killed under him and another wounded — A committee is appointed to consider what honors are due to the

memory of Gen. Wooster. There are different accounts of the day of his death. Some say Thursday, others Friday and others Saturday. I wish
that could be ascertained and that I could be informed of his age. I have had an account of the
election in the Hartford paper. A few lines from
you, with some account of the proceedings of the
Assembly will oblige your humble servant,

ROGER SHERMAN.

The HON. OLIVER WOLCOTT, Esq.

While the Americans were straining every nerve
to carry on the War of Independence, they were
distracted, not only by the controversy between
Connecticut and Pennsylvania, but by a dispute
about boundaries between New Hampshire and
New York. In a letter to Governor Trumbull, of
April 9, 1777, Mr. Sherman says: "The people in
the New Hampshire grants have petitioned Congress
to be acknowledged an independent State, and admitted to send delegates to Congress. The convention of New York has also remonstrated against
their proceedings, requesting Congress to interfere
for preventing the defection of the people on the
grants from that State. Nothing has been yet
acted on the affair." In the controversy, which
ended in the establishment of the State of Vermont,
Mr. Sherman took the part of the settlers.

In the first week of August, 1777, Mr. Sherman
attended, as a delegate from Connecticut, a convention of the States of New Hampshire, Massachusetts, Connecticut, Rhode Island, and New
York, held at Springfield, Mass., to consider the

state of the paper currency of said governments, the expediency of calling in the same by taxes or otherwise, and the best means of preventing the depreciation and counterfeiting of the same, also to consider the Acts relating to monopoly and oppression, and for preventing the transportation of certain articles from one State to another.

The convention recommended drawing in and sinking the bills of credit not upon interest, small change excepted, by taxes, or by exchanging them for Treasurer's notes, or for continental bills of credit, and not to emit any further bills, except for small change. The convention also recommended that the States provide for their own exigencies, and for the support of the war, as far as possible, by taxation, and in order to lighten the burdens and accommodate the taxes to the convenience of the people, and the more effectually to establish the credit of the continental currency, that these taxes be levied and assessed at the least once in every quarter of the year.

In reference to the monopoly Acts, the convention recommended their repeal, so far as they related to affixing the prices at which articles shall be sold, and penalties for not observing the same. At the same time provision was made that this repeal should not operate to the prejudice of the non-commissioned officers and soldiers. It also recommended the enactment of provisions against engrossing, and advised that the Acts against transporting certain articles out of the State be so framed that no unnecessary interruption be given to a free commercial intercourse between the States.

In a letter to William Williams, a member of Congress from Connecticut, dated Hartford, August 18, 1777, Mr. Sherman writes: "You have doubtless seen the result of the conference of the committees met at Springfield. I believe the measures recommended for supporting the credit of the paper currency, if adopted by all the States, will effectually conserve the end. I want to know the opinion of Congress upon it. If something is not immediately done, the currency will be worth nothing; but it may be easily supported by sinking the bills of the particular States, and taxing high and often to defray the expenses of the war. People in general are convinced of the necessity of it. Almost all dealing for common necessaries is carried on here by barter."

In a letter to Samuel Adams, of August 25, 1777, Mr. Sherman writes, after repeating statements similar to those in the letter to Mr. Williams: "I think it will be much better to carry on the war by taxes as much as can be borne, and the rest by loans in this country, than by foreign loans. It may be best to hire some money abroad to pay our debts due for the supplies that have been imported, and to pay for any further supplies that may be wanted, but not to sell Bills to merchants to import on their own account. We have very plentiful crops; people can now pay larger taxes, and seem generally willing to do it. I know no better way to preserve credit than to pay debts and not to run in debt more than is absolutely necessary. Confederation is likewise necessary to support the public credit of the United States, and if it is not done while the war lasts, I fear it will not be done at all."

Similar sentiments are repeated in a letter of September 22, 1777, from Mr. Sherman to William Williams. During the year 1777, Mr. Sherman was appointed on the following committees: February 11, on committee of seven to devise ways and means of supporting the credit of the continental currency, and supplying the treasury with money; March 13, on committee of five to confer with General Gates on the general state of affairs; April 23, on committee of six to consider means of speedily reinforcing General Washington's army; June 3, on committee of three to devise means to supply the army with shoes, hats, and shirts. June 5, Mr. Sherman was added to the Marine committee.

The campaign in the North this year ended in the battle of Saratoga, the turning-point in the Revolutionary War. When, on the 17th of October, 1777, General Burgoyne surrendered, General Wilkinson was despatched as a special messenger to carry the news to Congress. The messenger however travelled so slowly that the news reached Congress long before his arrival. Some one proposed that the messenger should be presented with a sword. Mr. Sherman suggested that a more appropriate present would be a pair of spurs.[1]

On the 15th of January, 1778, in accordance with the recommendations of Congress on the 22d of November, 1777, a convention of the States of New Hampshire, Massachusetts, Connecticut, Rhode

[1] Alexander Hamilton Papers, v. 26, p. 104.

Island, New York, New Jersey, and Pennsylvania, was held at New Haven, for the purpose of devising a plan for the regulation of prices. Mr. Sherman was a delegate from Connecticut, and was made chairman of the committee to prepare the report of the convention. This report was a very elaborate affair, and entered in great detail into a statement of prices recommended; but as the States generally declined to adopt it, this and similar efforts about the same time failed to have any practical effect.

In a letter to Benjamin Trumbull dated Philadelphia, August 18, 1778, Roger Sherman writes: "The affair of our currency is to be considered in Congress to-day. What will be done to restore and support its credit is uncertain. We can't lessen the quantity much while the army is kept up. I trust the fullest assurance ought and will be given for redeeming it in due time and for exchanging gold and silver for what shall be outstanding at the period fixed for its redemption at the expressed value. The whole that has been emitted is a little more than 60,000,000 dollars. I think a period of about 14 or 15 years should be fixed for sinking the whole. That taxes for about 6 million dollars per annum for 4 years, 5 million dollars for five years and four million dollars per annum for the residue of the period should be immediately laid to be collected as a sinking fund with liberty for each State to raise more than their annual quota and be allowed 6 per cent interest for the time they may anticipate the payment. That each of the States that have not called in their Bills do it immediately and refrain from further emissions and tax themselves for current expenses. Besides liberty may be given for the people to bring in as many of the Bills as they please into loan offices, with assurance that the whole that is brought in shall be burnt. That all unnecessary expenses be retrenched and the best economy introduced. That the future expense of the war be defrayed as far as may be by taxes and the residue by emissions — and if the war ceases this year, which I think not improbable, our finances may soon be put on a good footing. Provision ought to be made in the meantime by each State to prevent injustice to creditors and salary men."

On the 15th of October, 1778, Roger Sherman wrote to Governor Trumbull as follows: —

" The affair of finance is yet unfinished. The formation of a Board of Treasury is determined on but the officers are not yet appointed. To-morrow is assigned for their nomination. The members of Congress are united in the great object of securing the liberties and independence of the States; but are sometimes divided in opinion about particular measures. The Assembly of New York in their late session did not ratify the Confederation, nor has it been done by Maryland and Delaware States. These and some other of the States are dissatisfied that the western ungranted lands should be claimed by particular States, which they think ought to be the common interest of the United States, they being defended at the common expense. They further say that if some provision is not now made for securing lands for the troops who serve during the war, they shall have to pay large sums to the States who claim the vacant lands to supply their quotas of the troops.   Perhaps if the Assembly of Connecticut should resolve to make grants to their own troops and those raised by the State of Rhode Island, New Jersey, Delaware and Maryland in the lands south of Lake Erie and west of the land in controversy with Pennsylvania, free of any purchase money or quit rents to the Government of Connecticut, it might be satisfactory to those States, and be no damage to the State of Connecticut.   A tract of thirty miles east and west across the State would be sufficient for the purpose, and that being settled under good regulations would enhance the value of the rest; these would not be claimed as Crown lands, both the fee and jurisdiction having been granted to the Governor and Company of Connecticut.

" ROGER SHERMAN."

During the year 1778, Mr. Sherman was appointed on a committee of three on instructions to commissioners to foreign courts; on a committee of five to consider the report of the committee on finance; on committee of three on plan for procuring reinforcements to supply the place of men whose term of service would expire in the winter.

On the 12th of October, 1778, Congress passed resolutions recommending the States to suppress theatres, horse-racing, gaming, etc., and that the army officers discountenance profaneness and vice among the soldiers.   On the 16th of October, 1778, Congress passed a vote that no actor or encourager of plays should hold office under the United States.

The attempt of certain New Hampshire towns to withdraw from the jurisdiction of that State called forth the following patriotic letter from Mr. Sherman to Elisha Paine, October 31, 1778: —

SIR, — I take the liberty to address you on a subject which to me appears to be of a very dangerous and alarming nature. I am informed that the inhabitants in a number of towns in the State of New Hampshire on the east side of the Connecticut river, have withdrawn from the jurisdiction of that State and joined with the people on the grants on the west side of the river in forming a distinct State. The strength of the United States lies in their union. Their joint efforts under the smiles of Divine Providence have made a successful resistance to the power of Great Britain aided by foreign mercenaries; but if intestine divisions and contentions take place among them, will they not become an easy prey to a formidable enemy? I shall give no opinion in the case of the people on the New Hampshire grants upon the west side of Connecticut river, whether the States of New York or New Hampshire have the best right of jurisdiction over them or whether in case they belong to New Hampshire, and that State neglected to claim and support their jurisdiction in opposition to the claim of New York, it gave the people a right to form themselves into a distinct State, as these questions I suppose must at a proper time have a judicial determination. But for the people inhabiting within the known and acknowledged boundaries of any of the United States, to separate without the consent of the State to which they belong appears to me a very unjustifiable violation of the social compact, and pregnant with the most ruinous consequences. Sir, I don't know whether you live in one of the revolted towns, but as you are in that vicinity, I trust from acquaintance with your love of order and regard to the welfare of your country, you will use your influence to discourage everything that in your opinion may be prejudicial to the true interests of these States. If the present constitution of any of the States is not so perfect as could be wished, it may and probably will, by common consent be amended; but in present circumstances it appears to me indispensably necessary that civil government should be vigorously supported.

I hope you will excuse the freedom I have taken on this occasion, as my sole motive is the public good.   I am, with great esteem and regard,

Your humble servant

ROGER SHERMAN.

During the year 1779, Mr. Sherman was chosen on the following committees, viz.: on Indian affairs; to consider the report of the Board of Treasury on finance; on the treasury; to devise further ways and means for supplying the treasury.

On the 23d of June, 1780, he was chosen a member of the Treasury Board.   During the year 1780, he was also chosen on the following committees, viz.: on the western frontiers; to estimate the expenses of the present and the ensuing year, and to make provision for the same; on the instructions of Maryland to its delegates about the Act of Confederation.

During the year 1780, Mr. Sherman wrote the following letters to Governor Trumbull on the subject of the finances.

PHILADELPHIA, July 22d, 1780.

. . . I am sorry that the State of Connecticut have had occasion to emit so large a sum in Bills of Credit previous to their being furnished with the bills prepared by order of Congress, but am glad to hear that they have laid so large a tax to be paid in the new bills. I esteem that to be a very wise measure, to introduce the bills into circulation with full credit, and ought to be imitated by all the other States. I am fully persuaded that no way can be devised, in our circumstances, to support the value of a paper currency, but by taxing to the full amount of our expenditures after having emitted a sufficient sum for a medium of trade, which is limited by the resolution of Congress to ten millions of dollars for the thirteen States, and if the particular States extend their emission beyond their quotas of that sum, it will in my opinion give a fatal blow to the credit of the whole paper currency, and involve us in worse evils than we have heretofore experienced; therefore I think that no supposed necessity, or other consideration whatever, should induce any State in the least degree to exceed the limit fixed by the United States, by the resolution of the 18th of March last.

I am sensible that it was necessary to make some
state emissions, before those Bills were prepared,
but then I think they should be considered as part
of their quotas of the ten million dollars. The
resources of this Country are great, and may be
drawn out in so equable a manner by the wisdom
of the Legislatures of the several States as fully to
answer the exigencies of our affairs, without being
very burthensome to the people. It may be necessary to run in debt for some foreign articles, but
I think not for any that are to be procured in this
Country.

PHILADELPHIA, July 22d, 1780.

. . . It is with concern we observe the exigencies of the Public have been such as obliged
our State to issue large emissions of Paper Bills,
which with what will issue in pursuance of the resolution of the 18th of March last, may endanger
the public credit. The only way to avoid this evil
is speedily to draw in those bills by taxes, and not
suffer them on any account to reissue. Paper
money does its office when it goes out in payment,
and ought to be among the people as a medium of
trade, no longer than to find its way into their
pockets, and, like private security, should be destroyed when returned into the office it issued from.
This is doing business in sight of the people, and
every man who pays his tax knows he does it [in]
discharge of much of his public debt. But to me,
[to] issue bills taken in by loans and taxes, ac-
cumulates the public debt in a way not open to
the inspection of the people. They see the bills

are not redeemed, and are told they never will be. The credit of the State is scrupled and depreciation ensues. The people lose their confidence in Government. The laws are enervated, military operations prevented, justice impeded, trade embarrassed, the morals of the people corrupted, men of integrity in office abused and resigning, whilst peculators ride in coaches. These evils and the sources from whence they arise, so lately experienced, all serve to point out the way to avoid them in future. The design of Congress in limiting the amount of circulating bills within the United States will be wholly defeated by emissions from particular States, unless their amount is limited within the bound, and issued in lieu of the quotas assigned by Congress, and be in fact drawn in before the general currency issues.

PHILADELPHIA, Aug. 22, 1780.

. . . If every State would tax themselves to the extent of their abilities, relieving the poor as far as possible, we should find it the best resource in our power to obtain supplies, and save the Continent from that enthralment of debt which may be expected from loans. This doctrine, though trite, is no less important than true, and deserves the most serious attention. The current expenses of the war are chiefly of our own services, provisions, and manufactures, which do not much exceed our annual exports in time of peace. This alone is demonstration that our internal resources are nearly equal to our necessities and might with proper management be so applied as to prevent an enormous

8

national debt to foreigners, who may hereafter claim
the honor and merit of our whole salvation as due to
them, and surprise us with unexpected demands.

The news of the surrender of Lord Cornwallis
was sent to Governor Trumbull in the following
letter by Mr. Sherman and Mr. Law.

PHILADELPHIA, Oct. 25th, 1781.

SIR, — We have the honor now to transmit to
your Excellency an official account of the surrender of Lord Cornwallis and the army under his
command. The dispatches from General Washington were received yesterday morning, and at
two o'clock in the afternoon Congress went in a
body to the Lutheran Church where Divine service, suitable to the occasion, was performed by
the Rev. Mr. Duffield, one of the chaplains of
Congress. The Supreme Executive Council and
Assembly of this State, the Minister of France and
his Secretary, and a great number of the citizens
attended. In the evening the city was illuminated.
This great event, we hope, will prove a happy
presage of a complete reduction of the British
forces in these States, and prepare the way for the
establishment of an honorable peace.

Mr. Sherman was continued in Congress, by annual election, from September, 1774, to November,
1781. On October 13, 1783, he was again elected
for another year, making eight years of service in
the Continental Congress.

In May, 1783, Mr. Sherman and Richard Law,
Sherman's associate on the bench of the Superior

Court, were appointed, by the General Assembly of Connecticut, a committee " to revise the Statute Laws of this State, and make such alterations, additions, exclusions, and amendments, as they shall judge proper and expedient, collecting together into one all the statutes that have been made upon the same subject, reducing the whole into one regular system or code, in alphabetical order, and lay the same as soon as possible before the General Assembly."

This work was completed and laid before the General Assembly at its October session, 1783. At this session the same committee was directed " to continue to revise the laws of this State heretofore in force, to form a memorandum or table of such variations, abridgements, or enlargements, as they may think convenient, and lay the same before this Assembly, at their next meeting." This final revision was adopted by the General Assembly at an adjourned session, held for that purpose, at New Haven, January 8, 1784.

The following is a letter from Mr. Sherman to Mr. Law on the subject of the revision of the laws of Connecticut.

NEW HAVEN, July 25th, 1783.

DEAR SIR, — I received your letter with the last laws enclosed. I have now taken the whole of the act in Page 235 into my code; the first and last paragraphs cover civil actions and the residue with some additions, under the head of bail, which I have endeavored to regulate both in civil and criminal cases. I insert the act Page 608, next after the laws for settling testate and intestate estates, omitting the words, that respect future confiscations.

The maintaining the Light-house I have left for you. Perhaps it may come under the head of Ships or shipping. I have now completed my part of the laws, except a few blanks left for your opinion. I sent you a list of those I had then determined to take on. I don't know but I have included some others since. I have taken in under the head of Foreigners, four acts, viz: To prevent mischief, Infractions of the Law of Nations — Rendering speedy justice to those in alliance, and To prevent their holding lands. I have taken the Scale Act, and whatever concerns depreciation, and everything relating to dissenters. I think it would be well to make some additions to the Laws respecting Societies for regulating several Societies within the same bounds, of which I send a sketch.

I don't hear of the arrival of the Definite Treaty. I should not think it best to call the Assembly until that is received, with the recommendation of Congress upon it.

I have looked over the remaining Laws and arranged them as follows, that you may see which I have not taken. Mine contains 98 laws (those under the Title Lands but one) though containing several additions.

When you have arranged and revised your part, it will be best for us to meet and inspect the whole. I am sir, with esteem and respect,

Your humble servant,
ROGER SHERMAN.

P. S.   I have added a clause in the act for regulating civil actions concerning joint contracts that serving the process on those who belong to this State, shall be sufficient notice to obtain judgment against all.   Then follow some remarks about the regulation of New Gate prison and the List of Laws referred to in the above letter.

Copies of some of these laws having been sent to John Dickinson, he wrote the following letter of acknowledgment: —

SIR, — I feel myself indebted to you for your obliging politeness in furnishing me with copies of some of your laws; and I was sincerely sorry, that indisposition prevented me from presenting in person the thanks, which I now beg, you will be pleased to accept.

When you return to the Northward, I hope, I shall have the pleasure of seeing you, and should much regret your passing through this City, without my having that satisfaction.   With great and sincere esteem, I am, Sir,

Your most obedient and much obliged,

humble servant,

JOHN DICKINSON.

PHILADELPHIA, January 15th, 1784.
The HONORABLE ROGER SHERMAN, Esquire.

In January, 1784, Roger Sherman and James Wadsworth were authorized to convey to the United States all the land claimed by Connecticut lying westward of the west line of Pennsylvania, excepting a certain tract reserved for the use of

the State, and " to satisfy the officers and privates
in the Connecticut Line of the Continental army
the lands to which they are entitled by the Resolves of Congress."

On the 20th of January, 1784, Mr. Sherman
wrote to Lyman Hall, the Governor of Georgia,
the following account of the ratification of the
treaty of peace, and the necessity of an impost tax
to support the credit of government.

ANNAPOLIS, 20th of January, 1784.

SIR, — I sincerely congratulate you upon the
return of peace, whereby the rights we have long
contended for are fully established, on very honorable and beneficial terms.

The definitive treaty of peace between Great
Britain and the United States was ratified in Congress last week, and the ratification forwarded to
New York to go by a French packet which was to
sail this day. It was unanimously ratified by nine
States, no more being represented. A proclamation and recommendations pursuant thereto have
been agreed to, and ordered to be forwarded to the
several States by the Secretary. There are but
eight States now represented, one of the members
from Delaware went home last Saturday, on account of sickness in his family. There are several
important matters to be transacted interesting to
all the States. I hope that members will come on
from Georgia as soon as possible. The impost on
foreign goods recommended by Congress for raising a revenue for payment of the interest of the
money borrowed on the credit of the United States,

is fully complied with by the States of Massachusetts, New Jersey, Pennsylvania, Delaware, Maryland and Virginia; New Hampshire has likewise
agreed to it in a committee of the whole, but the
act was not completed when the delegates from
that State came away. The Assemblies of Connecticut and New York are now sitting. Congress
are in hopes to adjourn by the first of May, and
have a recess till next fall, in case all the States
transmit their act for enabling Congress to levy
and collect the duties personally for them to make
an ordinance for carrying it into effect, that being
a matter of the utmost importance for supporting
the national credit of the United States, and doing
justice to the public creditors both at home and in
Europe; and I apprehend it will be impracticable
to raise a sufficient revenue in the ordinary way of
taxing. Raising money by imposts takes it at the
fountain head and the consumer pays it insensibly
and without murmuring. I wish the result of your
State on that requisition may be transmitted as
soon as possible. The disposition and settlement
of the western territory is another object that will
come under the consideration of Congress. The
State of Virginia has ceded to the United States all
the lands claimed by that State northwest of the
Ohio on terms acceptable to Congress. Enclosed
is a copy of the act of Massachusetts for enabling
Congress to levy an impost which I think is well
guarded. I have also enclosed a letter from Governor Trumbull on public service. I am with
great esteem and respect,

Your humble servant
ROGER SHERMAN

The following letter from Benjamin Huntington to Roger Sherman gives an account of the adoption of the Revised Laws, and of the election of Mr. Sherman as Mayor of New Haven.

NEW HAVEN, Feb. 11th, 1784.

HONORED SIR, — I have been so happy as to board at your house since the session of assembly which rises this day having finished the revisal of the Laws with some alteration from the draughts made by the committee. Where the committee's alterations were not agreed to, the old Statutes are to stand as in time passed. The pay of the Supreme Court is not raised nor any alteration in Court or Counties excepting Colchester which is annexed [to] New London County. The impost not yet granted but much nearer to it than in October. The people at large begin to see their interest in the measure and I hope that by the May next they will be undeceived; about one third of the lower house are in favor of it now.

The New Haven and New London City bills are passed and the freemen of the city of New Haven are now in the upper house of the State house choosing their City magistrates and have made choice of a member of Congress for the Mayor and Deacon Howell, Deacon Bishop, Deacon Austin and Mr Isaac Beers are chosen Aldermen. Your little son, Oliver, hearing that his Papa was chosen Mayor was concerned and inquired who was to ride the Mare?

Mrs Sherman received some addresses on the subject of the election and by way of answer has fed some hungry bellies whilst others wanted money to buy powder to fire in honor of the Lord Mayor elect. Thus the emoluments of office are felt by her in your absence. The cannon are this moment firing in a most tremendous manner on the subject. I wish you could hear it. I am with esteem and respect

Your most humble servant,

BENJ. HUNTINGTON.

HONORABLE ROGER SHERMAN Esqr.

The following letter from Mr. Sherman to William Williams, dated May 4, 1784, gives the views of Mr. Sherman on an import duty, and some other matters.

ANNAPOLIS, 4th May, 1784.

DEAR SIR, — I received your letter of the 19th of April, yesterday with Mr Loomis's papers. · Shall attend to his affairs when I return to Philadelphia. I am obliged to you for the information contained in the close of your letter respecting the politics of our State. The States who have agreed to the impost recommended by Congress, are N. Hampshire, Massachusetts, N. Jersey, Pennsylvania, Delaware, Maryland, Virginia, and South Carolina; these have fully complied. We have not heard what New York and North Carolina have done in the late sessions of their Legislatures, but their delegates say that there is no reason to doubt but that they have complied with the requisition. Georgia, we find by the news papers has lately appointed delegates, but they have not arrived in Congress, and we are not informed what that State has done respecting the impost. Rhode Island delegates think their State will be the last that agrees to it, but that the last requisition is less exceptionable than the former. It appears to me that a general impost will be the best way for raising a revenue for the interest of the national debt, though I never wish to have the power in Congress to raise money extended beyond what may be necessary for the present debt, but never to raise any for current expenses. I am not able to furnish you with the journals of Congress for the last year, the volume is not completed. I understand by the Secretary that he has sent to Governor Trumbull all that have been printed. General Wadsworth and I in our late joint letter gave you an account of the principal matters done and expected to be done by Congress this session. All the States except Delaware and Georgia are now represented. It is not likely that Congress will agree to any answer to the address on commutation; the members are divided as to the style and tone in which it should be answered. Some were for transmitting a copy of the answer given to Massachusetts, or make an answer nearly like it. Others thought it would be best only to state what had been done and leave it to the House to make the inferences, as was done in the draught reported by the last committee of which we transmitted a copy, that would have been agreed to, if the question had been put without the yeas and nays, as several members told me they would have voted for it, in that case who now voted in the negative. I don't find any members that think that the commutation can be rescinded, or avoided without a violation of public faith, a majority approve of the measure.

I hope the western territory will sink a considerable part of the national debt; it is proposed to apply it only to the principal. You will see the plan for establishing new States, and the requisition for payment of arrears of interest and the current expenses, and a recommendation to the States lately passed for opposing the system adopted by Great Britain respecting commerce, in the printed journals that will be transmitted to the Governor. I sent some extracts to the Governor from the letters of our Ministers in Europe for his information and to be communicated to the General Assembly. I hope none of them will be published in the newspapers, as some things of that kind have been very improperly done in a neighboring State; Congress has lately laid an injunction to taking or publishing extracts from such letters without express permission.

The act of the General Assembly of our State respecting allowance for coast guards &c is now before a grand committee not reported on. We have not laid the act for making a cession of western territory before Congress, they have renewed the requisition to the States for that purpose, and we shall offer a cession a few days hence. I hope, Sir, that you or one of the other delegates will come forward to attend the committee of the States to be left in the recess of Congress. I am, Sir, with the most perfect respect and esteem

Your humble servant

ROGER SHERMAN.

HON. WILLIAM WILLIAMS Esqr.

Mr. Sherman was annually appointed a member of the Council of Safety of the State of Connecticut from 1777 to 1779, and again in 1782. There is no record of the proceedings of the Council, but it appears that Mr. Sherman was present at a great many meetings in the last half of 1777, and in the first half of 1779.

At the October session, 1785, of the General Assembly of Connecticut, Mr. Sherman was appointed one of a committee of five to inspect the copper coin manufactured in that State.

From November, 1784, till his election to the Constitutional Convention in 1787, Mr. Sherman enjoyed a period of comparative repose, devoting himself to the performance of his duties as Judge of the Superior Court, and as Mayor of the City of New Haven.

The following letter from Richard Henry Lee is of interest, as showing his regard for Mr. Sherman. He was mistaken in supposing that Mr. Sherman was not a member of Congress in 1780.

CHANTILLY IN VIRGINIA, Jan. 22, 1780.

DEAR SIR, — The very high sense that I entertain of your sound and virtuous patriotism will by no means suffer me to pass you by when I am distributing a pamphlet which I think it imports the friends of America to know the contents of. I apprehend that the faction in Congress would long since have made the most essential parts public, had not concealment been necessary to cover their own misdeeds. It was certainly due to the honor of Congress as well as to that of individuals, that the public should be disabused in points of great moment wherein they had been most boldly and wickedly mislead.

You may observe Sir, that I have taken care to omit such parts, as would if published, have tended to offend States that are now friendly to us. These things would have rendered the work much more complete to prove the vileness of that libel published on the 5th of December 1778, but I am sure there is no person injured by that, but who would rather choose to continue suffering such injury than to expose it by means that would be hurtful to the community.

It gave me great concern, my friend, to hear that you are not in Congress. I lament for the public good which I am sure is injured thereby. My mistake is great indeed if there ever was a time when more wisdom and virtue were wanting in the Great Council of America. I hope, dear sir, that it will not be long before you are again restored to that Assembly. Be so kind as present my best respects to Mr Hosmer and Mr Ellsworth and let them have the reading of this pamphlet.

It will give me pleasure to know that this letter with its enclosure has reached you safely, for this purpose a line directed for me to the care of the Post Master at Leeds Town in Westmoreland County, Virginia will find me. I am, dear Sir, with high esteem and great affection,

most sincerely yours,
RICHARD HENRY LEE.

The following is a letter from Roger Sherman

introducing Thomas Jefferson to Dr. Stiles, the President of Yale College : —

ANNAPOLIS, 11th May, 1784.

SIR, — I take the liberty to introduce to you the Honorable Thomas Jefferson Esqr. late Governor of Virginia, now a Minister Plenipotentiary of the United States for negotiating treaties of commerce with Great Britain and several other European Powers, in conjunction with Mr Adams, and Dr. Franklin. He is the bearer of this letter, and is now on his way to Boston, there to embark for Europe. He wishes to gain what acquaintance he can with the country as he passes through. He is a gentleman of much philosophical as well as political knowledge — and I doubt not you will be very agreeably entertained with his conversation. You will be pleased to introduce him to such other gentlemen in the City of New Haven as you may think proper. I am, Sir, with great esteem & respect

Your humble Servant,

ROGER SHERMAN.

DOCTR STILES.

CHAPTER VIII.

THE CONSTITUTIONAL CONVENTION.

THE Articles of Confederation provided no means of supplying the treasury of the government except by requisitions on the State governments. As the pressure of war was removed, the States paid less and less attention to those requisitions, until at last it became apparent that, unless Congress was clothed with adequate powers of taxa-. tion, the Union must fall to pieces. The remedy proposed was to give Congress the power to levy and collect a small tax on imports. To this all of the States consented but Rhode Island; and as the Articles of Confederation provided that no alteration should be made in them without the consent of the legislature of every State, it was in the power of the smallest State to frustrate the plans of all the others. In the Congress of 1782, a serious effort was made to change the decision of Rhode Island, but in vain.

Nothing more remained but to call a convention for the formation of a government truly national, to take the place of the league of States which had proved such a wretched failure. But it was very difficult, even with disunion and anarchy staring them in the face, to get the States to consent to such a convention. In the Congress of 1783,

Alexander Hamilton prepared a series of resolutions, setting forth the defects of the confederate government, and recommending the calling of a convention of the States to remedy those defects, and to clothe the government with such powers as experience had shown were essential to its existence. These resolutions were not presented for the reason endorsed on his draft in these words, " intended to be submitted to Congress in seventeen hundred and eighty-three, but abandoned for want of support." The fact is that, as Mr. Gerry stated in the Constitutional Convention of 1787, " the States were intoxicated with the idea of their sovereignty."

The Confederation was not only destitute of the power of taxation, it had no control of commerce. It was this latter defect which led to those movements which resulted in the Constitutional Convention of 1787. The first step in this direction was the attempt of Virginia and Maryland to establish a code of commercial regulations between themselves. This attempt made apparent the necessity of a uniform system to regulate the commerce of the entire country. Accordingly, in January, 1786, the legislature of Virginia passed a resolution to be sent to all the other States, inviting them to send deputies to a convention, for the purpose " of considering how far a uniform system of taxation in their commercial intercourse and regulations might be ncessary to their common interest and permanent harmony."

Four States, Connecticut, Maryland, South Carolina, and Georgia, failed to elect delegates.

The others elected delegates, but only those of five States, Virginia, Delaware, Pennsylvania, New Jersey, and New York, attended the convention, which assembled at Annapolis, September 11, 1786. Those who met were too few to accomplish the task in hand. But they did what, in the end, proved to be far better. They adopted an address, written by Alexander Hamilton, setting forth the evils afflicting the country, and recommending, as the only adequate remedy for them, that the States unite " in the appointment of commissioners to meet at Philadelphia on the second Monday in May next, to take into consideration the situation of the United States, to devise such further provisions as shall appear to them necessary to render the Constitution of the federal government adequate to the exigencies of the Union, and to report such an Act for that purpose to the United States in Congress assembled, as, when agreed to by them, and afterwards confirmed by the legislature of every State will effectually provide for the same."

This address, though nominally made to the legislatures of those States which the delegates represented, was sent to Congress, and to the legislatures of all the States. Fortunately, its suggestion was followed by all the States but Rhode Island, and the Constitutional Convention assembled at Philadelphia in May, 1787.

Among the many men, illustrious for character and public services, who composed the convention, two stand pre-eminent. Washington, whose name alone was with the people the most powerful argument in favor of any cause which he espoused, was made president of the convention. Franklin, the Nestor of the convention, bending under the weight of eighty-one years, was the most picturesque figure in that assembly. Two years before, he had returned from Europe, where his abilities as a scientific discoverer, as a diplomatist, and as a writer, were universally recognized, and were honored with the highest academic distinction which the universities of Oxford and Edinburgh had to bestow. Three members of the Stamp Act Convention of 1765 were there, — William S. Johnson, John Rutledge, and John Dickinson, the last the framer of the Articles of Confederation. A large proportion of those present had been members of the Continental Congress. The youthful and brilliant Hamilton, already distinguished as soldier, orator, and lawyer, and soon to take rank among the greatest of constructive statesmen, was one of the delegates from New York, and gave his earnest support to the cause of a strong, national government, of which Madison and Wilson were the foremost champions.

The delegates from Connecticut were Roger Sherman, William Samuel Johnson, and Oliver Ellsworth. Mr. Sherman was, next to Franklin, the oldest member of the convention, being at that time sixty-six years of age. In length and variety of public service Franklin alone surpassed him. In clearness of perception, soundness of judgment, and steadfastness of purpose, he had no superior in the convention. Johnson, who was only six years the junior of Sherman, was born at Stratford,

ᛁ.

Conn., and was the son of an Episcopal clergyman.
His scholarship had secured him the degree of
Doctor of Laws from Oxford. He was one of the
most learned lawyers and one of the most eloquent
orators in America. He spent nearly five years in
England in charge of an important law suit for the
State of Connecticut; and while there formed the
friendship of the famous Dr. Johnson, and associ-
ated freely with the leading statesmen of the Whig
party. He lacked the nerve necessary for a revolutionary period; and when the war broke out, he
retired from public life and devoted himself to
study. But notwithstanding he was an Episcopa-
lian in a severely Puritan commonwealth, and a
non-combatant among a people famous for their
fighting qualities, such was the respect entertained
for his integrity, abilities, and patriotism, that, as
soon as the war was over, he was placed in the most
important public positions. In the convention,
though not a frequent speaker, he always spoke
with marked ability, and was listened to with respectful attention. He was chairman of the committee of five, of which Hamilton, G. Morris,
Madison, and King were the other members, "to
revise the style of, and arrange the articles agreed
to by the House."

Oliver Ellsworth was several years younger than
his associates, having been born at Windsor, Conn.,
in 1745. A graduate of Princeton, he studied law
with Governor Griswold and Judge Root, and
speedily rose to the front rank of his profession.
He had been a member of the State legislature and
of the Continental Congress. He was an earnest

and forcible speaker, and in his business qualities, strong practical sense, and decided religious character, he resembled Roger Sherman, whom, as he told John Adams, he made his model. He was an effective debater in the convention; but his fame rests chiefly on the services which he afterwards rendered in the United States Senate, where, as John Adams says of him, he was "the firmest pillar of Washington's whole administration." His most enduring monument is the Judiciary Act of 1789. In 1796, he was appointed by Washington Chief Justice of the Supreme Court of the United States, and, in 1799, he was sent as envoy extraordinary to Paris, where, in connection with his colleagues, he negotiated a treaty with France.

During the latter part of Mr. Sherman's service in the Continental Congress he became strongly impressed with the necessity of a radical change in the Articles of Confederation. The following propositions found among his manuscripts were prepared by him, as embodying the amendments which he deemed necessary to be made to the existing government.

"That, in addition to the legislative powers vested in congress by the articles of confederation, the legislature of the United States be authorised to make laws to regulate the commerce of the United States with foreign nations, and among the several states in the union; to impose duties on foreign goods and commodities imported into the United States, and on papers passing through the post office, for raising a revenue, and to regulate the collection thereof, and apply the same to the payment of the debts due from the United States, and for supporting the government, and other necessary charges of the Union.

" To make laws binding on the people of the United States, and on the courts of law, and other magistrates and officers, civil and military, within the several states, in all cases which concern the common interests of the United States: but not to interfere with the government of the individual states, in matters of internal police which respect the government of such states only, and wherein the general welfare of the United States is not affected.

" That the laws of the United States ought, as far as may be consistent with the common interest of the Union, to be carried into execution by the judiciary and executive officers of the respective states, wherein the execution thereof is required.

" That the legislature of the United States be authorised to institute one supreme tribunal, and such other tribunals as they may judge necessary for the purpose aforesaid, and ascertain their respective powers and jurisdiction.

" That the legislatures of the individual states ought not to possess a right to emit bills of credit for a currency, or to make any tender laws for the payment or discharge of debts or contracts, in any manner different from the agreement of the parties, unless for payment of the value of the thing contracted for, in current money, agreeable to the standard that shall be allowed by the legislature of the United States, or in any manner to obstruct or impede the recovery of debts, whereby the interests of foreigners, or the citizens of any other state, may be affected.

"That the eighth article of the confederation ought to be amended, agreeably to the recommendation of congress of the — day of —.[1]

"That, if any state shall refuse or neglect to furnish its quota of supplies, upon requisition made by the legislature of the United States, agreeably to the articles of the Union, that the said legislature be authorised to order the same to be levied and collected of the inhabitants of such state, and to make such rules and orders as may be necessary for that purpose.

"That the legislature of the United States have power to make laws for calling forth such aid from the people, from time to time, as may be necessary to assist the civil officers in the execution of the laws of the United States; and annex suitable penalties to be inflicted in case of disobedience.

"That no person shall be liable to be tried for any criminal offence, committed within any of the United States, in any other state than that wherein the offence shall be committed, nor be deprived of the privilege of trial by a jury, by virtue of any law of the United States."

When Mr. Sherman entered the Constitutional Convention, he doubtless believed that some such amendments as were embodied in these propositions were all that was necessary to cure the defects of the existing Confederation. His associates

---

[1] Making the contribution of each State to the national treasury to be according to the number of inhabitants, instead of the value Date should be April 18, 1783.

from Connecticut agreed with him in this opinion. Substantially, this was the opinion of nearly one half of the convention. The other half were in favor of setting aside the Articles of Confederation altogether, and of substituting in their place a strong national government. While, in a general way, it was true that the convention was about equally divided between these parties, there was no such thing as a party organization among them. There were all shades of nationalists, and all shades of confederates, and some were partly the one, and partly the other. A more independent body of men never met together. While tenacious of their own opinions, they were largely men of open minds, and ready to change their opinions on the reception of further light. Their debates display remarkable ability, but, on the whole, what most impresses one is the sincere and earnest desire evinced to devise a scheme of government which should most largely promote the happiness and welfare of the people. The great struggle between the nationalists and the confederates took place over the question of representation in the national legislature. The story of that struggle, and of the compromise in which it ended, forms the most interesting and important part of the proceedings of the convention.

The debates in the Constitutional Convention divide themselves into three distinct periods: —

First. The debates in the Committee of the Whole on the state of the Union, which extended from May 30 to June 19.

From May 30 to June 13, the committee had

under consideration the fifteen resolutions of Randolph, which were proposed, and referred to the Committee of the Whole, on May 29, and which contained the leading principles which he thought should prevail in a National Constitution.

June 13, the committee reported in favor of the Randolph resolutions as they had been amended in debate. This may be called the national plan.

June 15, Mr. Patterson presented the resolutions known as the New Jersey or confederate plan. This plan was referred to the Committee of the Whole, and the national plan recommitted. These plans were debated till June 19, when the committee voted to rise and report in favor of the national plan.

Second. The debates in the convention on the national plan, which extended from June 19 to July 26, when a committee of detail of five members was appointed to prepare and report a Constitution conformable to the twenty-three resolutions adopted by the convention.

Third. The debates in the convention on the detailed plan, which extended from August 6 to September 16, when the Constitution was adopted. September 17, a few changes were made, the Constitution was signed, and the convention adjourned.

In the first period, which lasted only twenty days, the debates were brief and comparatively calm.

In the second period, which lasted thirty-seven days, the great struggle between the national and confederate parties took place which ended in the adoption of the compromise plan.

In the third period, which lasted forty-two days, the debate on details, which exhibited great diversity of opinion, was conducted without asperity. The slavery question excited a momentary feeling, but was soon disposed of.

The leaders of the nationalists in the debates were Madison, Wilson, Hamilton, and Gouverneur Morris. The leaders of the confederates were Patterson, Lansing, and Luther Martin. Those most active in effecting compromises between the contending parties were Sherman, Ellsworth, Franklin, and Dickinson.

The point on which there was the bitterest and most prolonged controversy was, as I have stated, the rule of suffrage in the legislature. The resolution on this subject was the second on Mr. Randolph's list. But when it was reached, at the request of Mr. Read, of Delaware, the consideration of it was postponed, " as the deputies from Delaware were restrained by their commission from assenting to any change in the rule of suffrage, and, in case such a change should be fixed on, it might become their duty to retire from the convention."

Accordingly the second resolution was not taken up till the other resolutions had been acted on. This second resolution provided " that the rights of suffrage in the national legislature ought to be proportioned to the quotas of contribution, or to the number of free inhabitants, as the one or the other rule may seem best in different cases." On the 9th of June the debate on the second reso-

lution began.   Mr. Brearly and Mr. Patterson,
of New Jersey, spoke in opposition, and Mr.
Wilson in favor of it.   June 11 the debate was
resumed.

Mr. Sherman proposed that the proportion of
suffrage in the first branch (the House of Representatives) should be according to the respective
numbers of free inhabitants; and that in the second
branch, or Senate, each State should have one vote
and no more.   He said, as the States would remain possessed of certain individual rights, each
State ought to be able to protect itself; otherwise
a few large States will rule the rest.   The House
of Lords in England, he observed, had certain
particular rights under the Constitution, and hence
they have an equal vote with the House of Commons, that they may be able to defend their
rights.

This was the first direct presentation of that compromise plan by which the conflicting claims of
the large and the small States were finally adjusted.
Twice before it had been suggested, in debates on
other questions.   May 31, during the discussion on
the mode of electing Senators, Mr. Sherman expressed himself in favor of an election of one member by each of the State legislatures.   June 2,
while discussing the mode of electing the Executive, Mr. Dickinson said, "As to the point of representation in the national legislature, as it might
affect States of different sizes, it must probably
end in mutual concession.   He hoped that each
State would retain an equal voice, at least in one
branch of the national legislature."   This plan

was modified in some of its details, as we shall hereafter see, but the compromise, as finally adopted, was, in substance, representation according to population in the House of Representatives, and equal representation of the States in the Senate. Roger Sherman was thus the first to propose this important compromise, and his merit consists in this, that, while the advocates of a strong general government were in favor of a representation in both Houses of the legislature based on population, and the advocates of a weak general government were in favor of an equal representation of the States in both Houses, Sherman, though sympathizing with the latter class, saw, at this early day, that it would be impossible to form a general government unless each side yielded a portion of its claims. The national principle must prevail in one House, and the confederate principle in the other. (To Roger Sherman belongs the credit, not only of introducing in the convention this compromise, which, as we have seen, was in substance the plan proposed by him eleven years before, in the debate on the Articles of Confederation, but also of bearing the brunt of the contest in its favor, through a long and severe struggle, till it was finally adopted.)

After a brief discussion, it was decided by a vote of nine to two that representation in the House should be in proportion to the whole number of free inhabitants and three-fifths of the slaves. New Jersey and Delaware were the only States voting in the negative.

Mr. Sherman then moved that the question be

taken whether each State shall have one vote in the second branch. "Everything," he said, "depended on this. The smaller States would never agree to the plan on any other principle than an equality of suffrage in this branch." Mr. Ellsworth seconded the motion, and the vote was five yeas to six nays.

Mr. Wilson then moved that the right of suffrage in the Senate ought to be according to the same rule as in the first branch. On this motion the vote was six yeas to five nays.

In the resolutions reported to the convention on June 13 by the Committee of the Whole, the national principle prevailed, except in the provision for electing the Senators by the State legislatures. The debate on those resolutions began June 20, and then the advocates of the confederate plan returned to the contest with renewed vigor. In the Committee of the Whole the resolution in favor of two Houses of the legislature was adopted without debate. But when that resolution came up in the convention, Lansing, Luther Martin, Sherman, and W. S. Johnson made elaborate speeches against it. The keynote of the opposition to a legislature of two Houses was struck in the opening remark of Mr. Lansing, "that the true question here was whether the convention would adhere to or depart from the foundation of the present confederacy."

Mr. Sherman seconded and supported Mr. Lansing's motion in favor of a single legislative House. He admitted two branches to be necessary in the State legislatures, but saw no necessity in a confederacy of States. The examples were all of a single council. Congress carried us through the war, and perhaps as well as any government could have done. The complaints at present are, not that the views of Congress are unwise or unfaithful, but that their powers are insufficient for the execution of their views. The national debt, and the want of power somewhere to draw forth the national resources, are the great matters that press. All the States were sensible of the defect of power in Congress. He thought much might be said in apology for the failure of the State legislatures to comply with the Confederation. They were afraid of leaning too hard on the people by accumulating taxes; no constitutional rule had been, or could be observed in the quotas; the accounts also were unsettled, and every State supposed itself in advance rather than in arrears. For want of a general system, taxes to a due amount had not been drawn from 'trade, which was the most convenient resource. As almost all the States had agreed to the recommendation of Congress on the subject of an impost, it appeared clearly that they were willing to trust Congress with power to draw a revenue from trade. There is no weight, therefore, in the argument drawn from a distrust of Congress; for money matters being the most important of all, if the people will trust them with power as to them, they will trust them with any other necessary powers. Congress, indeed, by the Confederation, have in fact the right of saying how much the people shall pay, and to what purpose it shall be applied; and this right was granted to them in the

expectation that it would in all cases have its effect.
If another branch were to be added to Congress,
to be chosen by the people, it would serve to embarrass.   The people would not much interest
themselves in the elections; a few designing men
in the large districts would carry their points; and
the people would have no more confidence in their
new representatives than in Congress. He saw no
reason why the State legislatures should be un-
friendly, as had been suggested, to Congress. If
they appoint Congress, and approve of their
measures, they would be rather favorable and partial to them.   The disparity of the States in point
of size, he perceived, was the main difficulty.   But
the large States had not yet suffered from the
equality of votes enjoyed by the smaller ones.   In
all great and general points, the interests of all the
States were the same.   The State of Virginia, notwithstanding the equality of votes, ratified the Confederation without even proposing any alteration.
Massachusetts also ratified without any material
difficulty.   In none of the ratifications is the want
of two branches noticed or complained of.   To
consolidate the States, as some had proposed,
would dissolve our treaties with foreign nations,
which had been formed with us as confederated
States.   He did not, however, suppose that the
creation of two branches in the legislature would
have such an effect.   If the difficulty on the subject of representation cannot be otherwise got over,
he would agree to have two branches, and a pro-
portional representation in one of them, provided
each State had an equal voice in the other.   This

was necessary to secure the rights of the lesser States, otherwise three or four of the large States would rule the others as they please. Each State, like each individual, had its peculiar habits, usages, and manners, which constituted its happiness. It would not, therefore, give to others a power over this happiness, any more than an individual would do, when he could avoid it.

Mr. Mason, Mr. Wilson, and Mr. Madison very ably supported the resolution in favor of two Houses of the legislature; and the vote stood: yeas, seven; nays, three; Maryland divided. The vote of Connecticut was in the affirmative.

The debate on the rules of suffrage in the two branches began on June 27, and was continued till July 16, when the compromise plan was adopted by a vote of five to four. When the debate had lasted two days, and the prospect of harmonious action seemed to be diminishing rather than increasing, Dr. Franklin moved that the convention be opened each day with prayer. This motion was seconded by Mr. Sherman. It did not come to a vote, apparently from fear that it might excite alarm among the people. On the 28th of June, in discussing the resolution that the suffrage in the first branch should be according to an equitable ratio, Mr. Sherman said, the question is, not what rights naturally belong to a man, but how they may be most equally and effectually guarded in society. And if some give up more than others, in order to obtain this end, there can be no room for complaint. To do otherwise, to require an equal concession from all, if it would create danger to the rights of some, would be sacrificing the end to the means. The rich man who enters into society along with the poor man gives up more than the poor man; yet, with an equal vote, he is equally safe. Were he to have more votes than the poor man, in proportion to his superior stake, the rights of the poor man would immediately cease to be secure. This consideration prevailed when the Articles of Confederation were formed.

On the 29th of June, it was decided by a vote of six to four that the rule of suffrage in the first branch (the House of Representatives) ought not to be according to that established by the Articles of Confederation. Connecticut, New York, New Jersey, Delaware voted in the negative, and Maryland was divided. On this day, Mr. Sherman's associate, Mr. Johnson, made the following admirable speech on behalf of the compromise plan: —

"The controversy must be endless whilst gentlemen differ in the grounds of their arguments: those on one side considering the States as districts of people composing one political society, those on the other considering them as so many political societies. The fact is that the States do exist as so many societies, and a government is to be formed for them in their political capacity, as well as for the individuals composing them. Does it not seem to follow, that if the States, as such, are to exist, they must be armed with some power of self-defence? This is the idea of Col. Mason, who appears to have looked to the bottom of this matter. Besides the aristocratic and other interests, which ought to have the means of defending themselves, the States have their interests as such, and are equally entitled to like means. On the whole, he thought that, as, in some respects, the States are to be considered in their political capacity, and, in others, as districts of individual citizens, the two ideas embraced on different sides, instead of being opposed to each other, ought to be combined — that in one branch the people ought to be represented, in the other, the States."

After this vote was taken, Mr. Ellsworth moved that the rule of suffrage in the second branch (the Senate) be the same with that established by the Articles of Confederation. Mr. Baldwin, of Georgia, "thought the second branch ought to be the representation of property, and that in forming it, therefore, some reference ought to be had to the relative wealth of their constituents, and to the principles on which the Senate of Massachusetts was constituted."

The debate on Mr. Ellsworth's motion was resumed on the 30th of June. In the course of this debate, Mr. Madison said that the difference in interest between the States depended not upon their size, but upon their being slave-holding or non-slave-holding States. The remedy for this difference which had occurred to him was that, instead of proportioning the votes of the States, in both branches, to their respective numbers of inhabitants, computing the slaves in the ratio of five to three, they should be represented in one branch according to the number of free inhabitants only, and in the other according to the whole number, counting the slaves as free. By this arrangement the Southern scale would have the advantage in one House, and the Northern in the other.

Mr. Sherman, in reply to the charge that the States had not complied with the requisitions of Congress, said, " Congress is not to blame for the faults of the States. Their measures have been right, and the only thing wanting has been a further power in Congress to render them effectual."

Mr. Wilson proposed one Senator for every 100,000 souls, the States not having that number to be allowed one.

Dr. Franklin proposed an equal number of Senators from each State; that in all questions touching the sovereignty of the States, or whereby the authority of the States over their own citizens may be diminished, or the authority of the general government within the States increased, and in the appointment of civil officers, each State should have equal suffrage; that in money bills the delegates of the several States shall have suffrage in proportion to the contribution of their States to the Treasury. The debate on this day was very heated, Mr. Bedford, of Delaware, stating that the small States, rather than agree to the national plan, would prefer a foreign alliance.

July 2, the vote on Mr. Ellsworth's motion was taken, and it was lost by an equal division, five to five.   Connecticut, New York, New Jersey, Delaware, Maryland, aye ; Massachusetts, Pennsylvania, Virginia, North Carolina, South Carolina, nay ; Georgia divided.

Up to this time Georgia had voted with the Nationalists. It is an interesting fact, that the Georgia delegate, whose affirmative vote on this occasion divided that State, and thus destroyed the majority of the nationalists on this question of representation, and made the compromise which was finally adopted a necessity, was Abraham Baldwin, who was born and educated in Connecticut, and who removed to Georgia about three years before this convention was held. His vote at this critical juncture gives an added emphasis to the phrase "the Connecticut Compromise," which Mr. Bancroft has made so familiar.

Mr. C. Pinckney proposed that the representation of the States in the Senate should vary according to population, but that the larger States should not have their full proportion.

Gen. C. C. Pinckney proposed a committee of one from each State to report a plan of compromise. This seemed to be felt by most to be a necessity.

Mr. Randolph said he would agree that, in the choice of an Executive, each State should have an equal vote. Vote for the committee: yeas, nine; nays, two.

July 5, the committee of eleven reported two propositions:

1. That in the House of Representatives there be one representative for every 40,000 inhabitants; each State to have at least one; all money bills to originate in the House, and not be amended in Senate; no money to be drawn from the Treasury but in pursuance of appropriations originated in the House.

2. In the Senate each State to have an equal vote.

Mr. Madison, in a note (5 Elliot, 274) says that this compromise was proposed by Dr. Franklin; that Mr. Sherman, who took the place of Mr. Ellsworth, proposed that each State should have an equal vote in the Senate, provided that no decision therein should prevail unless the majority of States concurring should also comprise a majority of the inhabitants of the United States, but it was not much deliberated on or approved in the committee. Mr. Madison says a similar provision was proposed in the debates on the Articles of Confederation. I can find no confirmation of this last statement. Probably Mr. Madison had in mind the proposition reported by Mr. Adams, to which reference has been made in speaking of those debates, and in which proposition Mr. Sherman, eleven years before the Constitutional Convention, provided for combining an equal representation of States with a proportionate representation of individuals.

The debate which followed on this day and the next related principally to the question whether giving to the House the sole right to originate money bills was really any concession to the large States. It was finally voted, five to three, that the clause relating to money bills should stand as a part of the report.

July 7, the question was taken up: Shall the clause allowing each State one vote in the second branch (the Senate) stand as a part of the report?

Mr. Sherman supposed it was the wish of every one that some general government should be established. An equal vote in the second branch would, he thought, be most likely to give it the necessary vigor. "The small States have more vigor in their government than the large ones; the more influence, therefore, the large ones have, the weaker will be the government. In the large States it will be most difficult to collect the real and fair sense of the people; fallacy and undue influence will be practiced with the most success, and improper men will most easily get into office. If they vote by States in the second branch, and each State has an equal vote, there must be always a majority of States as well as a majority of the people on the side of public measures, and the Government will have decision and efficacy. If this be not the case in the second branch, there may be a majority of States against public measures, and the difficulty of compelling them to abide by the public determination will render the Government feebler than it has ever yet been." The vote on this question stood: yeas, six; nays, three. Pennsylvania, Virginia, South Carolina, nay; Massachusetts and Georgia, divided.

From the 9th to the 14th of July, the debate was on a variety of questions growing out of the provision relating to the number of members in the House of Representatives, such as slave representation, census, and representation of new States.

On the 14th of July, Mr. Rutledge proposed to reconsider the two propositions touching the originating of money bills in the first, and the equality of votes in the second branch.

Mr. Gerry favored the reconsideration, with a

view, not of destroying the equality of votes, but of providing that the States should vote per capita, which, he said, would prevent the delays and inconveniences that had been experienced in Congress, and would give a national aspect and spirit to the management of business.

This proposition of Mr. Gerry's that the Senators vote per capita, though not acted upon at this time, was renewed by Gouverneur Morris and Mr. King on July 23, and was then adopted. This was the last step in the controversy, and one of the most important. It must have seemed to the Nationalists a much greater concession than the giving to the House of Representatives the exclusive right to originate money bills. It removed from the proceedings of the Senate all appearance of State action, and, as Mr. Gerry said, it gave a national aspect and spirit to the management of business. Only the extreme State rights men, like Luther Martin, opposed it, and, on the final vote, Maryland was the only State voting in the negative. For this suggestion Mr. Gerry is entitled to no small share of credit.

The reconsideration proposed by Mr. Rutledge having been agreed to, Mr. Pinckney moved that, instead of an equality of votes, the States should be represented in the Senate as follows: New Hampshire, two; Massachusetts, four; Rhode Island, one; Connecticut, three; New York, three; New Jersey, two; Pennsylvania, four; Delaware, one; Maryland, three; Virginia, five; North Carolina, three; South Carolina, three; Georgia, two. Total, thirty-six. This motion was seconded by Mr. Wilson.

Mr. Sherman urged the equality of votes, as a security not so much for the small States, as for the State governments, which could not be preserved unless they were represented and had a negative in the general government. He had no objection to the members in the second branch voting per capita, as had been suggested by Mr. Gerry.

Strong speeches were made by King, Madison, and Wilson against giving to the States an equality of votes in the Senate. Vote on Mr. Pinckney's motion: yeas, four; nays, six.

On the 16th of July, the vote was taken on the whole report as amended, including equality of votes in the Senate, and resulted in five yeas and four nays. Massachusetts divided.

July 23, Gouverneur Morris and Mr. King moved that the Senators vote per capita. Mr. Ellsworth said he had always approved of voting in that mode. It was agreed to that the number of Senators be two from each State.

Mr. L. Martin was opposed to voting per capita, as departing from the idea of the States being represented in the second branch. Mr. Carroll was not struck with any particular objection against the mode, but he did not wish so hastily to make so material an innovation.

The vote on the whole motion, viz.: "The second branch to consist of two members from each State, and to vote per capita," was: yeas, nine; nay, one (Maryland).

From this review of the proceedings in the Federal Convention on the rule of suffrage in the two Houses of the national legislature, we perceive:

(1) That the first motion that the States have an equal vote in the Senate was made in the Committee of the Whole, on June 9, by Roger Sherman, and was seconded by Oliver Ellsworth, and that this motion was negatived by a vote of five yeas to six nays.

(2) That immediately after this vote was taken James Wilson moved that the right of suffrage in the Senate be the same as in the House of Representatives (that is, according to population), and that this motion prevailed by a vote of six yeas to five nays.

(3) That on the 13th of June the national plan was reported by the Committee of the Whole, which provided that the rule of suffrage in both Houses should be according to population.

(4) That in the debate in the convention on this national plan, on June 29, Oliver Ellsworth moved that the rule of suffrage in the Senate be the same with that established by the Articles of Confederation. After a long debate, the vote was taken on this motion on July 2, and resulted in an equal division of the convention, five yeas and five nays, and Georgia divided.

(5) That, to break this deadlock, a committee of eleven, one from each State, was appointed to see if they could not agree on a compromise plan.

On July 5, the committee of eleven, of which Mr. Sherman was a member, reported a plan, which was, in substance, that in the House of Representatives representation be according to population; that money bills originate in the House, which shall not be altered or amended in the Senate; and that in the Senate each State shall have an equal vote. After a long debate and various amendments, which only affected the representation in the House of Representatives, the compromise plan, giving the States an equal vote in the Senate, was, on July 16, adopted by a vote of five yeas to four nays, Massachusetts being divided.

(6) That the final action on this subject was taken on the 23d of July, when it was decided, by a vote of nine yeas to one nay, that there be two Senators from each State, and that they vote per capita.

Besides the three main plans for representation in the two Houses, which I have called the national, the confederate, and the compromise plans — by the first of which representation in both Houses was to be according to population; by the second, the States were to have an equal vote in both Houses; by the third, the States were to be represented according to population in the House, and to be equally represented in the Senate — besides these three main plans, a variety of other plans were suggested in the course of the debate. They were, as we have seen, the plans of Mr. Baldwin, of Mr. Madison, of Mr. Wilson, of Dr. Franklin, of Mr. Pinckney, and of Mr. Sherman in the committee of eleven.

September 15, the last day of the debate, Mr. Sherman moved a proviso to the Article on Amendments, "that no State shall, without its consent, be affected in its internal police, or deprived of its equal suffrage in the Senate." The part relating to equal suffrage in the Senate was adopted.

This plan of a double representation in our national legislature, of population in one House and of States in the other, has generally been spoken of as a masterstroke of statesmanship. We have seen that it was simply the result of a compromise. It originated in a groundless fear that the larger States would combine to oppress the smaller ones. It was in vain that Madison, and Wilson, and Hamilton pointed out that States would be led to act together, not from similarity in size, but from unity in interest, and that there was no such unity of interest in what were then the large States (Massachusetts, Pennsylvania, and Virginia) as to lead them to oppress the smaller ones. As we read the debates, we cannot help believing that a man of such strong sense as Roger Sherman must have felt the force of these arguments. That he did so seems apparent from the fact that toward the close of the debate he defended the equal representation of the States in the Senate on the ground that it was necessary to preserve the rights, not of the small States against the large States, but of all the States against the general government.

Experience has shown that there never was the slightest danger that the large States would combine to oppress the small ones; and that there was more danger to the national government from the State governments than to the State governments from the national government. But while these fears of the early advocates of State rights were groundless, Sherman and his associates were doubtless right in their belief that the majority of the people were in favor of an amendment of the Articles of Confederation rather than of a purely national government, and that there was danger that they would reject a Constitution which did not give to the States an equal representation in at least one House of the national legislature. And so they insisted on a compromise which gave us not an ideally perfect national government, but the best perhaps which the people were willing to bear.

Madison and his associates were right in pointing out that the danger to the nation was from the State-rights sentiment rather than from the national sentiment. Accordingly we find that the first mutterings of discontent were in the Kentucky nullification resolutions and in the Hartford Convention. Disloyalty took a more serious form, in Jackson's time, in the nullification proceedings in South Carolina. It culminated, in our own day, in secession and civil war.

The constitution of the Senate as the representative of the States did not produce the good anticipated, as the large States were never hostile to the small States, and the negative of the Senate was never invoked to guard the States against injurious legislation by the House of Representatives. Neither did it produce the evil feared, as the action of the Senate was never anti-national. It did, however, produce what the advocates of a strong national government most desired, a small body of picked men, whose intelligence, character, and length of service have made them a fit check on the popular branch of the legislature, and a safe depository of the treaty-making power. We never think of the Senate as the guardian of State rights, but as the noblest embodiment of the legislative wisdom of the nation.

During the early debates in the convention, Roger Sherman showed himself in favor of amending the Articles of Confederation rather than of forming a strictly national government. He expressed himself to this effect on the first day he took his seat in the convention. Luther Martin said in his report to the Maryland legislature that the members of the convention who prepared the resolutions for amending the Articles of Confederation presented by Patterson were principally of the Connecticut, New York, New Jersey, Delaware, and Maryland delegations.

Sherman favored the election of both Representatives and Senators by the State legislatures rather than by the people, though he finally acquiesced in the election of Representatives by the people. He thought the President should be elected by the national legislature, and should be absolutely dependent on it and removable by it at pleasure.[1] He thought Representatives and Senators should be paid by the State and not by the national legislature, but finally proposed that they be paid five dollars a day out of the national treasury, and that any further emoluments be added by the States.

He thought the judges should be removed by the President, on the application of the Senate and

[1] The resemblance between this plan and the Cabinet Government described in Bagehot's English Constitution will be noticed.

House. He opposed inferior courts as a needless expense, as the State courts would answer the same purpose. Finally, he was willing the legislature should create them, but wished the State courts to be used when it could be done with safety to the general interest. He, however, expressed more confidence in the national judiciary than some did, and believed it a better tribunal for determining controversies between the States than the old method under the Confederation.

He favored the ratification of the Constitution by the State legislatures rather than by conventions of the people. To the clause relating to amendments, he moved to add that " no amendments shall be binding unless consented to by the several States."

In the plan for choosing a President by electors, it was provided that, in case of failure to choose, the Senate should choose a President out of the five highest candidates. It was thought this would strengthen the aristocratic influence of the Senate too much; so it was proposed that the choice should be by the legislature. Mr. Sherman then suggested that in that case the vote should be by States — " in favor of the small States, as the large States would have so great an advantage in nominating the candidates." Finally he suggested the plan — which was adopted — of a vote by the House of Representatives, each State having one vote.

When the proposition for the election of Representatives by the people was first under discussion (May 31), Mr. Sherman opposed election by the people, insisting that it ought to be by the State

legislatures. " The people," he said, " immediately should have as little to do as may be about
the government. They want information, and are
constantly liable to be misled."

When this matter was brought up the second
time (June 6), Mr. Sherman said : —

" If it were in view to abolish the State governments, the elections ought to be by the people. If
the State governments are to be continued, it is
necessary, in order to preserve harmony between
the national and State governments, that the elections to the former should be made by the latter.
The right of participating in the national government would be sufficiently secured to the people
by their election of the State legislatures."

When the clause that the President should be
chosen by the national legislature was under discussion (July 17), Mr. Sherman thought that the
sense of the nation would be better expressed by
the legislature than by the people at large.   " The
latter will never be sufficiently informed of characters, and besides will never give a majority of votes
to any one man. They will generally vote for
some man in their own State, and the largest State
will have the best chance for the appointment.   If
the choice be made by the legislature, a majority
of voices may be made necessary to constitute an
election."

In the speech above referred to, made on June 6,
Mr. Sherman took a very limited view of the powers of the general government.   " The objects of
the Union," he thought, " were few — first, defense
against foreign danger; secondly, against internal

disputes and a resort to force; thirdly, treaties with foreign nations; fourthly, regulating foreign commerce and deriving revenue from it. These, and perhaps a few lesser objects, alone rendered a confederation of the States necessary. All other matters, civil and criminal, would be much better in the hands of the States. The people are more happy in small than in large States. States may, indeed, be too small, as Rhode Island, and thereby be too subject to faction. Some others were, perhaps, too large, the powers of government not being able to pervade them. He was for giving the general government power to legislate and execute within a defined province."

He was opposed to the appointment by the general government of the general officers of the militia. He was opposed to a tax on exports. When it was proposed to give the President an absolute veto power, Mr. Sherman said he "was against enabling any one man to stop the will of the whole. He thought we ought to avail ourselves of his wisdom in revising the laws, but not to permit him to overrule the decided and cool opinions of the legislature." [1] The awkward plan of giving the national legislature the power to negative State laws contrary to the Constitution was opposed by Mr. Sherman on the ground that such a power involves a wrong principle — to wit, that a law of a State contrary to the Articles of the Union would, if not negatived, be valid and operative.

---

[1] See the discussion of this matter in the correspondence between John Adams and Roger Sherman, in the Appendix.

In view of the part which slavery has played in our national history, it strikes one as strange, at first, that it should have played so small a part in the Federal Convention. But at that time slavery was not confined to the Southern States, and anti-slavery sentiments were not confined to the Northern States. Gouverneur Morris made a speech denouncing slavery which would have done credit to Wendell Phillips. But he was ably supported by Mason and Madison. Georgia and South Carolina were the only States that upheld it. Virginia and Maryland had already abolished the slave-trade. It was natural, therefore, that the members of the convention should suppose that in a few years slavery would come to an end in most, if not all the States. Mr. Ellsworth undoubtedly expressed the general belief when he said, " Slavery, in time, will not be a speck in our country."

The view which Mr. Sherman took of the matter was thus expressed by him. He disapproved of the slave-trade; yet, as the States were now possessed of the right to import slaves, as the public good did not require it to be taken from them, and as it was expedient to have as few objections as possible to the proposed scheme of government, he thought it best to leave the matter as we find it. He observed that the abolition of slavery seemed to be going on in the United States, and that the good sense of the several States would probably by degrees complete it.[1]

One of the most surprising things in these de-

[1] For further illustration of Mr. Sherman's views on slavery, see Index, title Slavery.

bates is the hostility shown by some of the members to new States, and the absurd attempt to restrict their representation in the national legislature. Gouverneur Morris was the leader in this movement, which was strongly condemned by Mason and Madison.

This hostility found its formal expression in the motion made by Mr. Gerry, on the 14th of July, " that, in order to secure the liberties of the States already confederated, the number 'of representatives in the first branch of the States which shall hereafter be established shall never exceed in number the representatives from such of the States as shall accede to this confederation."

Mr. Sherman made the only speech in opposition to this motion. He thought there was no probability that the number of future States would exceed that of the existing States. " If the event should ever happen, it is too remote to be taken into consideration at this time. Besides, we are providing for our posterity, for our children and our grandchildren, who would be as likely to be citizens of new Western States as of the old States. On this consideration alone we ought to make no such discrimination as is proposed by the motion."

And yet four States — Massachusetts, Connecticut, Delaware, and Maryland — voted in favor of Mr. Gerry's motion; Pennsylvania was divided, and only five States voted against the motion.

In expressing the opinion that there was no probability that the number of future States would exceed that of the existing States, Mr. Sherman of course had reference to the limits of the country as then existing.

In discussing the articles prohibiting the States from doing certain acts, Mr. Sherman, in connection with Mr. Wilson, moved to insert, after the words " coin money," the words, " nor emit bills of credit, nor make anything but gold and silver coin a tender in payment of debts; " making these prohibitions absolute, instead of making the measures allowable, as in the 13th article, with the consent of the legislature of the United States.

Mr. Gorham thought the purpose would be as well secured by the provision of article 13, which makes the consent of the general legislature necessary; and that, in that mode, no opposition would be excited; whereas, an absolute prohibition of paper money would rouse the most desperate opposition from its partisans.

Mr. Sherman thought this a favorable crisis for crushing paper money. If the consent of the legislature could authorize emissions of it, the friends of paper money would make every exertion to get into the legislature in order to license it.

The motion prevailed by a vote of eight to one.

There was a long argument as to whether representation in the first branch should be according to population, or wealth, or payment of taxes. Dr. Johnson, in favoring population, proposed to include the blacks equally with the whites. He said " that wealth and population were the true, equitable rules of representation; but he conceived that these two principles resolved themselves into one, population being the best measure of wealth."

He concluded, therefore, that the number of people ought to be established as the rule, and that all descriptions, including blacks *equally* with the whites, ought to fall within the computation."

The strongest speech made by Mr. Ellsworth in the convention was in the form of two questions, addressed to Wilson and Madison at the close of two able speeches by those gentlemen, in which the Continental Congress was severely criticised, and the plan of giving the States an equal representation in the Senate was condemned as unjust and unsafe.

" Mr. Ellsworth asked two questions. One of Mr. Wilson, whether he had ever seen a good measure fail in Congress for want of a majority of States in favor. He had himself never known such an instance. The other of Mr. Madison, whether a negative lodged with a majority of States, even the smallest, could be more dangerous than the qualified negative proposed to be lodged in a single executive magistrate, who must be taken from some one State."

It is a singular fact that those delegates who favored the strongest form of a national government were also in favor of electing both branches of the legislature and the President, either directly or indirectly, by the people; while their opponents, who thought their views tended to monarchy or aristocracy, were unwilling to give this power to the people, as incapable of exercising it aright.

Another noticeable fact is that some of the ablest men in the convention proposed some of the unwisest measures. Franklin proposed that neither

the Senators nor President should receive any salary.   Gouverneur Morris, as we have seen, favored
an unjust discrimination against the Western States.
Hamilton proposed that the President and Senators
should hold their office during good behavior,
though he afterwards changed his views on that
subject.   Madison at one time voted in favor of a
presidency during good behavior.

Mr. Sherman, as we have seen, fell into errors,
like others; but, in the end, he gave in his adhe-
sion to those measures which were essential to the
formation of a strong general government.   He
showed the highest qualities of a statesman, in
knowing when to compromise, and when to be
firm.   He insisted upon an equal representation of
the States in the Senate; but to obtain this he was
ready to give up many things which he at first advocated, such as a single legislative House, and the
election of Representatives as well as Senators by
the State legislatures.   While inflexible in his determination to give the States the power which he
deemed essential to protect them from the general government, he was equally firm in his refusal
to give the States the power to emit bills of credit,
which he deemed injurious to the general welfare.

On the 17th of September, the convention closed
its labors, after a session of nearly four months.
The Constitution was signed by all the members
present, except Randolph, Mason, and Gerry.   No
member was perfectly satisfied with it, but it was felt
that, under the circumstances, it was the best that
could be formed.   With the exception of those who
refused to sign, all went home with the purpose of

putting forth their best efforts to secure its adoption. As the years have gone by, the strength and the excellence of the Constitution have become more and more apparent until at last we have come to regard it with something of the sacred veneration with which Burke regarded the British Constitution. Of the members who signed the Constitution, Mr. Sherman is the only one who also signed the three other great national compacts, namely: the Articles of Confederation, the Declaration of Independence, and the Association of 1774.

In the Senate of the United States, on the 20th of February, 1847, John C. Calhoun said "that it was owing mainly to the States of Connecticut and New Jersey that we had a federal instead of a national government; the best government instead of the most intolerable on earth. Who are the men of those States to whom we are indebted for this admirable government? I will name them; their names ought to be engraved on brass and live forever. They were Chief Justice Ellsworth and Roger Sherman, of Connecticut, and Judge Patterson, of New Jersey. To the coolness and sagacity of these three men, aided by a few others not so prominent, we owe the present Constitution."

In 1861, the followers of Calhoun discovered, to their dismay, that they had to deal, not with a federal, but with a national government. The State of Connecticut may justly take pride in the fact, that it was largely owing to the wise and conciliatory spirit of Roger Sherman that the convention which framed our National Constitution was not held in vain.

CHAPTER IX.

THE CONSTITUTION ADOPTED.

IT is remarkable that some of the most distinguished leaders of the revolution were either hostile or indifferent to the adoption of the National Constitution, without which the revolution would have been of no avail. In Virginia, Patrick Henry and Richard Henry Lee were among the strongest opponents of the Constitution, and in Massachusetts, Samuel Adams did not give his assent to it till the last moment.

The smallest State in the Union, Delaware, was the first to ratify, and its ratification was unanimous. Pennsylvania, one of the largest States, was the next to follow, with a vote of two to one in favor of ratification. New Jersey and Georgia speedily followed, each with a unanimous vote for the Constitution. The contest was close in Massachusetts, but the friends of the Constitution finally prevailed by a majority of nineteen in a convention of three hundred and fifty-five. The issue was long in doubt in Virginia, and but for the influence of Washington even the small majority of ten for ratification could hardly have been obtained. In the New York Convention, the opponents of ratification were at first in a majority of two to one; and nothing apparently but the genius of Hamilton could have obtained from that convention a majority of three in favor of the Constitution.

In Connecticut, the opposition to the Constitution was led by General Wadsworth; but, as was stated in the New Haven Gazette, " All the objections to the Constitution vanished before the learning and eloquence of a Johnson, the genuine good sense and discernment of a Sherman, and the Demosthenean energy of an Ellsworth." The vote for ratification was one hundred and twenty-eight to forty. Sketches of the speeches of Johnson and Ellsworth were published in the papers, but none of Sherman's have been preserved.

A series of articles on the Constitution was published by Mr. Sherman in the papers, which are said to have materially influenced the public mind in favor of its adoption. Soon after the convention had concluded its labors, Mr. Sherman expressed his opinion of the Constitution which had been agreed upon, in a letter to General Floyd. " Perhaps," he remarks, " a better could not be made upon mere speculation; it was consented to by all the States present in convention, which is a circumstance in its favor, so far as any respect is due to them. If, upon experience, it should be found deficient, it provides an easy and peaceable mode of making amendments. If it should not be adopted, I think we shall be in deplorable circumstances. Our credit as a nation is sinking; the resources of the country could not be drawn out to defend against a foreign invasion, nor the forces of the Union, to prevent a civil war. But, if the Constitution should be adopted, and the several

States choose some of their wisest and best men, from time to time, to administer the government, I believe it will not want any amendment. I hope that kind Providence, which guarded these States through a dangerous and distressing war to peace and liberty, will still watch over them and guide them in the way of safety."

In the absence of any speeches of Mr. Sherman, the following documents doubtless give substantially the arguments that he made use of in the Connecticut Convention. The first is the letter addressed to Governor Huntington by Roger Sherman and Oliver Ellsworth as delegates to the Constitutional Convention. It was not signed by Dr. Johnson, as he was then in Congress, in New York.

NEW LONDON, September 26, 1787.

SIR, — We have the honor to transmit to your excellency a printed copy of the Constitution formed by the Federal Convention, to be laid before the legislature of the State.

The general principles which governed the Convention in their deliberations on the subject are stated in their address to Congress.

We think it may be of use to make some further observations on particular parts of the Constitution.

The Congress is differently organized; yet the whole number of members, and this State's proportion of suffrage, remain the same as before.

The equal representation of the States in the Senate, and the voice of that branch in the appointment to office, will secure the rights of the lesser, as well as of the greater States.

Some additional powers are vested in Congress, which was a principal object that the States had in view in appointing the Convention. Those powers extend only to matters respecting the common interests of the Union, and are specially defined, so that the particular States retain their sovereignty in all other matters.

The objects for which Congress may apply moneys are the same mentioned in the eighth article of the Confederation, viz, for the common defence and general welfare, and for payment of the debts incurred for those purposes. It is probable that the principal branch of revenue will be duties on imports. What may be necessary to be raised by direct taxation is to be apportioned on the several States, according to the number of their inhabitants; and although Congress may raise the money by their own authority, if necessary, yet that authority need not be exercised, if each State will furnish its quota.

The restraint on the legislatures of the several States respecting emitting bills of credit, making any thing but money a tender in payment of debts, or impairing the obligation of contracts by *ex post facto* laws, was thought necessary as a security to commerce, in which the interest of foreigners, as well as of the citizens of different States, may be affected.

The Convention endeavored to provide for the energy of government on the one hand, and suitable checks on the other hand, to secure the rights of the particular States, and the liberties and properties of the citizens. We wish it may meet the approbation of the several States, and be a means of securing their rights, and lengthening out their tranquillity. With great respect, we are, sir, your excellency's obedient, humble servants,

ROGER SHERMAN.
OLIVER ELLSWORTH.

His Excellency, GOVERNOR HUNTINGTON.

The next document, found among Mr. Sherman's manuscripts, is entitled, "Observations on the new Federal Constitution." It does not appear whether this paper was prepared for publication, or as a memorandum for a speech before the Convention. The substance of this and the next paper were afterward embodied in an article published in the New Haven Gazette.

"Observations on the new Federal Constitution.

"A conviction that the present Confederation is deficient to give respectability and security to the United States was the motive with the several States to appoint a convention to make amendments.

"It was deficient in the organization of the government, and with respect to the powers necessary for the common defence and general welfare of the Union.

"One principal defect in the government was the want of a Supreme Executive power. Congress exercises that power when sitting, and a committee of the States in the recess of Congress, which has been found to be very inadequate for the purposes of government. The frequent changing the members of that body and their being vested with legislative as well as executive authority, renders their administration slow, unstable, and precarious.

"But the want of sufficient power was still a greater evil — they had power to enter into engagements, but no power to fulfil them, and there is no security in trusting to the legislatures of the several States to provide for the exigencies of the Union upon requisition. The want of a power to regulate commerce with foreign nations and among the several States, and to enforce a due observation of treaties, has been very detrimental to the interests of the States and the cause of lessening their national credit. These defects will be supplied by the new Constitution if adopted. There are some other powers vested in the general government which relate to the common interests of the Union, and are particularly defined, so that each State retains its sovereignty in what concerns its own internal government, and a right to exercise every power of a sovereign State not delegated to the government of the United States. And although the government of the United States in matters within its jurisdiction is paramount to the Constitutions and laws of the particular States, yet all acts of the Congress not warranted by the Constitution would be void, nor could they be enforced contrary to the sense of a majority of the States. When the general government acts within its proper jurisdiction, it will be the interest of the legislatures of the several States to support it, and they will be a check sufficiently powerful to prevent unconstitutional incroachments on the rights and privileges of the particular States, but the jurisdiction of each will be so easily distinguished that there will be no great danger of interference.

"In order to a well regulated government the legislature should be properly constituted, and vested with plenary powers for all the purposes for which it is instituted, to be exercised for the public good as occasion may require. The greatest possible security that a people can have for the enjoyment of their civil rights and liberties, is that no laws can be made to bind them or taxes be imposed on them without their consent by representatives of their own choosing — this was the great point contended for in our controversy with Great Britain, and this will be fully secured to us under the new Constitution. The rights of the people will be secured by a representation in proportion to their numbers in one branch of the Congress, and the rights of the several States by their equal representation in the other branch. This will be a much greater security than a declaration of rights or restraining clauses on paper.

"A farther security will be that the representatives, and the people they represent, will have one common interest, and will participate in the benefits and burdens of the public measures. •

"The President and Vice President as well as the members of Congress, though chosen for fixed periods, will be re-eligible as often as the electors shall think proper, which will be a great security for their fidelity in office, and will give much greater stability and energy to government than an exclusion by rotation, and will always be an operative and effectual security against arbitrary government, either monarchical or aristocratic. There is as much security in the new Constitution as in the present against keeping up standing armies in time of peace; it can't be done without the consent of Congress, with this additional security that it will require the concurrence of two branches, and that no law appropriating money for that purpose can be in force for more than two years.

"The liberty of the press not being the regulation of Congress will be in no danger. There are but few powers vested in the new government but what the present Congress have power to do or require to be done. The new powers are to regulate commerce, provide for a uniform practice with respect to naturalization, bankruptcies, and forming and training the militia, and for the punishment of certain crimes against the United States, and for promoting the progress of science in the mode therein pointed out. These appear to be necessary for the common benefit of the Union, and can't be effectually provided for by the particular States; therefore the objection that the convention exceeded the authority given by the States is groundless, for, though they have formed a new instrument including the former and additional powers, yet it is no more than an amendment of the present Constitution in those matters wherein it was really deficient.

"The objects of expenditure are the same as under the present Constitution, and why should this system be more expensive than the present? The number of the members of Congress is the

same — that number may be increased with the
increase of the people, but then it is probable that
the wealth of the State will be proportionably
increased.   The executive is vested in a single
person, whose support will not probably exceed
the present allowance to the President of Congress
and the pay of a committee of the States.   The subordinate officers need not be more numerous, nor
have larger salaries than at present; the expense
of collecting the impost will be transferred from
the particular States to the United States, but need
not be greater than at present. — The principal
sources of revenue will be imposts on goods imported, and sale of the western lands, which probably will be sufficient to pay the debts and expenses
of the United States if properly managed, so long
as peace continues; but should there be occasion
to resort to direct taxation, each State's quota will
be ascertained according to a rule which has been
approved by eleven of the States, and should any
State neglect to furnish its quota, Congress may
raise it by a tax in the same manner as the State
ought to have done.   And what remedy more
easy and equitable could be devised to obtain the
supplies from a delinquent State?   Some have
objected that the representation will be inadequate,
but the States have never thought fit to keep up
the full representation they are entitled to in Congress; and of what possible advantage can it be
to have a very large Assembly to transact the few
general matters that will come under the direction
of Congress, sufficient information may be had
from the legislatures of the several States in the

matters that the members of Congress are not
personally acquainted with. The regulating the
time, place, and mode of elections seems to be as
well secured as possible. The legislature of each
State may do it, and if they neglect to do it properly, it may be done by Congress, and what possible motive can either have to injure the people in
the exercise of that right? The qualifications of
the electors will remain as fixed by the constitutions or laws of the several States.

"The power of the President to grant pardons
extends only to offences against the United States,
with exception of impeachments, which is a sufficient security for seclusion of offenders from office;
therefore no great mischief can be apprehended
from that quarter. — The partial negative of the
President on the acts of Congress and the rescission
in consequence thereof may be very useful to prevent laws being passed without mature deliberation.
— The Vice President, while he acts as President of
the Senate, will have nothing to do in the executive department, his being elected by the suffrage
of all the States will incline him to regard equally
the interests of all — and when the members of the
Senate are equally divided on a question, who so
proper to give a casting voice, as one who repre-
sents all the States?"

The next paper is a letter, dated December 8,
1787, which repeats, with some variations, the
arguments set forth in the preceding paper, and
contains, in addition, the following statements. To
the objection that there was no Bill of Rights in
the Constitution, Mr. Sherman replies: —

"Declarations of rights in England were charters granted by Princes, or acts of Parliament made to limit the prerogatives of the crown, but not to abridge the powers of the legislature. — These observations duly considered will obviate most of the objections that have been made against the Constitution."

In reference to. the judicial powers conferred by the Constitution, he says: — "It was thought necessary in order to carry into effect the laws of the Union, and to preserve justice and harmony among the States, to extend the judicial powers of the confederacy; they cannot be extended beyond the enumerated cases, but may be limited by Congress, and doubtless will be restricted to such cases of importance and magnitude as cannot safely be trusted to the final decision of the courts of the particular States; the Supreme Court may have a circuit through all the States to make the trials as convenient and as little expensive to the parties as may be; and the trial by jury will doubtless be allowed in cases proper for that mode of trial, nor will the people in general be at all affected by the judiciary of the United States; perhaps not one to a hundred of the citizens will ever have a cause that can come within its jurisdiction, for all causes between citizens of the same States, except where they claim lands under grants of different States, must be finally decided by the courts of the State to which they belong."

Some of the States, in connection with their act of ratification, passed resolutions recommending certain amendments to the Constitution. To these

Mr. Sherman was strongly opposed, and published the following article on the subject: —

OBSERVATIONS.

On the alterations proposed as amendments to the new Federal Constitution.

Six of the States have adopted the new Constitution without proposing any alterations, and the most of those proposed by the conventions of other States may be provided for by Congress in a code of laws without altering the Constitution. If Congress may be safely trusted with the affairs of - the Union, and have sufficient power for that purpose, and possess no powers but such as respect the common interest of the States (as I have endeavored to show in a former piece), then all the matters that can be regulated by law may be safely left to their direction, and those will include all that I have noticed, except the following, which I think on due consideration will appear to be improper or unnecessary.

1. It is proposed that the consent of two-thirds or three-fourths of the members present in each branch of the Congress shall be required for passing certain acts.

On which I would observe, that this would give a minority in Congress power to control the majority, joined with the concurrent voice of the President, for if the President differs, no act can pass without the consent of two-thirds of the members in each branch of Congress; and would not that be contrary to the general principles of republican government?

12

2. That impeachments ought not to be tried by the Senate, or not by the Senate alone.

But what good reason can be assigned why the Senate is not the most proper tribunal for that purpose? — The members are to be chosen by the legislatures of the several States, who will doubtless appoint persons of wisdom and probity, and from their office can have no interested motives to partiality. The House of Peers in Great Britain try impeachments, and are also a branch of the legislature.

3. It is said that the President ought not to have power to grant pardons in cases of high treason, but the Congress.

It does not appear that any great mischief can arise from the exercise of this power by the President (though perhaps it might as well have been lodged in Congress). The President cannot pardon in case of impeachment, so that such offenders may be excluded from office notwithstanding his pardon.

4. It is proposed that members of Congress be rendered ineligible to any other office during the time for which they are elected members of that body.

This is an objection that will admit of something plausible to be said on both sides, and it was settled in convention on full discussion and deliberation, there are some offices which a member of Congress may be best qualified to fill, from his knowledge of public affairs acquired by being a member. Such as minister to foreign courts, &c. and on accepting any other office his seat in Congress will be vacated, and no member is eligible to any office that shall have been instituted or the emoluments increased while he was a member.

5. It is proposed to make the President and Senators ineligible after certain periods.

But this would abridge the privilege of the people, and remove one great motive to fidelity in office, and render persons incapable of serving in offices on account of their experience, which would best qualify them for usefulness in office — but if their services are not acceptable, they may be left out at any new election.

6. It is proposed that no commercial treaty should be made without the consent of two-thirds of the Senators, nor any cession of territory, right of navigation or fishery, without the consent of three-fourths of the members present in each branch of Congress.

It is provided by the Constitution that no commercial treaty shall be made by the President without the consent of two-thirds of the Senators present, and as each State has an equal representation and suffrage in the Senate, the rights of the States will be as well secured under the new Constitution as under the old; and it is not probable that they would ever make a cession of territory or any important national right without the consent of Congress. The king of Great Britain has by the Constitution a power to make treaties, yet in matters of great importance he consults the Parliament.

7. There is one amendment proposed by the convention of South Carolina respecting religious tests, *by inserting* the word *other* between the

words *no* and *religious* in that article, which is
an ingenious thought, and had that word been inserted, it would probably have prevented any
objection on that head.   But it may be considered
as a clerical omission and be inserted without calling a convention; as it now stands the effect will
be the same.

On the whole it is hoped that all the States will
consent to make a trial of the Constitution before
they attempt to alter it; experience will best show
whether it is deficient or not; on trial it may appear that the alterations that have been proposed
are not necessary, or that others not yet thought
of may be necessary; every thing that tends to disunion ought to be avoided.   Instability in government and laws tends to weaken a State and render
the rights of the people precarious.

If another convention should be called to revise
the Constitution, 'tis not likely they would be more
unanimous than the former; they might judge differently in some things, but is it certain that they
would judge better?   When experience has convinced the States and people in general that alterations are necessary, they may be easily made, but
attempting it at present may be detrimental, if not
fatal, to the union of the States.

The judiciary department is perhaps the most
difficult to be precisely limited by the Constitution,
but Congress have full power to regulate it by law,
and it may be found necessary to vary the regulations at different times as circumstances may differ.

Congress may make requisitions for supplies
previous to direct taxation, if it should be thought
expedient, but if requisitions be made, and some

States comply and others not, the non-complying States must be considered and treated as delinquents, which will tend to excite disaffection and disunion among the States, besides occasioning delay; but if Congress lay the taxes in the first instance, these evils will be prevented, and they will doubtless accommodate the taxes to the customs and convenience of the several States.

Some suppose that the representation will be too small, but I think it is in the power of Congress to make it too large, but I believe it may be safely trusted with them. Great Britain contains about three times the number of the inhabitants in the United States, and according to Burgh's account in his political disquisitions, the members of Parliament in that kingdom do not exceed one hundred thirty-one [from the counties?], and if sixty-nine more be added from the principal cities and towns, the number would be two hundred, and strike off those who are elected by the small boroughs, which are called the rotten part of the Constitution by their best patriots and politicians, that nation would be more equally and better represented than at present, and if that would be a sufficient number for their national legislature, one-third of that number will be more than sufficient for our federal legislature, who will have a few general matters to transact. But these and other objections have been considered in a former paper, before referred to. I shall therefore conclude this with my best wishes for the continuance of peace, liberty, and union of these States.

A CITIZEN OF NEW HAVEN.

CHAPTER X.

THE SUPERIOR COURT.

AT the January session, 1789, of the Connecticut Assembly, Roger Sherman was chosen a Representative in Congress. As this office and that of Judge of the Superior Court of the State were made incompatible by the laws of the State, Mr. Sherman resigned the latter office, which he had held, by annual election, for twenty-three years. That he should have been continued in this high office for so long a period, during a portion of which he had as associates such men as William Samuel Johnson and Oliver Ellsworth, the ablest men at the bar, shows the high esteem in which he must have been held by the legal profession, as well as by the community at large.

In the biography of Roger Sherman in Sanderson's "Lives," it is said of his services as a judge: "It is uniformly acknowledged by those who have witnessed his conduct and abilities on the bench, that he discovered, in the application of the principles of law and the rules of evidence to the cases before him, the same sagacity that distinguished him as a legislator. His legal opinions were received with great deference by the profession, and their correctness was almost universally acknowledged."

In another passage in the same biography, Mr. Sherman's judicial qualifications are thus described : —

"The genius and talents of Mr. Sherman were particularly calculated for eminent usefulness in the judiciary department. Cool, attentive, deliberate, and impartial, skilled in all forms and principles of law, he was not liable to be misled by arts of sophistry, or the warmth of declamation. He formed his opinions on a careful examination of every subject, and delivered them with dignity and perspicuity. His decisions were too firmly founded on correct and admitted principles to be readily shaken, and he necessarily enjoyed, in his important judicial station, a confidence and esteem highly honorable to himself, as well as to the professional gentlemen by whom those sentiments were entertained.

"But, although the testimonies of individuals, whose profession and opportunities enabled them to decide, with peculiar exactness, upon the judicial character of Mr. Sherman, are almost affirmatively unanimous, yet that unanimity was not confined to the limits of the forum. The public at large, and especially that portion of it which, during the long period that he held his official station, had been interested in the proceedings of the court, entertained the same sentiments in relation to his abilities, his purity, and his integrity."

Very few of the opinions of the Superior Court of that early day have been preserved. But from the records of that court we select a few opinions which, being in Mr. Sherman's handwriting, were evidently prepared by him.

N. London County ⎱ Mumford vs. Avery
Sept. Term 1786   ⎰ Action of Account.

The defendant's motion in arrest is judged insufficient.

The only exception to the declaration is that Action of Account will not lie, in this case, because a certain sum of money, and certain bills of exchange are alleged to have been received to be delivered over to the plaintiff, for which Action of Assumpsit would be the proper remedy, and not Action of Account.

But it is the opinion of the court that Action of Account will lie in any case where a person has received monies to the use of another, especially if it be received of a third person to be delivered over to the plaintiff, and although Action of Assumpsit might be brought for the same, yet an Action of Account is most favorable for the defendant.

Hartford County ⎱
March Term 1788 ⎰ The deft's plea in bar
Coomes vs. Prior ⎰ insufficient.

In a former action between the same parties wherein the present plaintiff was defendant, a verdict was found and a judgment rendered against him on his plea of title to the land now demanded, but that was only an action of trespass for the recovery of damages. This being an action for the recovery of the land is of a higher nature, therefore a recovery in that ought not to be a bar to this, for the party may be able to produce further evidence in support of his title than was produced on the former trial, and this is admissible by the uniform practice of the courts of law in this State, as well as in England in favor of Estates of inheritance. See 4 Bacon's Abridgment, 119. Therefore we are of opinion that the defendant's plea is insufficient.

Middlesex County
July Term   } The Plaintiff's Replication adjudged
Marshall *v.* Miller {   sufficient.
and Henshaw.

In this case the defendants jointly promised to pay a sum of money to the plaintiff by a note in writing under their hands, but Henshaw, one of the defendants, being insolvent, was by an act of the legislature discharged from all his debts on his delivering up all his estate for the benefit of his creditors, which he had complied with, and now the question is whether this note is thereby discharged, on which judgment is rendered against Miller, the other defendant for the whole debt. If one joint obligor is discharged by an act of the obligee, it is presumed that he hath received satisfaction, and therefore is a discharge of the obligation, but if one of the joint obligors dies or is discharged by an act of the legislature which does not extend to the other, no such presumption ariseth and therefore the other is liable alone to pay the debt. See the rules and principles of law on this point considered and stated more fully in a late case determined in this county between Mortimer and Caldwell.

Fairfield County
Aug. Term 1788
Blackman *v.* Fairchild.
} Plaintiff's Replication insufficient.

The action is on a promissory note; — which the defendant pleads was an arbitration note, and that the instructions to the arbitrators were a *written* award, which they have not made. The plaintiff replies that their instructions were a *verbal* award and to indorse down the note to the sum they should find due, both of which he states their performance of; and traverses "that their instructions were to make a written award, otherwise than by indorsing down said note," which is not a direct traverse, but argumentative only, and therefore ill. No issue could be joined upon it without the defendant's affirming over differently from what he had pled in bar, which he was not bound to do. The defendant's averment that the instructions were a written award, was a material one, and it behoved the plaintiff to submit as a question of law to the court, whether the doings of the arbitrators amounted to a written award, or of fact to the jury, whether such were their instructions, but he has done neither.

For which reasons we think his replication insufficient.

(The following dissenting opinion is in the handwriting of Roger Sherman, except the end of it, which is in that of Judge Law.)

Fairfield County   ) Judgment for the Defendant
August Term 1788   }   that the Plaintiff's reply
Blackman *v.* Fairchild.)   is insufficient.

We dissent from the judgment because it is admitted that the plaintiff in his replication hath set forth a good and legal parol submission and award, and he hath traversed the only material fact alleged in the defendant's plea in bar viz., that the arbitrators were instructed to make and publish their award *in writing*, with the addition of these words in a parenthesis; viz, (" otherwise than by endorsing down said note ") which is the only exception taken to the reply which words we are of opinion are merely surplusage, and no way repugnant to the other matters contained in the plaintiff's replication and therefore do not vitiate it. But the defendant ought to have joined the traverse by reaffirming the said fact as alleged in his plea in bar, which would have laid a sufficient foundation for a fair trial and legal judgment in the case. And the law delights in establishing pleadings as well as awards when it can be done consistent with substantial justice, any circumstantial defects or informalities notwithstanding.

(The opinion so far is in the handwriting of Roger Sherman; the rest of it is in that of Judge Law, as follows:) The plaintiff by setting forth in his replication, — in what manner the award was to be made, thereby strips the pleading of an and   that might otherwise have been made had he directly joined issue upon the traverse tendered — viz, whether the instructions were to make a written award, — this question of law upon such instructions might then arise before the jury, whether such an award was a written one or parol, as it   partly of both, being a mode peculiar to our practice and unknown in the British Rules — whereas the plaintiff has now fairly disclosed that question to the court unless the defendant will give it up.

Windham County   ⎞ The Plaintiff's reply
Jan. adj. Term 1789 ⎬   Sufficient.
Hamlin v. Fitch.   ⎠

For the reasons rendered in the same case on a motion in arrest of judgment. The contract which is alleged in the defendant's plea to be usurious was not a loan of money, goods, wares or commodities within the description of the Statute against usury but was a bargain respecting certain final settlement certificates of uncertain value, there being no time fixed or funds provided for their payment, and their current value was fluctuating, and did in fact depreciate between the time of the defendant's receiving the certificates, and the time fixed for the payment of them the value of the one thousand hard dollars secured by the other note — They were issued by government as securities for the nominal amount in hard money, and if the plaintiff had sold them to the defendant and taken his security for the payment of the nominal sum in hard money it would have been a much more unequal bargain than that now in question, but no one would contend that it would have been a usurious contract, and although the note is to repay the same certificates or others of like tenor date and value with lawful interest. Yet the value of both principal and interest were in hazard of depreciation, and the law regards the substance more than the form of a contract. The Statute of this State prohibits the taking more than the *value* of six pounds for the forbearance of one hundred pounds for a year, but it does not prohibit the taking more in quantity of any commodity of *uncertain value*, than at the rate of six per cent per annum. For instance, if a man lends twenty bushels of corn before harvest when the market price is four shillings per bushel, and receives forty bushels in payment after harvest when corn is but two shillings per bushel, he receives no more than the value of the principal lent, although he receives double the quantity.

The following principles are advanced by the Judges as law in the case of Murray against Harding, 2 Blackstone's Reports page 863. Degrey, Chief Justice. "It is essential to a loan that the thing borrowed is at all events to be restored. If that be *bona fide* put in hazard, it is no loan, but a contract of another kind." 865 — Blackstone, Justice, "I do not know an instance, where the principal is *bona fide* hazarded, that the contract has been held to be usurious." "If the price be inadequate to the hazard, it may be an imposition, and under some circumstances relievable in equity; but it cannot be legal usury." The other Judges concurred. We are therefore of opinion that judgment be given for the plaintiff.

LAW.
SHERMAN.

Judge Ellsworth concurred in opinion, but was absent when these reasons were assigned.

December 2, 1772, Mr. Sherman wrote to Thomas Cushing, of Boston, the following letter, in reference to equity proceedings in Massachusetts and Connecticut: —

SIR, — I should be glad to be informed how matters of equity are determined in your Province, also your method of proceeding on petitions before the General Assembly, whether the parties are ever admitted to be heard *viva voce* before the whole Assembly or before either House. In this Colony matters of equity are determined by the Assembly, and the parties are admitted to be heard at large before both Houses as in trials before the Executive Courts, but as business of that kind increases it is become very burthensome and expensive for the whole Assembly to sit to hear them, and we have had some thoughts of erecting a Court of Chancery — but 'tis feared by many that that will be attended with inconveniences, and as your Province is much larger than this Colony and you have hitherto done without a Court of Chancery, a few lines from you on your method of proceeding in those affairs will much oblige your humble servant,

ROGER SHERMAN.

The Revised Laws of Connecticut, prepared by Mr. Sherman and Mr. Law in 1784, constituted the Superior Court a Court of Equity.

CHAPTER XI.

SERVICES IN CONGRESS. — FIRST SESSION, 1789.

PART I. — IMPOST LAW, &c.

ON being notified of his election as a representative in Congress, Mr. Sherman addressed the following letter to Governor Huntington.

NEW HAVEN, Jan. 7th, 1789.

SIR, — I have a grateful sense of the honor done me by the freemen of this State in electing me one of their representatives in the Congress of the United States. This fresh instance of their confidence lays me under an additional obligation to devote my time to their service. The trust I esteem very weighty and important in the present situation of public affairs. I could therefore have wished that their choice had been fixed on some other person in my stead, better able to sustain the weight and perform the services of that office, especially as I hold another in the State which as the law now stands is incompatible with holding this at the same time. I wish to employ my time in such service as may be most beneficial and acceptable to my country. Much of my time since the commencement of the late war has been employed at a distance from home, and as I have a numerous family to provide for, it would be most agreeable to me to be in a situation wherein I might pay some attention to their affairs. But if the honor-

able the Legislature shall think fit to provide that
my acceptance of this office shall not vacate my
office in the Superior Court until their further
pleasure shall be made known, I will accept the
trust to which I have been elected by the freemen,
(I do not wish to hold any office otherwise than
subject to their pleasure) but if in their wisdom
they shall not think fit to make such provision, I
shall desire a little further time to consider and advise on the matter. I have the honor to be with
great respect your excellency's most obedient
humble servant,

ROGER SHERMAN.

His Excellency, GOVERNOR HUNTINGTON.

Although the legislature of Connecticut did not
make the provision proposed by Mr. Sherman in
the above letter, he decided to accept the position
of Representative in Congress, and resigned his
position on the bench of the Superior Court.
March 5, 1789, Mr. Sherman took his seat in the
House of Representatives. A quorum was not
present till April 1, when a speaker was elected.
April 6, the form of oath to be taken by the
Representatives, as provided by the Constitution,
was agreed upon; and on the same day the pre-
sence of a quorum in the Senate was notified to the
House, and the House was informed of the readiness of the Senate to count the votes for President
and Vice-President. April 7, it was ordered that
the Chief Justice of the State of New York be
requested to attend the House on the next day,
for the purpose of administering the oath to the

members, as provided by the Constitution. On April 8, the oath was administered to the members present.

As soon as the oath was administered to the members, the House resolved itself into a Committee of the Whole on the state of the Union, and began the consideration of certain provisions relating to import duties and tonnage, introduced by Mr. Madison. As the treasury was nearly empty, and as it was agreed on all hands that the revenue should be raised by impost duties, and not by direct taxation, this first tariff bill passed with comparatively little discussion. No question was raised as to the propriety, or the constitutionality, of so arranging the duties as to protect home manufactures. The principal points discussed were as to the effect of certain duties on different parts of the country.

April 11, this subject being under consideration, Mr. Sherman gave it as his opinion that in fixing the duties on particular articles, if they could not ascertain the exact quantum, it would be better to run the risk of erring in setting low duties than high ones, because it was less injurious to commerce to raise them than to lower them; but nevertheless he was for laying on duties which some gentlemen might think high, as he thought it better to derive revenue from impost than from direct taxation, or any other method in their power. He moved that the article of rum should be charged with fifteen cents per gallon.

The duty on nails, spikes, tacks, and rods being objected to, Mr. Sherman said: "The gentle-

men object to these articles because they are
necessary and cannot be furnished in quantities
equal to the demand; but I am of opinion, if they
cannot now be had in such plenty as is wished for,
they may be in a very short time. Every State
can manufacture them, although they cannot make
nail rods. Connecticut has excellent iron ore of
which bars are made; but she gets nail rods from
this city; others can do the like; and until every
State can supply themselves by their own industry,
for which purpose they have everything at their
hands, it may not be amiss for the government to
get some revenue from the consumption of foreign
nails."

It was proposed to make discriminating duties
on spirits, in favor of nations in alliance with us.
Mr. Sherman said: "I would rather make a discrimination on any other article than ardent spirits,
the importation of which does not deserve encouragement from any part of the world." Later
he said: "Molasses is an article principally imported from the colonies of nations in alliance; a
discrimination therefore in favor of such molasses
would be a substantial benefit, and he recommended it in lieu of that on brandy."

It was claimed by some that the duties were too
high. To which Mr. Sherman replied: —

"If gentlemen prevail in getting the duties low-
ered to what the late Congress proposed, they will
find themselves obliged to have recourse to direct
taxation for a million and a half or two millions of
dollars. It then only remains for us to consider,
whether it will be more agreeable to the people to re-

duce the impost in this manner, and raise the deficiency by direct taxes. If these duties are to be considered as a tax on the trading part of the community alone, they are improper; but this I believe is not the case; the consumer pays them eventually, and they pay no more than they choose, because they have it in their power to determine the quantity of taxable articles they will use. A tax left to be paid at discretion must be more agreeable than any other. The merchant considers that part of his capital applied to the payment of the duties the same as if employed in trade, and gets the same profit upon it as on the original cost of the commodity.

"As to the tax on distilled spirits, it will be felt as little as any other whatever; and from this source we are to expect a very considerable proportion of the revenue. . . . The duty on it cannot be said to be unequal, as it has been contended on other articles: it is pretty generally consumed throughout the United States. The State I belong to is at a considerable distance from the West Indies, yet she consumes no inconsiderable quantity, much more than I wish she did. The gentleman from South Carolina seems to suppose that the duty will bear harder upon his State than upon others. I cannot think it will be the case; but if they consume more, they should agree to a high duty, in order to lessen the consumption.

"One gentleman had observed that there is not money enough to pay all the duties imposed in this bill; but is it not as easy to introduce money as merchandise? When there is a demand for it, the merchants will bring it in, for they can as well bring less of a commodity and more money; so that, if this should take place, the objection will be done away.   It is in this way that we must be supplied with cash, because we have neither gold nor silver mines to draw from; if we get it, it must be imported, and will be imported, if it is more advantageous than the importation of other articles.

"I think we ought to rely a great deal on the virtue of our constituents; they will be convinced of the necessity of a due collection of the revenue; they will know that it must be done in this way, or it will be by direct taxation.   I believe the people will prefer this mode of raising revenue, and will give all the assistance in the execution of the law that is in their power; and as the mercantile part of the people will see that it is equally laid, though it be something higher than the States have hitherto required, they will submit themselves to our ordinance, and use their influence to aid the collection."

It having been asserted that the people would be unable to pay so high duties as then proposed, Mr. Sherman said : —

"I believe the people are able to pay as much as the necessities of the government require; if they are not, we shall never restore the public credit, which is one of the chief ends of our appointment.   I believe they are not only able but willing to contribute sufficient for this purpose.   The resources of this country are very great if they are properly called into action; and although they may not be so great as those of Britain, yet it should be remembered that that nation has occasion for twelve times as much revenue as the United States.

"Gentlemen have had recourse to popular opinion in support of their argument. Popular opinion is founded in justice, and the only way to know if the popular opinion is in favor of a measure is to examine whether the measure is just and right in itself. I think whatever is proper and right, the people will judge of and comply with. The people wish that the government may derive respect from the justice of its measures; they have given it their support on this account. I believe the popular opinion is in favor of raising a revenue to pay our debts, and if we do right, they will not neglect their duty; therefore the arguments that are urged in favor of a low duty will prove that the people are contented with what the bill proposes. The people at this time pay a higher duty on imported rum than what is proposed in this system, even in Massachusetts; it is true it is partly laid by way of excise, but I can see no reason against doing it in this way as well as the other. . . . When gentlemen have recourse to public opinion to support their arguments, they generally find means to accommodate it to their own; the reason why I think public opinion is in favor of the present measure is because this regulation in itself is reasonable and just.

"I think if we should not support public credit now we have the ability, the people will lose all confidence in the government. When they see public bodies shrink from their duty what can be expected but they will neglect theirs also? It cannot be for the interest of the people of the United States that they should continue to pay a high interest, and suffer an accumulation of the principal of the national debt till some distant period. Will any gentleman assure us that the people will then be better able to pay it off than at present? Have they any certain evidence that we shall grow richer as we delay the establishment of our credit and the payment of our debts? I think they have not; therefore it is best to get out of debt as fast as possible, and while we have the command of funds amply sufficient for that purpose."

It having been proposed to limit the time of the continuance of the import duties, Mr. Sherman said, " He wished a limitation to the law in general terms, such as until the debt, foreign and domestic, is discharged. He thought a short term would make an unfavorable impression upon the minds of the public creditors, and tend in a great measure to cloud the happy prospects that began to brighten the political hemisphere of this country."

April 21, the duties on tonnage being under consideration, Madison advocated a discrimination in favor of those nations having commercial treaties with the United States. His remarks were especially directed against Great Britain, whose commercial policy towards the United States he attacked with great severity. Mr. Sherman said he would trouble the committee no further than just to remark, that the policy of laying a high tonnage on foreign vessels, whether in treaty or not in treaty, was at best but a doubtful point.

The regulation is certainly intended as an encouragement to our own shipping; but if this is not to be the consequence of the measure, it must be an improper one. If a large duty is laid on foreigners coming into our ports, they will be induced to counteract us by increasing the restraint which our vessels already labor under in theirs. But sixty cents will surely be too high in the present case, if it is proposed to lay more on foreigners not in treaty. Not seeing, therefore, any advantage resulting from high duties on tonnage, he should vote against the sixty cents.

May 4, this same subject being under consideration, Mr. Sherman said, " He was opposed to the discrimination. In his opinion, the great principle in making treaties with foreign powers was to obtain equal and reciprocal advantages to what were granted, and in all our measures to gain this object the principle ought to be held in view. If the business before the House was examined, it would appear to be rather founded on principles of resentment, because the nation of Great Britain has neglected or declined forming a commercial treaty with us. He did not know that she discriminates between these States and other powers who are not in treaty with her, and therefore did not call upon us for retaliation; if we are treated in the same manner as those nations, we have no right to complain. He was not opposed to particular regulations to obtain the object which the friends of the measure had in view; but he did not like this mode of doing it, because he feared it would injure the interest of the United States."

In the debate on this subject on June 27, Mr. Sherman said, " He was well convinced there was a large and decided majority in both Houses, and that it was the universal voice of the Union, that America should meet commercial restrictions with commercial restrictions; but there might be some disagreement about the best way to effect this point. He did not think it the voice of the people that Congress should lay the commerce of a nation under disadvantages merely because we had no treaty with them. It could not appear a solid reason in the minds of gentlemen, if they considered the subject carefully; therefore it was not the proper principle for the government to act upon. He would mention one that appeared to him more equitable, namely, lay a heavy duty upon all goods coming from any port or territory to which the vessels of the United States are denied access; this would strike directly at objects which the honorable gentlemen had in view, without glancing upon other ports to which we are allowed access."

On the 13th of May, Mr. Parker, of Virginia, moved to impose a duty of ten dollars on each slave imported. He hoped such a duty would prevent, in some degree, this irrational and inhuman traffic.

Mr. Sherman approved of the object of the motion, but he did not think this bill was proper to embrace the subject. He could not reconcile himself to the insertion of human beings as an article of duty among goods, wares, and merchandise. He hoped it would be withdrawn for the present, and taken up hereafter as an independent subject.

Mr. Parker hoped Congress would do all that lay in their power to restore to human nature its inherent privileges, and, if possible, wipe off the stigma under which America labored. The inconsistency in our principles with which we are justly charged should be done away, that we may show by our actions the pure beneficence of the doctrine we hold out to the world in our Declaration of Independence.

Mr. Sherman thought the principles of the motion, and the principles of the bill, were inconsistent; the principle of the bill was to raise revenue, and the principle of the motion to correct a moral evil. Now, considering it is an object of revenue, it would be unjust, because two or three States would bear the whole burden, while he believed they bore their full proportion of all the rest. He was against receiving the motion into this bill, though he had no objection to taking it up by itself on the principles of humanity and policy; and therefore would vote against it if it was not withdrawn.

On the 20th of April, Mr. Sherman wrote to Pierpont Edwards, of New Haven, giving him an account of the arrival of the Vice-President, &c.: —

NEW YORK, April 20th, 1789.

SIR, — The Vice President of the United States arrived this afternoon about 4 o'clock escorted by the cavalry of this city, and attended by a number of gentlemen of distinction, in their coaches, chariots and other carriages.

The President is expected the latter end of this week or the beginning of next when our Federal Government will be completely organized. A bill for laying and collecting a general impost, and several other bills are preparing in the House of Representatives; but it is probable that much impost will be lost on this spring's importations by the delay of the members to meet on the day appointed.

On the 14th of May, Mr. Sherman wrote the following letter to Oliver Wolcott: —

NEW YORK, May 14, 1789.

SIR, — As the proceedings of Congress are daily published in the papers in this city, and from them in the papers of the other States, I cannot give your honor any new information respecting them. Much time was lost by the non-attendance of members at the beginning of the session, so that seasonable provision could not be made by an impost law to embrace the spring importations.

The House of Representatives entered upon that subject immediately after they formed, and have agreed upon the rates of the impost on the various articles, in doing which they had respect to revenue, and the encouraging the manufactures of these States. Much time was necessarily taken up in adjusting those rates to suit the circumstances of the different parts of the Union. A spirit of harmony and accommodation has been manifested, and the business has been done to general satisfaction, except as to the duty on molasses which at first was fixed at 6 cents per gallon, which gave great dissatisfaction to the members from Massachusetts and occasioned much debate, till at length it was altered to 5 cents. It was the general sense of the House that were it not for the distillation of that article into rum it ought to be lower, but as a considerable branch of the revenue was to be derived from distilled spirits it was urged, that if molasses was not rated in a greater proportion to imported rum than some other articles, it would tend to diminish the revenue on that branch by increasing the manufacture of it in the country, and so lessening the importation; and that it would operate unequally on the different parts of the Union, as in those parts where the distillery is not carried on the people would pay a higher tax on the spirits which they consume than the citizens of the other States.

All classes of citizens here appear to be well pleased with the new Government, and especially with the President's address.

There has been a joint committee to consider what style shall be annexed to the offices of President and Vice President, who reported that it is not proper to annex any style or title other than the style of office in the Constitution, which was unanimously approved by the House and dissented to by a majority of the Senate — on which a committee of conference was appointed, and the committee from the Senate agreed to report that the address of the Senate should be made to the President, only by the style of office.

The House have this day agreed to engross the bill for laying duties on goods imported, which is

to be read a third time to-morrow — having previously agreed to a deduction of 10 per cent of the
duties on goods imported in vessels built in the
United States and belonging to citizens thereof.

The freedom of the City of New Haven was
conferred on John Adams as he passed through
the city in April, 1789, on his way to the inauguration of President Washington. The following correspondence shows his appreciation of the honor,
and his personal esteem for Mr. Sherman: —

Pierpont Edwards to John Adams.

NEW HAVEN, April 27th, 1789.

SIR, — The absence of the Honorable Roger
Sherman our Mayor necessitated the measure of
presenting you the freedom of this city authenticated by our Senior Aldermen. Having had an
opportunity to communicate with Mr. Sherman, I
now do myself the honor to enclose you a Diploma
authenticated according to the usages of this city,
under the signature of our Mayor, City Clerk, and
the Seal of the City.

The honor of expressing the very great respect
with which they regard your character, and the
sincere affection which they have for your Person,
actuated them to enroll your name in the Registry
of their Citizens. They hope that this step may
meet with your approbation. I have the honor
to be, with very great respect, your excellency's
most obedient, and very humble

Ser.

PIERPONT EDWARDS.

John Adams to Roger Sherman.

NEW YORK, May 14, 1789.

MY DEAR FRIEND: — Inclosed is a letter of thanks to our fellow citizens of New Haven and to Mr Edwards, for the most endearing compliment I ever received. I suppose myself chiefly indebted to your friendship for the favorable representation of my character among your neighbors which has produced this obliging result. I hope it will not be long before we shall have an opportunity to renew our former acquaintance and intimacy: in the meantime let me pray your acceptance of my sincere thanks for the Diploma under your Mayoralty and Signature; and that you will take the trouble of transmitting the enclosed letter, which I leave open for your perusal, to Mr Edwards.

With the most cordial affection and the highest esteem, I have the honor to be, dear sir, your most obedient and most humble servant,

JOHN ADAMS.

The following letter, from Governor Lyman Hall, of Georgia, to Roger Sherman, shows the anxiety felt by some as to the success of the new government.

GEORGIA, 10th June, 1789.

DEAR SIR, — I have advised my son, who will hand you this, to wait on you, with my respectful compliments and to pay particular attention to such hints and advice as he may receive from you for the guide of his conduct, upon a plan of im-

provement, during his stay in N. York, which if
his health will permit, may be for some considerable time.

I know your benevolent heart, and I can rely
with confidence, that in this instance, I shall experience your friendship. My son will tell you all
the news from this part of the world.

I am heartily glad that Congress are on business, but give me leave to say, you ought to lay a
scheme to bring in N. Carolina and Rhode Island,
as soon as may be, either by Convention, (which
will give them opportunity to come in with a decent face, which I believe is in part all they wish)
or, perhaps some other mode may succeed equally
well, at all events they must be brought in — Consequences otherways, I could not hint, but your
own mind must suggest, alarming and dangerous,
at least to the tranquillity, if not to the existence
of the Union. — Revolt of other States has been
hinted — Hush —

I am sorry that the whole Congress (a bad example) cannot agree to pray together — you understand me —

I am, Dear Sir, respectfully your most obedient
& humble servant,

L. HALL.

PART II. — AMENDMENTS TO THE CONSTITUTION.

At the time of the adoption of the Constitution,
the conventions of five States recommended
amendments, as also did a minority in the conven-

tions of two other States. The feeling in Virginia was so strong on this point, that Mr. Madison felt bound to introduce in the House a series of amendments which he had prepared. Accordingly, on June 8th, Mr. Madison stated that he proposed to bring forward certain amendments to the Constitution.

Mr. Sherman: "I am willing that this matter should be brought before the House at a proper time. I suppose a number of gentlemen think it their duty to bring it forward; so that there is no apprehension it will be passed over in silence. Other gentlemen may be disposed to let the subject rest until the more important objects of government are attended to; and I should conclude, from the nature of the case, that the people expect the latter from us in preference to altering the Constitution; because they have ratified that instrument in order that the government may begin to operate. If this was not their wish, they might as well have rejected the Constitution, as North Carolina has done, until the amendments took place. The State I have the honor to come from adopted this system by a very great majority; because they wished for the government; but they desired no amendments. I suppose this was the case in other States; it will therefore be imprudent to neglect much more important concerns for this. The executive part of the government wants organization; the business of the revenue is incomplete, to say nothing of the judiciary business. Now, will gentlemen give up these points to go into a discussion of amendments, when no advantage can arise from them? For my part, I question if any alteration which can be now proposed would be an amendment in the true sense of the word, but, nevertheless, I am willing to let the subject be introduced. If the gentleman only desires to go into committee for the purpose of receiving his proposition, I shall consent; but I have strong objections to being interrupted in completing the more important business; because I am well satisfied it will alarm the fears of twenty of our constituents where it will please one."

Mr. Madison then moved that a select committee be appointed to consider and report such amendments, as are proper for Congress to propose to the legislatures of the several States, conformably to the fifth article of the Constitution. He stated what amendments he thought should be made, supporting them by an elaborate speech.

Mr. Sherman: "I do not suppose the Constitution to be perfect, nor do I imagine if Congress and all the legislatures on the continent were to revise it that their united labors would make it perfect. I do not expect any perfection on this side of the grave in the works of man; but my opinion is, that we are not at present in circumstances to make it better. It is a wonder that there has been such unanimity in adopting it, considering the ordeal it had to undergo; and the unanimity which prevailed at its formation is equally astonishing; amidst all the members from the twelve States present at the federal convention, there were only three who did not sign the instrument to attest their opinion of its goodness. Of the eleven States who

have received it, the majority have ratified it without proposing a single amendment. This circumstance leads me to suppose that we shall not be
able to propose any alterations that are likely to
be adopted by nine States; and gentlemen know,
before the alterations take effect, they must be
agreed to by the legislatures of three-fourths of
the States in the Union. Those States which have
not recommended alterations will hardly adopt
them, unless it is clear that they tend to make the
Constitution better. Now, how this can be made
out to their satisfaction I am yet to learn; they
know of no defect from experience."

August 13. The first article of the amendments
proposed ran thus: — "In the introductory paragraph of the Constitution, before the words 'We
the people,' add 'Government being intended for
the benefit of the people,' and the rightful establishment thereof being derived from their authority
alone."

Mr. Sherman: "I believe, Mr. Chairman, this is
not the proper mode of amending the Constitution.
We ought not to interweave our propositions into
the work itself, because it will be destructive of the
whole fabric. We might as well endeavor to mix
brass, iron and clay, as to incorporate such hetero-
geneous articles, the one contradictory to the
other. Its absurdity will be discovered by com-
paring it with a law. Would any legislature endeavor to introduce into a former act a subsequent
amendment, and let them stand so connected?
When an alteration is made in an act, it is
done by way of supplement: the latter act always

14

repealing the former in every specified case of difference.

"Besides this, sir, it is questionable 'whether we have the right to propose amendments in this way. The Constitution is the act of the people, and ought to remain entire. But the amendments will be the act of the State governments. Again, all the authority we possess is derived from that instrument; if we mean to destroy the whole, and establish a new Constitution, we remove the basis on which we mean to build. For these reasons, I will move to strike out that paragraph and substitute another."

The paragraph proposed was to the following effect:

Resolved by the Senate and House of Representatives of the United States in Congress assembled, That the following articles be proposed as amendments to the Constitution, and when ratified by three-fourths of the State legislatures shall become valid to all intents and purposes as part of the same.

Under this title the amendments might come in nearly as stated in the report, only varying the phraseology so as to accommodate them to a supplementary form.

Mr. Gerry said that this was a dispute about form.

Mr. Sherman: " If I had looked upon this question as mere matter of form, I should not have brought it forward or troubled the committee with such a lengthy discussion. But, sir, I contend that amendments made in the way proposed by the committee are void. No gentleman ever knew an addition and alteration introduced into an existing law, and that any part of such law was left in force; but if it was improved or altered by a supplemental act, the original retained all its validity and importance in every case where the two were not incompatible. But if these observations alone should be thought insufficient to support my motion, I would desire, gentlemen, to consider the authorities upon which the two Constitutions are to stand. The original was established by the people at large, by conventions chosen by them for the express purpose. The preamble to the Constitution declares the act: but will it be a truth in ratifying the next Constitution which is to be done perhaps by the State legislatures, and not conventions chosen for the purpose? Will gentlemen say it is 'We the people' in this case? Certainly they cannot; for, by the present Constitution we, nor all the legislatures in the union together, do not possess the power of repealing it. All that is granted us by the fifth article is, that whenever we shall think it necessary, we may propose amendments to the Constitution, — not that we may propose to repeal the old, and substitute a new one.

"Gentlemen say, it would be convenient to have it in one instrument, that people might see the whole at once; for my part, I view no difficulty on this point. The amendments reported are a declaration of rights; the people are secure in them, whether we declare them or not; the last amendment but one provides that the three branches of government shall each exercise its own rights.

This is well secured already; and in short I do not see that they lessen the force of any article in the Constitution: If so there can be little more difficulty in comprehending them whether they are combined in one or stand distinct instruments."

Mr. Sherman's motion did not prevail. On August 21st, he renewed his motion, and it prevailed by a two-thirds vote.

August 14th, the second amendment was under consideration, which provided that there should be one representative for every thirty thousand until the number shall amount to one hundred; after which the proportion shall be so regulated by Congress that the number of representatives shall never be less than one hundred, nor more than one hundred and seventy-five; but each State shall always have at least one representative.

Mr. Sedgwick moved to strike out one hundred and seventy-five and insert two hundred.

Mr. Sherman said, if they were now forming a Constitution he should be in favor of one representative for forty thousand rather than thirty thousand.

The objects of the Federal Government were fewer than those of the State Government; they did not require an equal degree of local knowledge; the one case, perhaps, where local knowledge would be advantageous, was in laying direct taxes; but here they were freed from an embarrassment, because the arrangements of the several States might serve as a pretty good rule on which to found their measures.

So far was he from thinking one hundred and

seventy-five insufficient, that he was about to move for a reduction, because he always considered that a small body deliberated to better purpose than a greater one.

Later, Mr. Sherman said, — He was against any increase. He thought if a future House should be convinced of the impropriety of increasing this number to above one hundred, they ought to have it at their discretion to prevent it; and if that was likely to be the case, it was an argument why the present House should not decide. He did not consider that all that had been said with respect to the advantages of a large representation was founded upon experience; it had been intimated, that a large body was more incorruptible than a smaller one; this doctrine was not authenticated by any proof; he could invalidate it by an example notorious to every gentleman in this House; he alluded to the British House of Commons, in which, although it consisted of upwards of five hundred members, the minister always contrived to procure votes enough to answer his purpose.

The proposition as amended by Mr. Sedgwick was carried by a vote of twenty-seven to twenty-two.

August 15. The fourth proposed amendment was that " No religion should be established by law, nor shall the equal rights of conscience be infringed."

Mr. Sherman thought the amendment altogether unnecessary, inasmuch as Congress had no authority whatever delegated to them by the Constitution to make religious establishments; and moved therefore to have it struck out.

Mr. Livermore proposed that the amendment should be made to read, " shall make no laws touching religion, or infringing the rights of conscience," which passed by a vote of thirty-one to twenty.

On a proposition authorizing the people to instruct " their representatives," Mr. Sherman said, " It appears to me that the words are calculated to mislead the people, by conveying an idea that they have a right to control the debates of the legislature. This cannot be admitted to be just, because it would destroy the object of their meeting. I think, when the people have chosen a representative, it is his duty to meet others from the different parts of the union, and consult, and agree with them to such acts as are for the general benefit of the whole community. If they were to be guided by instructions, there would be no use in deliberation; all that a man would have to do, would be to produce his instructions, and lay them on the table, and let them speak for him. From hence, I think it may be fairly inferred, that the right of the people to consult for the common good can go no further than to petition the legislature, or apply for a redress of grievances. It is the duty of a good representative to inquire what measures are most likely to promote the general welfare, and, after he has discovered them, to give them his support. Should his instructions, therefore, coincide with his ideas on any measure, they would be unnecessary; if they were contrary to the conviction of his own mind, he must be bound by every principle of justice to disregard them."

The proposition was negatived by a vote of ten yeas to forty-one nays.

August 18. The ninth proposed amendment was, "The powers not delegated by the Constitution, nor prohibited by it, to the States, are reserved to the States respectively."

Mr. Tucker moved to amend this proposition by adding the word "expressly," so as to read "the powers not expressly delegated by this Constitution."

Mr. Madison objected to this amendment, because it was impossible to confine a government to the exercise of express powers; they must necessarily be admitted powers by implication, unless the Constitution descended to recount every minutia. He remembered the words "expressly" had been moved in the convention of Virginia, by the opponents to the ratification, and, after full and fair discussion, was given up by them, and the system allowed to retain its present form.

Mr. Sherman coincided with Mr. Madison in opinion, observing that corporate bodies are supposed to possess all powers incident to a corporate capacity, without being absolutely expressed.

Mr. Tucker's motion was negatived.

August 21. The House having taken into consideration the amendments to the Constitution, as reported by the Committee of the Whole, Mr. Sherman renewed his motion for adding the amendments to the Constitution by way of supplement; which was agreed to by two thirds of the House.

The first proposed amendment was rejected, because two thirds of the members present did not support it.

Mr. Sherman moved to alter the clause in reference to the delegation of powers by adding to it the words, " or to the people; " so that it would read " the powers not delegated to the United States by the Constitution, nor prohibited by it to the States, are reserved to the States respectively, or to the people."

This motion was adopted without debate.

Mr. Burke proposed as an amendment that "Congress shall not alter, modify, or interfere in the times, places, or manner of holding elections of senators, or representatives, except when any State shall refuse or neglect or be unable, by invasion or rebellion, to make such election."

Mr. Sedgwick moved to amend the motion by giving the power to Congress to alter the times, manner, and places of holding elections, provided the States made improper ones.

Mr. Sherman observed, that the convention were very unanimous in passing this clause; that it was an important provision, and if it was resigned it would tend to subvert the government. .

The motions of Mr. Burke and Mr. Sedgwick were determined in the negative.

Two thirds of the House finally agreed to seventeen amendments. The Senate reduced the number to twelve. Only ten of these, which were in the nature of a bill of rights, were ratified by the legislatures of three fourths of the States, and so became a part of the Constitution. Mr. Livermore doubtless expressed a very prevalent opinion when he pronounced these ten amendments " of no more value than a pinch of snuff, since they went to secure rights never in danger."

June 25. The following clause in a bill for establishing the Treasury Department was under consideration, viz.: Making it the duty of the Secretary to digest and report plans for the improvement and management of the revenue and the support of the public credit.

Mr. Sherman thought the principle held up by the clause was absolutely necessary to be received. It was of such a nature as to force itself upon them; therefore it was in vain to attempt to elude it by subterfuge. It was owing to the great abilities of a financier, that France had been able to make the exertions we were witnesses of a few years ago, without embarrassing the nation. This able man, after considerably improving the national revenue, was displaced; but such was the importance of the officer, that he has been restored again. . . . It is the proper business of this House to originate revenue laws: but as we want information to act upon, we must procure it where it is to be had; consequently we must get it out of this officer, and the best way of doing so must be by making it his duty to bring it forward.

September 25. Mr. Boudinot moved that the President be requested to appoint a day of Thanksgiving for the many signal favors of Almighty God, especially by affording them an opportunity peaceably to establish a constitution of government for their safety and happiness.

Mr. Sherman justified the practice of thanksgiving on any signal event, not only as a laudable one in itself, but as warranted by a number of precedents in Holy Writ: for instance, the solemn thanksgivings and rejoicings which took place in the time of Solomon, after the building of the temple, was a case in point. This example he thought worthy of Christian imitation on the present occasion; and he would agree with the gentleman who moved the resolution.

The motion was opposed by Burke, who did not like this mimicking European customs. Tucker intimated that it would be as well to wait for some experience of the effects of the Constitution before returning thanks for it. He thought the question of a thanksgiving ought to be left to the State authorities, as they would know best what reason the people had to be pleased with the new government.

The resolution was carried; and Messrs. Boudinot, Sherman, and Sylvester were appointed a committee on the part of the House. In compliance with this resolution, in which the Senate concurred, the President appointed Thursday, November 26th, 1789, as our first national Thanksgiving day.

The first session of the first Congress came to an end September 29th, 1789. A few days before the adjournment, Mr. Sherman wrote to Gov. Huntington the following letter, giving him an account of the work done during the last four months of the Congress.

᷍

New York, Sept. 17th, 1789.

Sir; Your excellency has doubtless seen the amendments proposed to be made to the Constitution as passed by the House of Representatives, Enclosed is a copy of them as amended by the Senate wherein they are considerably abridged and I think altered for the better.

The present session draws near to a close, the 22d inst. being the time fixed by both Houses for adjournment. Some bills for laws and other business begun will be continued to next session; but the arrangements that will be completed will enable the Executive to administer the Government in the recess of Congress. It was impossible to make any special appropriation for paying the interest of the public debt without further information than can be obtained at present. The Secretary of the Treasury will be directed to make proper statements and report to the next session.

The salaries of some of the officers are higher than I thought was necessary or proper considering the state of the finances and the just and meritorious demands of the creditors who have long been kept out of their dues, especially such of them as originally loaned their money, or rendered services or specific supplies, and still hold their securities. I don't know whether any discrimination will or ought to be made between them and others, but if there should I think it ought not to be made for the benefit of the public, but of the original creditors who were necessitated to sell their securities at a discount. I was absent when the bill for fixing the compensation of the members and officers of Congress was brought in and passed the House. The Senate concurred with an alteration that in the year 1795 the pay of a Senator should be augmented one dollar a day, on this principle that a Senator ought to have higher pay than a Representative, though they were willing to dispense with it during their continuance in office, a great majority of the House of Representatives thought the principle not admissible, but on conference rather than lose the bill it was agreed by way of accommodation to limit the continuance of the law to seven years, so that the extra pay of a Senator will continue but one year.

The pay is fixed at one dollar a day more than was last stated by the legislature of the State of Connecticut which is perhaps as economical a State as any in the Union, and I suppose the members from that State would have been content with that allowance, if they had to provide only for themselves, but the members from those States who had formerly allowed eight dollars a day thought it hard to be reduced to six, but mutual concession was necessary. It is important that a full representation be kept up, and it is well known that in Connecticut as well as in other States, it was difficult out of seven members to keep up a representation by two, and some could not be induced to attend at all.

The judiciary bill which had passed the Senate was this day concurred with by the House of Representatives with some small alterations. The salaries of the Judges have been this day reported but not considered by the House. The enclosed papers contain the news of the day. I have the honor to be with great respect, your excellency's most obedient humble servant,

ROGER SHERMAN.

In the previous month of June, Mr. Sherman's son William had died. The following letter on this subject was written to him by his daughter Elizabeth.

NEW HAVEN, June 29, 1789.

HOND. SIR; It is an hour of trying affliction with us. We all need your advice and counsel in this affecting moment. Mama has been graciously supported beyond our expectation. Thus we have reason to praise God in the midst of this most severe chastisement. It is by her desire that I write to inform you the particulars of the death and interment of my deceased brother. He appeared to have his senses and was able to speak until about six hours before his death.

Doctor Stiles, Doctor Wales and Mr. Austin all visited and conversed with him concerning the state of his mind. He expressed penitence for sins and his belief of a necessity of the atonement by Christ and seemed sincerely to desire to be enabled by the grace of God to repent of all his sins and accept of salvation upon the terms offered in the Gospel, and the last words he was heard to utter appeared to be an earnest prayer to his Creator for the salvation of his soul and at 3 o'clock on Saturday he was buried. His daughter Betsy attended as a mourner at the funeral. Mama got for her and for the rest of us hats, gloves, buckles, handkerchiefs and everything necessary for mourning except gowns. Those we borrowed. They were black silk. Now Mama wishes to know what you think proper to get for the family and whether you do not think best to get for them and for his Betsy suits of black silk and she also wishes if possible to have you come home even if you cannot stay but two days. Roger and Oliver have dark coats and other dress that is very decent. John and Isaac have no dark coats. They have black underdresses, stockings, gloves and all else that is necessary and Mama wants to know if they had not best have some dark coats. Roger has been to Mr Tomlinsons and took some patterns of the lute strings which I have enclosed. They are half yard wide. The large piece is 11/8 per ell. The other 9/6 per ell York currency, and he will make his usual deduction from the above prices. At the same place is some English taffety for 7 pounds per piece Y. C. and marked price.

from yours affectionately,

ELIZA SHERMAN.

N. B. We cannot find any broad cloths here. If you think best to get any I suppose you can get enough in New York.

Mama is happy to inform you that Isaac has been a great comfort to her and all the family in our present distress.

The following is a letter from Mr. Sherman to Simeon Baldwin on the same subject.

NEW YORK, June 29th, 1789.

SIR, — I received your letter of the 24th on the evening of the 25th and that of the 26th on the evening of the 28th — I am greatly obliged to you for the attention you gave to my son William in his sickness, and the early and circumstantial account given me respecting him in your letters. I had thought of returning home on receipt of your first letter but had no opportunity by land or water until it was too late to see him alive or to attend his funeral. The first account I had of his death was by a letter from my son Isaac last Saturday evening. I wish this sudden and sorrowful event may be sanctified to all the family — that we may always be prepared for so great and important a change, by choosing the good part that can never be taken away from us.

These with my love to you and Mrs. Baldwin, from your affectionate Parent,

ROGER SHERMAN.

The following letter to Simeon Baldwin gives an account of the method of applying for office, at that early day.

NEW YORK, July 21st, 1789.

DEAR SIR, — Enclosed is last Saturday's paper. The Collecting Bill passed the House and was sent to the Senate last Friday — the Judiciary Bill passed the Senate the same day — and has been once read in the House — Two persons have applied for the office of Surveyor in New Haven, Mr

Phips who was a Lieutenant under Capt. Harding in the Navy of the United States — and Capt. William Munson, who I suppose have applied to the President in common form, which is by letter mentioning the office to which they wish to be appointed, and their past services and sufferings as a ground of claim — and if the President is not personally acquainted with their character, their letter is accompanied with a certificate from persons of distinction, certifying their qualifications, and they sometimes in their letters refer the President to members of Congress, or other persons residing at the Seat of Government for information.   The district Court and the circuit Court will have two Sessions in a year in Connecticut to be held at Hartford and New Haven alternately and may hold special Court at other places.   I am in health and hope to come home as soon as the Judiciary Bill. passes.

Yours respectfully,

ROGER SHERMAN.

The following letter to his wife shows that the cares of State did not make Mr. Sherman unmindful of domestic economy.

NEW YORK, July 23, 1789.

DEAR WIFE, — I received Roger's letter of the 20th inst wherein he mentions that you had a poor turn that day but was so far recovered as to ride out.   If your state of health makes it necessary, I will return home immediately, otherwise I shall stay a little longer.   The bill establishing courts

passed by the Senate is now before the House, and
I am on a committee for considering amendments
to the Constitution. The bill for fixing the pay of
the members is depending and undetermined — I
wish you to write me by the first post.

I received my clothes in the green box — The
new jacket fits well. Coppers have taken a sudden fall here to 48 for a shilling York money, if we
have any on hand I think it best to keep them for
the present. I believe it would answer to take in
good flax well dressed for spinning at a reasonable
price — the crop won't be so good this year as
last.

Yours, &c.,
ROGER SHERMAN.

I had a letter from Mr Gibbs dated the 19th he
says that sister and all friends are well — They
lately made an excursion into the country and
found our friends at Concord well.

R. S.

On Mr. Sherman's return home, he wrote the
following letter to Richard Law, who had been his
associate on the bench, and in revising the laws of
Connecticut.

NEW HAVEN, Oct. 3, 1789.

DEAR SIR; — Congress closed the session last
Tuesday, having made such arrangements as will
enable the Executive to administer the Government. They could not obtain sufficient information to make any appropriations for the interest of
the public debts, but have directed the Secretary

of the Treasury to report the necessary statements for that purpose, to the next session.

The Judiciary Act passed with but *little altera-tion from the original draft.* · I suppose you will be furnished with a copy of it. You are appointed District Judge for Connecticut. The salary is something more than you now receive from the State and can't be diminished.

Your honor will have the appointment of a Clerk who must reside at Hartford or New Haven. Simeon Baldwin, Esq., of this city, with whom you are well acquainted, would execute the office well, and I believe, to good acceptance, if he should be appointed. If your honor shall think fit to confer that office on him the favor will be gratefully acknowledged by him, and

Your sincere friend and humble servant,

ROGER SHERMAN.

The Diary of George Washington, from 1789 to 1791 gives the following account of his visit to New Haven in October, 1789.

Saturday, Oct. 17, 1789.

From Milford we took the lower road through West Haven, part of which was good and part rough, and arrived at New Haven before two o'clock; we had time to walk through several parts of the city before dinner. By taking the lower road we missed a committee of the Assembly, who had been appointed to wait upon and escort me into town — to prepare an address — and to conduct me when I should leave the city as far as they should judge proper.· The address was presented at 7 o'clock, and at 9, I received another address from the Congregational clergy of the place. Between the receipt of the two addresses I received the compliment of a visit from the Gov. Mr Huntington — the Lt. Gov. Mr Wolcott — and the Mayor, Mr Roger Sherman.

Sunday, 18th.

Went in the forenoon to the Episcopal Church, and in the afternoon to one of the Congregational meeting houses. Attended to the first by the Speaker of the Assembly, Mr Edwards, and a Mr Ingersoll, and to the latter by the Governor, the Lieut. Governor, the Mayor, and Speaker.

These gentlemen all dined with me, (by invitation,) as did Gov. Huntington, at the house of Mr Brown, where I lodged, and who keeps a good tavern. Drank tea at the Mayor's, Mr Sherman.

It was on this occasion that Mr. Sherman's daughter Mehetabel opened the door for the President, as he was leaving. Washington, putting his hand on her head, remarked, — " You deserve a better office, my little lady." " Yes, sir," she replied with a curtsey, " to let you in." This young lady afterwards became Mrs. Evarts. Her son, the Hon. William M. Evarts told me he had often heard his mother repeat this story.

PART III. — PUBLIC CREDIT.

SECOND SESSION.   Jan. 4, 1790 — Aug. 12, 1790.

The second session of Congress met on the 4th
of January, 1790. On the 14th of January the
Secretary of the Treasury submitted a plan for the
support of the public credit, which was made the
order of the day for January 28th. In the mean .
time, on January 20th, the motion to direct the
Secretary of the Treasury to report some regulation for the distribution of western lands being
under consideration, Mr. Sherman said, that he
thought the best way to manage this business was
to refer it to the Secretary of the Treasury as was
proposed.   He said that the unappropriated land
in the western territory was the great fund of
wealth which, if properly disposed of, might ex-
tinguish the national debt, and be peopled by a
valuable class of citizens; but if, from a mistaken
policy, it was thrown away upon foreign adven-
turers or speculators, the public would get nothing
for it as had been the case heretofore, in the sale
of large districts, where the expenses attending the
surveys &c., left very little profit to the United
States.   It is true, such measures may induce a
number of foreigners to come among us; but then
it ought to be remembered that such are generally
persons of different education, manners, and customs from the citizens of the Union, and not so
likely to harmonize in a republican government as
might be wished; consequently any considerable

accession of this class of settlers might tend to disturb the harmony and tranquillity and embarrass
the operations of the government. He thought it
was worthy of inquiry whether America stood in
need of emigrants to people her territory. He
supposed the notorious rapid population of the
present inhabitants was of itself sufficient for the
purpose. It must have struck the observation of
every gentleman that they were daily throwing off
vast numbers, and extending the settlements into
that country which some gentlemen seemed to
think could not be too early cultivated. ˙ But,
nevertheless, he was willing to let foreigners come
in gradually, and in the same way he was inclined
to dispose of the lands. He thought it would be
most judicious to lay off a district at a time, re-
serving some lots, which, with the increasing population of the surrounding ones, would increase in
value, and ultimately these reserved lots would bring
more into the Treasury than the others. He wished
the business to go to the Secretary of the Treasury,
because he supposed he had the most information
respecting it.

January 28. The report of the Secretary of
the Treasury on the means of supporting public
credit was under consideration. It proposed two
things. First, that all idea of discrimination
among the public creditors, as original holders
or transferees, ought to be done away; second,
the assumption of the State debts by the general
government.

Mr. Sherman hoped the business would be conducted in such a way as to be concluded before

the end of the present session. As to obtaining
the sense of the State legislatures, he did not think
that necessary. The people appointed the members of this House, and their situation enabled
them to consult and judge better what was for the
public good, than a number of distinct parts, void
of relative information, and under the influence of
local views. He supposed that Congress contained
all the information necessary to determine this or
any other national question. As to the first observation of the gentleman from Georgia, that specu-
lations had been carried on to a great extent, he
had only to observe, that this had been the case
from the time when the public securities were first
issued, and he supposed they would continue until
the holders were satisfied with what was done to
secure the payment.

As to the State debts, it was a subject which he
apprehended would not be ultimately decided
till the sense of the people is generally known;
and on this occasion, it might be well to be acquainted with the sense of the State legislatures;
he hoped, therefore, that it would be. But with
regard to the. foreign and domestic continental
debts, he did not hesitate to say, it was proper for
Congress to take them into consideration as
speedily as possible; for the sooner they are discussed, the sooner will the House make up their
judgment thereon. He believed they were possessed of all the facts they could be possessed of,
and therefore any great delay was improper.

February 9. Mr. Sherman: "I think whatever
doubts there may be with respect to the advan-

tage or disadvantage of a public debt, we can none of us hesitate to decide that provision of some kind ought to be made for what we have already incurred. It is true, if we were about now to borrow money, it would be highly prudent to consider whether the anticipation would not be repaid by a speedy collection of taxes or duties to the amount; but when a debt is incurred beyond our present ability to discharge, we ought to make some provision for its gradual extinction, and, in the interim, pay punctually the interest; now this resolution goes no further.

" Some of the propositions which follow go further than this. They propose perpetual annuities, and talk of irredeemable stock. This is more than I am willing to agree to. I think it prudent for us to get out of debt as soon as we can; but then I do not suppose we can raise money enough to pay off the whole principal and interest in two, three, or ten years. If I am right in this, we ought to agree to some mode of paying the interest in the interim."

February 9. The report of the Secretary of the Treasury relating to the domestic debt being under consideration, Mr. Sherman said: " I do not differ much in principle from the gentleman who spoke last, from Pennsylvania, Mr. Scott, but I do not extend my views so far as he extends his, in the exercise of the power which he contends is vested in this body. I look upon it, that legislators act in a threefold capacity; they have the power to make laws for the good government of the people, and a right to repeal and alter those

laws as public good requires; in another capacity,
they have a right to make contracts; but here I
must contend, that they have no right to violate,
alter, or abolish; but they are obliged to fulfil
them. The legislature stands in another capacity, what is called judicial, between the Union at
large and those creditors with whom she has entered into stipulations; there can be no other
solemn judge on such occasions, because no court
of law is capable of giving redress; they cannot
issue an execution against the sovereign power,
and enforce their decrees; therefore, any creditor
who has money due him from the State has a
right, by petition, to apply to the legislature, who
has the sole power of doing him justice. When
applied to in that manner, the legislature has a
right to examine, or appoint another to examine,
how far the claim is just or unjust; this power has
been exercised, with respect to the greatest part of
the claims against the United States. There has
been a liquidation of these accounts, and the specie
value has been ascertained of the depreciated security. When bills of credit were first emitted, it
was declared that they should be redeemed with
specie, indeed they passed as such at first; but
the opinion of their real value was changed by
common consent; those that were put into the
continental loan offices were always payable in
the same species of money. If they had been
paid in paper currency, the owners of them would
have suffered a loss and injury; in justice, therefore, to the holders, the government agreed to fix
the value of the loans according to the current

rate of paper bills, at the time they were left in
the office; all certificates were ordered to be liquidated in this manner; the same could not be done
in favor of those who had left their other property
with the public, and took the continental bills as
a security; because they passed as a circulating
medium, and went from one hand to another, by
which means every one who received them, and
kept them, though a small space of time, suffered
loss; in that way it operated as a tax, and perhaps as equitable and as just a one as could have
been any way apportioned; therefore it could not
have been supposed equitable, that the last posses-
sor should receive for these bills the nominal sum
in specie. The government, therefore, interfered
in order to do justice; but when they had entered
into a contract, founded on specie value, liquidated
and ascertained, I do not see but the public are
bound by that contract, as much as an individual,
and that they cannot reduce it down in either
principal or interest, unless by an arbitrary power,
and in that case there never will be any security
in the public promises. If we should now agree
to reduce the domestic debt to four per cent the
world may justly fear that we may, on some future
occasion, reduce it to two. If this government
once establishes such a principle, our credit is
inevitably gone forever. I presume the gentleman does not found his motion upon the idea that
there has been fraud and injustice committed on
the one side, or imbecility or oversight on the
other; if there was, it would be a good reason
why an inquiry should take place in such cases.

But though the legislature may judge of accounts exhibited against the government, and determine on them, their power ought not to be extended to judge of those already acknowledged; unless it be for the special reasons which I have just mentioned. From these considerations, I should be · inclined to vary the motion for amendment, and insert the word liquidated before domestic debt, so as to provide permanent funds for the payment of interest on the liquidated part of the debt only."

February 23, 1790. The assumption of the State debts being under consideration, Mr. Sherman said if we can make provision for these debts it would be a desirable object to assume them. It will at the same time ease the State of a very great burden, and put all ranks of creditors upon the same footing, and this last will have the effect to prevent speculation; inasmuch as there will be but one uniform object for men to trade in, there will be no difficult variety in the nature of stock. But at the same time, I think the debts to be assumed ought to consist of those only which were incurred for the common or particular defence during the last war, and not those debts which the State may have incurred for the support of its government, the protection and encouragement of its manufactures, or for maintaining and opening highways, clearing the obstructions in the navigation of rivers, or any other local purpose undertaken merely for the benefit of one or two States.

Mr. Sherman said, in reply to certain objections by Mr. Stone: " It appears to me that the objections of the gentleman from Maryland are not

sufficient to prevent our adoption of this proposition. His first objection is that it will give a
greater degree of importance to the general government, while it will lessen the consequence of
the State governments. Now, I do not believe
that it will have that effect. I consider both
governments standing on the broad basis of the
people. They were both constituted by them for
their general and particular good. The Representatives in Congress draw their authority from
the same source as the State legislatures; they
are both of them elected by the people at large,
the one to manage their national concerns, and the
other their domestic, which they find can be better done by being divided into lesser communities
than the whole Union; but to effect the greater
concerns they have confederated; therefore everything which strengthens the Federal Government
and enables it to answer the end for which it was
instituted, will be a desirable object with the people. It is well known we can extend our authority
no further than to the bounds the people have
assigned. If we possess this power, doubtless the
people will send others to correct our faults, or,
if necessary, alter the system; but we have every
reason to believe the people will be pleased with it,
and none suppose that the State governments will
object. They are the supreme power within their
own jurisdiction; and they will have authority over
the States in all cases not given to the general
government, notwithstanding the assumption of
the State debts. If it was a question between two
different countries, and we were going to give the

British Parliament power, by assuming our debts, of levying what taxes they thought proper, and the people of America were to have no voice in the appointment of the officers who were to administer the affairs of the government, the experiment would be dangerous to the country; but as the business is to be conducted by ourselves, there can be no ground for apprehension. The people of the United States are like masters prescribing to their servants the several branches of business they will each have to perform. It might not comport with their interests if the Federal Government was to interfere with the government of particular States; while on the other hand, it would injure their interests to restrict the general government from performing what the Federal Constitution allows them. It is the interest of each and of the whole that they should be separate within their proper limits.

"Another objection is that we are to pay the whole by imposts, and that this mode will be unequal. I apprehend that this is not well founded, because the consumers of the imported goods get the benefit of the use, and the consumption is in a great degree proportioned to the abilities of the citizens. The rich man, with his dependents, consumes more; there is more waste too in such a family than in the economy and frugality of the poor. If this is a fact, the rich contribute revenue in a proportion, and of consequence the burden of the tax is borne generally and equally by those who derive benefit from the late Revolution.

"Another objection is that we were not authorized by the Constitution to assume the State debts. By the confederation Congress were authorized to raise money; but not being able to effect this in an immediate and direct manner, they did it mediately through the intervention of the State governments; so that in fact these debts were to be looked upon as the absolute debts of the Union; however, I should have no objection to qualify the mode of expressing our opinion in such way as to confine the assumption to those debts alone which were contracted by the States for the common defence. Those debts, as was observed by the gentleman from Pennsylvania, will ultimately be assumed, and it is as well to be charged with them in the first instance, especially as if doing so in the first instance will promote the general good.

"Another objection is that the debts of the States are of different value. I take it, sir, that no debt will be assumed but what is liquidated and reduced to specie value, and although we differ in nominal accounts, a dollar is everywhere equal. As to the inequality of the market rate, it may have been occasioned by some States not having made equal provisions for their debts when compared to the provisions of other States; but as the debts are all equally meritorious, an equality of provision ought to be made. That some creditors have hitherto suffered is no reason why they should continue to suffer; so I can see no weight in this objection. But he supposes that some creditors will prefer holding the State for their money rather than the United States; if it should be the case, it will make no difference on the final settlement, because the States will only be debited for that part of the debt which their creditors had subscribed into the general fund. But I can see no good reason for supposing that the creditors of the States will refuse to subscribe. They have an election, it is true, but the terms must appear to them so advantageous, considering all things, as to induce them to accept the plan.

"I have no difficulty in my mind respecting the assumption, but as to the time of doing it I am not so well satisfied. I have not a doubt of our ability, because if the whole debt must be paid by general efforts of the State and general governments, the same money may be raised, with greater ease, by the general government alone."

April 12. On assuming the State debts.

Mr. Sherman: "When I see the House so equally divided on an important subject, it gives me great concern on account of the threatening aspect it has on the peace and welfare of the government.

"The support of public credit by a provision for doing justice to the creditors of the United States was one great object that led to the establishment of the present government; and should it fail of doing justice to so great a proportion of them as are involved in this provision, it would lose the confidence of many of its best friends, and disappoint the expectations of the people in general.

"I consider the debts incurred by the several States in support of the war, and for the common defence and general welfare, as the debts of the United States, and that those creditors have as

just and meritorious a claim on the Union for payment as any creditors whatever. A great part of
them were assumed by the States in behalf of the
United States in consequence of the requisitions of
Congress.

" I shall not now go into a particular discussion
of the proposition before the committee, (everything
having been already said that may reflect light on
the subject,) but shall only state the reasons for
which I shall give my vote in the affirmative.

" The measure appears to me both just and poli-
tic ; just in respect to the creditors whose debts
are due for services and supplies rendered in support of the common cause of the Union, which
therefore ought to be paid out of the same common funds as the other creditors of the United
States, and although some of the States would be
able to provide for their creditors as well as the
United States, yet that is not the case as to those
whose exertions, sufferings, and burdens have been
much greater than the others, and it would not
give satisfaction to assume the debts of some
States and not of others.

" The measure will be just in respect to the
several States, because each will bear only its just
proportion of the present burden, and their past
exertions and expenditures will be equitably adjusted in the final settlements of their accounts for
which effectual provision is to be made by some
act that provides for the assumption of the debts.

" The policy of the measure consists in its tendency to promote justice and harmony and confidence in the government in lifting the burdens of

a number of States who, from their situation and circumstances during the war, were necessitated to make greater exertions, and subjected to greater sufferings and expenditures, than the other States, and by putting all the funds necessary for paying the debts under one direction, to facilitate the collection and render them more productive and less embarrassing to Congress. The principal resource for pay (the impost) is in possession of the general government.

"But if the State debts are not assumed, the States which have heretofore borne the greatest burdens will be left still to sustain those unequal and grievous burdens, or their creditors will be left without any provisions for satisfying their claim, either of which would be unreasonable and occasion great uneasiness, which will tend to embarrass and obstruct the measures of government.

"It has been said, let those States wait until their accounts with the United States shall be settled, and then receive security for the balances that may be due to them. But why should those States be subjected to greater burdens at present than the other States? As it is not known which are debtor or creditor States, why not bear the burden equally until that can be ascertained? If there is to be no settlement, I think it is a conclusive argument that the whole public debt should be assumed by the United States. It ought to be presumed that the States have made exertions according to their abilities and in due proportion, until the contrary appears, and that can no otherwise appear but by a settlement of the accounts; and until that is done I can see no good reason why any State should bear more than its just proportion of the existing debts, whether contracted by the United States, or by the individual States, if incurred for the common defence or general welfare of the Union. It is said there is no rule to establish or ascertain the quotas of the several States; but I think the rule is fixed by the resolution of the late Congress of the 22d of November, 1777, and the other of June 1778, and the provision in the new Constitution for apportioning direct taxes."

Vote on the assumption, 29 for, 31 against.

On the 21st of April, Mr. Sherman suggested the assumption of certain specific sums for each State; and being called upon to ascertain in what proportion he meant to fill up the blanks, he read the following as a statement of the debts owing by the States, and the proportion he wanted to have assumed.

Assumption of the State Debts, not exceeding the sums in the last column, Due as per Secretary's Report.

Sums to be assumed.		Dollars.
New Hampshire	300,000	300,000
Massachusetts	5,226,801	4,000,000
Connecticut	1,951,173	1,600,000
New York	1,167,575	1,000,000
New Jersey	788,680	750,000
Pennsylvania	2,200,000	2,000,000
Delaware		100,000
Maryland	800,000	750,000
Virginia	3,600,743	3,000,000
North Carolina		1,600,000
South Carolina	5,386,232	4,000,000
Georgia		200,000
		$19,300,000

The bill as finally passed, Aug. 4, 1790, provided for the assumption of the State debts as follows.

New Hampshire	300,000
Massachusetts	4,000,000
Rhode Island	200,000
New York	1,200,000
Connecticut	1,600,000
New Jersey	800,000
Pennsylvania	2,200,000
Delaware	200,000
Maryland	800,000
Virginia	3,500,000
North Carolina	2,400,000
South Carolina	4,000,000
Georgia	300,000
	$21,500,000

Tuesday, May 25. Mr. Gerry's motion on the assumption of the State debts being under consideration, Mr. Sherman summed up the argument as follows: " The question now under consideration is, whether the State debts that have been contracted for the benefit of the Union shall be assumed by the United States. This is an essential part of the system reported by the Secretary of the Treasury for funding the national debt. The substance of the arguments in favor of the assumption are: —

" 1. That the debts were contracted on behalf and for the benefit of the United States and therefore justice requires that they should be assumed.

" 2. That some States have taken upon themselves greater sums than others, and beyond their just proportions or abilities to pay.

" 3. That the funds out of which these debts

ought to be paid, are by the Constitution put under the direction of the Federal Government; and
this has been done by the authority of the people
since the debts were contracted, and for the express purpose of paying the debts of the United
States, of which these are a part, and therefore
ought to follow the funds.

" 4. That the imposts and excises, so far as excises may be necessary, can be best managed
under one direction.

" 5. That equal justice ought to be done to all
the creditors, but this cannot be done by the individual States, some of them being unable to
make the necessary provision, they being burdened beyond their quota, and deprived of their
former revenues.

" 6. That the measure is founded in good policy,
as well as justice, as it will promote harmony among
the different classes of creditors, and among the
several States, and attach them to the government and facilitate its operations.

" I shall now take notice of some of the principal
objections.

" 1. It is said that the accounts of the several
States with the United States ought to be settled.
I agree that no payment ought to be made to the
States until their accounts are settled.   But that
ought not to affect the rights of individuals, who
have liquidated claims for services or supplies rendered for the benefit of the Union, whether the
contract was made with a member, or an officer
of the United States.   It is not in the power of
these creditors to compel a settlement, nor ought

their claims to be postponed or affected for want of
such settlement; but such of the securities as may
be the property of a State are on a different footing.

"2. It is objected that when the States took the
debts on themselves, they expected to pay them.
This cannot be admitted without some explanation: by the confederation all charges of war, &c.
incurred for the common defence and general welfare, were to be paid out of a common treasury,
which was to be supplied by the several States,
paying in their respective quotas, and a final ad-
justment of the accounts was to be made; and
the individual States expected that all the sources
of revenue would remain in their hands, out of
which they expected to pay their quotas of all the
debts and expenses of the Union: but by a revolution in government, the revenues are put under
the power of the Federal Government, for the express purpose of paying the debts, so that the
mode of payment is materially altered, and the
obligation transferred from the individual States
to the United States.

"3. It is objected that this is a new project —
and not mentioned in the Constitution. The nov-
elty of it is no just objection against adopting it —
if the measure be just. It was mentioned in the
general convention — but it was not thought necessary or proper to insert it in the Constitution, for
Congress would have sufficient power to adopt it
if they should judge it expedient.

"4. It is said that the States most urgent for this
measure are not incapacitated by adopting the
new Constitution for paying their debts.

"Answer. The States most burdened with debts, and the only ones who expected to have sums greater than their quotas assumed, are Massachusetts and South Carolina; and these depended chiefly on impost, of which they are now wholly deprived.

"Connecticut does not wish or expect to have more of her debt assumed, than her just quota of the whole sum to be assumed, so that no other State will bear any greater burden on her account.

"The debt of New Hampshire will not amount to half the sum of her quota of the debts proposed to be assumed, but she has been in favor of the measure on principles of justice and national policy.

"But a very fallacious argument has been advanced respecting the ratio in which some States contribute to the common funds by way of imposts; and it comes with a very ill grace from the gentleman who advanced it, because it is so fully refuted by the report of a committee of the late Congress, of which committee he was a member. It appears on the Journal of the 29th April, 1783, page 203, whereby it is shown that the several States contribute by a general impost, in proportion to the number of their inhabitants, whether the articles are imported, and the duties paid, in the State in which they are consumed or not, as the tax is ultimately paid by the consumers. [Here a part of the Journal was read.]

"5. It is objected that it will be difficult to discriminate the State debts contracted for the Union, from their other debts. But what necessity is there for such a discrimination, if only certain sums are assumed, and the States charged with them? The whole will be adjusted among the States on the settlement of their accounts; besides, their debts for other purposes are inconsiderable.

" 6. Objection: if only part of the State debts be assumed, equal justice will not be done to all the creditors.

" Answer. The small sums that will remain of the debts of any of the States can, and doubtless will, be as well provided for by the respective States as those assumed will by the United States.

" It is proposed to assume the whole of the debts of the States of New Hampshire, New York, New Jersey, Pennsylvania, Delaware, Maryland, Virginia, and Georgia; and the small sums that will remain of the debts of Massachusetts, Connecticut, North Carolina, and South Carolina can easily be provided for by those States.

" 7. It has been objected that Virginia has made greater exertions in complying with the specie requisitions of Congress, and in sinking a considerable part of the principal of her debts, since the peace, and therefore it would be inequitable to increase her burden by assuming the debts of other States which have not made like exertions.

" The answer is, that it is not proposed to lay any additional burden on that State. The amount of the State debts to be assumed will not exceed $23,000,000; the debt of Virginia to be assumed amounts to $3,681,000, which is something more than that State's quota of the whole sum to be assumed, in proportion to its number of representatives; so that the interest of Virginia would be no

otherwise affected by the assumption than by trans-
ferring its debt from its particular fund to the common funds. It is also proposed to assume of the
debts of Connecticut and North Carolina the just
amount of their respective quotas of the whole
sum proposed to be assumed.

" 8. It is objected, that the debts of Georgia are
not on interest. If anything to the purpose can be
inferred from this objection, it is in favor of the
assumption; for, if the debts are just, they ought
immediately to be paid, or put on interest.

" 9. It is objected that the debt of the United
States will be so increased by the assumption of
the State debts, as to make direct taxes or excises
necessary to be laid by Congress, which would be
odious to the people.

" Answer. The assumption of the State debts is
a part of the plan reported by the Secretary of the
Treasury. — He does not propose direct taxes, nor
excises, further than those that have already been
adopted by the House — and I think some reliance
ought to be had on the opinion of the officer whom
government have placed at the head of the department of finance.

" The whole of the debts must be paid by the
citizens of the United States; they do now exist,
and government is under obligation to do justice
to all creditors. The people have put all the
sources of revenue in the power of Congress, for
that purpose, and will doubtless be satisfied with
their administration of them. The resources of the
nation will be abundantly sufficient, if prudently
managed, to pay the annual interest of the debt

and gradually to discharge the principal within a reasonable time. The western territory, if properly disposed of, will sink a considerable part of the national debt. It was observed that excises are the most expensive taxes to collect; but Dr. Smith, on the Wealth of Nations, says, that in Britain the collection of excises costs at the rate of but five per cent, but that imposts at the rate of ten per cent; this is according to my best recollection. I have not the book now before me.

" 10. It is objected, that the securities will probably centre in large towns, or get into the hands of foreigners. — I think it is probable that the securities will centre in the hands of such citizens in the several States as shall choose to live on the interest of their capital, and in the hands of corporate bodies instituted to promote science and other useful purposes; but the securities will not get out of the possession of the original owners without their consent, nor (if well funded) will they be induced to part with them for less than their just value, and it is reasonable that they should be left at liberty to dispose of their own property.

" 11. It is objected, that funds are not to be provided for the State debts this session, and we do not know what may be the opinions of our successors.

" Answer. The provision is proposed to be made by the present Congress at their next session.

" 12. Objection: the House are divided in sentiment, and it will be safer to negative the proposition than to adopt it by a small majority. — It

appears to me that the greatest safety will be on
the other side.   There is no dispute about the justice of the claims of the creditors, the only point
in dispute is, which would be the most expedient
mode of payment, and which would be most agreeable to the public opinion.   My reasons for supposing that it will be safer to adopt a measure by
a small majority than to negative it, is, because
people are more influenced by their feelings than
by speculative reasonings, or nice calculations.   If
the debts are assumed, what inconveniences will
the people feel from it?   And, if they reason upon
it, they will find that no injustice will ultimately
take place, but all will be set right by a liquidation
of the accounts.   But if the State debts are not assumed and the creditors are not provided for by
the States, or if the States are subjected to heavy
direct taxes in making the provision, these evils
will be severely felt, and must create uneasiness
and complaints which may prove very prejudicial
to the administration of government.

" 13. It is said that 'several of the legislatures
have lately been in session and have not applied to
Congress or instructed their representatives to obtain an assumption of the State debts.'

" I think their opinions cannot be inferred from
their silence on the subject. — In matters that
concern only the particular interest of a State, the
State may properly instruct their representatives,
who in such case would act only as agents for
the State: but in matters which concern the Union
in general, such interference might be of dangerous
tendency; for all the members ought to be at per-

fect liberty to act their best and unbiased judgment upon public measures, according to the light
and information that may be obtained by a public
discussion of them in the House, which may not
be known to the legislatures of the particular
States. I have endeavored briefly to give the
reasons which have induced me to be in favor of
this measure, and to obviate the objections that
have been made to it, which I submit to the opinion of the committee, without troubling them with
any observations."

The bill providing for the assumption of the
State debts, notwithstanding the strenuous opposition of Mr. Madison, was finally carried by a compromise arrangement, by which the permanent
seat of government was to be fixed on the Potomac,
in consideration of enough southern votes being
secured to pass the bill for assuming the State
debts. Mr. Sherman voted against the Potomac
site.

PART IV. — THE SLAVE TRADE.

On the 11th of February, 1790, an address was
presented from the Quakers of Pennsylvania, New
Jersey, Delaware, and the western part of Maryland and Virginia, on the "licentious wickedness
of the African trade for slaves." A similar address was presented from the Society of Friends
of the City of New York.

Mr. Sherman suggested a reference to a committee of one member from each State, because

several States had already made some regulations on the subject.

This was objected to principally by the representatives from South Carolina and Georgia.

Mr. Sherman then observed that the petitioners from New York stated that they had applied to the legislature of that State to prohibit certain practices which they considered to be improper, and which tended to injure the wellbeing of the community; that the legislature had considered their application, but had applied no remedy, because they supposed that power was exclusively vested in the general government under the Constitution of the United States; it would therefore be proper to commit that petition, in order to ascertain what are the powers of the general government in the case.

The next day, February 12th, a memorial of the Pennsylvania Anti-Slavery Society, signed by Benjamin Franklin as President, was presented, asking Congress to devise means for the abolition of slavery. This called forth an exciting debate, in which the advocates of slavery, though opposed by such men as Madison and Parker from Virginia, as well as by the northern representatives, made up in violence and denunciation what they. lacked in numbers. They attacked the motives of their opponents, and claimed that the Bible and the universal practice of mankind were on their side.

Mr. Sherman endeavored to calm the agitation by saying that he could see no difficulty in committing the memorial; because it was probable the committee would understand their business,

and perhaps they might bring in such a report as
would be satisfactory to gentlemen on both sides
of the House.

Finally, on the 15th of February, it was voted
by forty-three to fourteen that the petitions should
be sent to a committee.

On the 8th of March, this committee made their
report, in which, after setting forth the Constitutional restrictions on the subject, they stated that
Congress had authority to interdict the African
trade, so far as it is or may be carried on by citizens of the United States for supplying foreigners,
and to make provisions for the humane treatment
of slaves in all cases while on their passage to the
United States, or to foreign parts, so far as it respects citizens of the United States. The House,
in committee of the whole, adopted this report in
substance.

March 9th, it was moved that the report of the
committee be recommitted. Mr. Sherman opposed this motion. He said that this report was
agreeable to his ideas; it was prudent, humane,
and judicious.

After considerable debate, on March 23d, it
was voted by twenty-nine to twenty-five that the
report of the committee, and also the report of the
committee of the whole, be inserted in the Journal.

The second session of Congress adjourned on
the 12th of August, 1790.

Mr. Sherman's desire for the abolition of slavery
is expressed in a letter to Gov. Huntington, March
7, 1792, where, referring to the massacres resulting
from the negro revolt in Hayti, he writes, — "This

shows the bad effects of slavery, and I hope it will
tend to its abolition."

Mr. Sherman's brother Josiah died in 1789.
The widow wrote to some of her friends to see
what assistance could be obtained to enable her
son Roger Minott Sherman to continue his studies
at Yale. It was apparently in response to this
appeal that Mr. Sherman wrote the following
letter to his nephew.

NEW YORK, April 28, 1790.

DEAR NEPHEW, — I would have you continue
your studies and remain at my house as you have
done hitherto. I hope you will be provided for
so as to complete your education at College, and
lay a foundation for future usefulness. When I
return home I shall take such further order respecting it as may be proper. I shall afford you
as much assistance as under my circumstances
may be prudent.

I am your affectionate uncle

ROGER SHERMAN.

Mr. Sherman died a year after his nephew graduated; but before he died he doubtless saw the
promise of that distinguished career, which added
new lustre to the Sherman name. Senator Hoar
has sent me the following interesting statements in
reference to this eminent lawyer.

"Roger Minott Sherman, son of Mr. Sherman's
brother Josiah, was born in Woburn, Mass., May
22, 1773. Mr. Sherman was much attached to
him and defrayed the cost of his education. He

was an inmate of Mr. Sherman's family while a
student at Yale College. He was graduated in the
year 1792. He was one of the ablest lawyers and
advocates New England ever produced, probably
having no equal at the bar of New England except
Jeremiah Mason and Daniel Webster. I attended
a dinner of the Alumni of Yale College some years
ago. President Woolsey sat on one side of me,
and Dr. Leonard Bacon on the other; and right
opposite at the table was the Rev. Dr. Atwater,
then I believe of Princeton, but formerly Mr.
Sherman's pastor in Fairfield. President Woolsey
said that Roger Minott Sherman came nearer his
conception of Cicero than any other person he
ever heard speak. They used frequently to invite
him to deliver public addresses at the College.
But he never would accept the invitation. After
refusal, the invitation would be renewed again in
a few years with like result.

"To the above estimate of Mr. Sherman, Dr.
Bacon and Mr. Atwater agreed.

"When I was in the Law School at Harvard,
Prof. Simon Greenleaf told the class in one of his
lectures that he was once travelling through Connecticut in a carriage on a summer journey, and
came to a town, I think Fairfield, which was the
county seat. He stopped to get his dinner and
rest his horses. While the horses were being fed
he went into the court-house, intending to stay only
a few minutes, and found Roger Minott Sherman
arguing a case before the Supreme Court with
Judge Gould on the other side. He was so much
interested in the discussion that he stayed through

the afternoon. Mr. Sherman and Judge Gould were engaged on opposite sides in nearly all the cases. Prof. Greenleaf was so much interested in their masterly arguments that he remained and attended court during the entire week. I do not remember his exact language, but he, in substance, gave an estimate of Mr. Sherman as a profound lawyer and able advocate, not less exalted than President Woolsey had given of him as an orator.

"Some slight account of Roger Minott Sherman will be found in Goodrich's Recollections.

"Mr. Evarts once told me that there was an important controversy involving the title to a valuable cargo in which a lawyer in Hartford was on one side, and a member of the bar of the city of New York on the other. The New York lawyer went to Hartford to negotiate about the case. The Hartford lawyer had obtained the opinion of Roger Minott Sherman for his client and held it in his hand during the conversation, labeled on the outside, "Opinion of Roger Minott Sherman," and moved it about under the eye of his opponent. The opinion was in fact that the Hartford man's client had no case. But the New York lawyer supposed that if the man had got Roger Minott Sherman's opinion, and seemed to set so much store upon the document, it was favorable to the party who had consulted him. He was much alarmed and settled the case on favorable terms to his antagonist.

"Mr. Sherman was famous for the quickness of his wit. A story went the rounds of the papers in my youth, which may or may not have any truth in it, but which I will record. It is said that he was once arguing a case against Nathaniel Smith, a very able but rather coarse lawyer. Mr. Smith had discussed the question of law with the subtlety for which he was distinguished. Mr. Sherman said to the court that he thought his brother Smith's metaphysics were out of place in that discussion; that he was not adverse to such refinement at a proper time, and would willingly, on a fit occasion, chop logic and split hairs with him. Smith pulled a hair out of his own head, and holding it up, said, — 'Split that.' Sherman replied, quick as lightning, 'May it please your honor, I did n't say bristles.' "

The following is the passage from L. G. Goodrich's "Recollections of a Lifetime," referred to by Senator Hoar (Vol. I. p. 47).

. "Roger Minot Sherman was distinguished for acute logical powers and great elegance of diction, — words and sentences seemed to flow from his lips as if he were reading from the Spectator. He was a man of refined personal appearance and manners; tall, stooping a little in his walk; deliberate in his movements and speech, indicating circumspection, which was one of his characteristics. His countenance was pale and thoughtful, his eye remarkable for a keen penetrating expression. Though a man of grave general aspect, he was not destitute of humor. He was once travelling in West Virginia, and stopping at a small tavern, was beset with questions by the landlord, as to where he came from, whither he was going, etc. At last said Mr. Sherman, 'Sit down, sir, and I will tell you all about it.' The landlord sat down. ' Sir,' said he, ' I am from the Blue Light State of Connecticut.' The landlord stared. ' I am a deacon in a Calvinistic church.' The landlord was evidently shocked. ' I was a member of the Hartford Convention.' This was too much for the democratic nerves of the landlord; he speedily departed, and left his lodger to himself."

PART V. — NATIONAL BANK.

THIRD SESSION. — Dec. 6, 1790–March 3, 1791.

The third session of Congress began December 6, 1790. On the 3d of January, 1791, Mr. Sherman wrote the following letter to Governor Huntington, giving him an account of the matters pending before Congress.

PHILADELPHIA, Jan. 3rd, 1791.

SIR, — There are diverse weighty matters before Congress to be considered and acted upon this session; such as making further provisions for paying the interest of the national debt; establishing a National Bank; a Land Office; a Mint; weights and measures; regulating the Militia; the Post Office; the coasting trade; the election of President; and to provide in case of vacancy of the offices both of President and Vice President; some further provisions in the judiciary department as to fees, process and execution, and some regulations respecting commercial affairs. These have been already entered upon. Others may occur, besides applications from private persons. There have been several petitions preferred from public creditors for a greater allowance of interest than is provided by the Act providing for the public debt, on which the Senate have resolved that it is inexpedient to make any alteration, in which all concurred except one. I believe the House will concur in the same sentiment by a great majority.

I hope Congress will be able to finish the business by the first of March next, so as not to call a meeting under the new election.

Our loss of brave officers and men in the late western expedition is great, and much to be lamented. No authentic accounts of the particular circumstances of the action have been received, further than what was at first transmitted by General Harmar, which your Excellency has doubtless seen in the newspapers. The enclosed paper of Dec. 22 contains the Secretary's plan of a Bank. That of Dec. 27, the supplementary funds for which a bill is prepared and brought in. That of the first of January contains the copy of a letter from London of the 4th of Nov. giving an account of a pacification between Britain and Spain.

Your Excellency will be furnished with the acts of Congress by the Secretary of State. There has been but one law completed this session, and that is only a short one to supply a deficiency in one of the last session.

The weather has been very cold here. Teams

pass the Delaware on the ice opposite to this City, and there is snow sufficient for good sleighing in the country. The market is good and plentiful.

The House provided here for the accommodation of Congress is quite as convenient as that at N. York. The galleries are not quite so commodious.

I am Sir with much respect your Excellency's obedient humble servant,

ROGER SHERMAN.

The most important matter discussed in this short session of three months was the bill for a National Bank. Although no speeches were made by Mr. Sherman on this subject, so far as the record shows, he gave the bill his hearty support. In the course of the debate he wrote on a slip of paper a statement of his views on the subject, which he handed to Mr. Madison; and Mr. Madison, in a note at the bottom, indicated his objections. This interesting document, which came from Mr. Madison's papers, in which the arguments on both sides of this important question are given in a nut-shell, is in the possession of Hon. G. F. Hoar. The following is a copy.

"You will admit that Congress have power to provide by law for raising, depositing and applying money for the purposes enumerated in the Constitution

X (and generally of regulating the finances).

"That they have power so far as no particular rules are pointed out in the Constitution to make such rules and regulations as they may judge necessary and proper to effect these purposes. The only question that remains is — Is a bank [a necessary and] a proper measure for effecting these purposes? And is not this a question of expediency rather than of right?

"Feb. 4, 1791. This handed to J. M. by Mr. Sherman during the debate on the constitutionality of the bill for a National Bank. The line marked X given up by him on the objection of J. M. The interlineation of 'a necessary &' by J. M. to which he gave no answer other than a smile."

The following letter, of Feb. 11th, 1791, from Mr. Sherman to William Williams, is of a more personal and confidential character than most of his correspondence.

PHILADELPHIA, Feb. 11th, 1791.

DEAR SIR, — I received your much esteemed favor of 1 instant yesterday, I should have commenced a correspondence with you before this time, had it not been that the proceedings and debates in Congress were more fully communicated in the newspapers than they could be by letter, as well as all other occurrences of importance.

But I seldom see the papers from Connecticut or hear much of the politics of that State : in the time of the war I always received by your letters the most full account of public measures and also of the motives and springs of action from which they originated, and the principal agents by which they were effected, to my great satisfaction. I shall ever retain a grateful remembrance of our

You will admit That Congress
have power to provide by Law,
for raising, depositing & apply
ing money for the purposes
enumerated in the constitution.

X & generally of regulating the Finances

That they have power so far as no particular
rules are pointed out, in the constitution
to make such rules & regulations as they
may judge necessary & proper to effect
these purposes. The only question that
remains is- Is a Bank a proper measure
for effecting these purposes?
And is not this a question of expediency
rather than of right?

74.1791. This handed to J. M. by Mr Sherman, during the
debate on the constitutionality of the Bill for a national
Bank - the line marked X given up by him on the
objection of J. M - The interbretation of "necessary"by
J. M. to which he gave no answer when the whole

former friendship while we were fellow laborers in the common cause of our country in several departments. I am also very sensible of the indefatigable exertions of your brother, the late sheriff, in the service of the United States, and his sharing in the common calamity by a delay and depreciation of his pay.

Your nephew at Hartford executed the office of Deputy Sheriff to good satisfaction when he attended the Superior Court, and I believe to general satisfaction in other respects. And I wish that the United States may avail themselves of his services in the collection of the revenue. I am not in the line of appointment to offices. I mentioned him to Mr Trumbull who concurs with me as to his qualifications. The new revenue bill has not yet passed the Senate: it is like to undergo considerable alterations in that House, and what offices will be ultimately established is not yet known to me. I shall bear in mind your request.

You and I have borne the burden and heat of the day, but the most faithful and painful services are soon forgotten when they are passed, and young persons are rising up who would be willing to crowd us off of the stage to make room for themselves, but they can't deprive us of the consolation arising from a consciousness of having done our duty.

A bill for establishing a National Bank has passed both Houses, and a bill to admit Kentucky into the Union. Vermont has adopted the Constitution and applied for admission, their application is referred to a committee by each House.

This session will end the third day of March. The House of Representatives have passed a bill fixing the time for the next meeting of Congress to the first Monday in November next. I am Sir with great respect and esteem,

Your friend and humble servant,

ROGER SHERMAN.

PART VI. — SENATE. May 1791 — July 1793.

At the May session, 1791, of the Connecticut Assembly, Mr. Sherman was appointed United States Senator, in the place of William Samuel Johnson resigned. This position Mr. Sherman held till his death in July, 1793. As the sessions of the Senate during this time were secret, we have no account of his speeches in that body.

On the 21st of November, 1791, Mr. Sherman wrote the following letter to Governor Huntington.

PHILADELPHIA, Nov. 21, 1791.

SIR, — The President's speech at the opening of the present session of Congress gives a favorable view of public affairs, and particularly that the revenues are likely to be adequate to their objects, so that no additional burdens need be imposed on the people.

Both branches of Congress are nearly full, and have so arranged the principal business of the session that each have taken a proportion of it, and are forwarding it with the usual despatch.

The House of Representatives after some days

debate, have passed a vote for fixing the number
of Representatives for the next, and succeeding
elections, under the present census, at one for
every 30000 inhabitants, which will make the whole
to be about 112. The members were divided on
the question, 35 being for it and 23 against it, two
members that were for a less number, who were
present at the debate, were absent when the vote
was taken. I understand that some members intend
to move to lessen the number when the bill is considered in the House. I am not able to make any
conjecture what will be the opinion of the Senate
on the subject.

It appears to me that no advantage can be derived from so great an increase of the number
sufficient to countervail the expense. As the jurisdiction of Congress is limited to a few objects
that concern the States in general, a less number
might give the necessary information, and more
conveniently transact the public business. Increasing the number will not increase the powers
of that branch of the legislature, but it will lessen
the weight and the responsibility of each individual member. I wish that the number was so fixed
by the Constitution as not to be varied by Congress. When the Constitution was formed the
number of the Representatives was in proportion
to the number of Senators as five to two. At that
rate the Representatives should be increased at the
next election to 75, which being apportioned to
the several States, would not lessen the number
first assigned to Connecticut, nor vary their proportion of suffrage in either House from that of

allowing one vote to each State. If the Constitution should be altered so as always to preserve the like proportion between the numbers in each House as at first, I think it would be a real amendment; and the expense would be about 40000 dollars per annum less, than if the amendment heretofore recommended should be ratified; which sum might be applied toward sinking the national debt.

We have no late accounts from the hostile Indians in the territory northwest of the Ohio; a treaty with the Cherokee nation has been lately concluded which will probably secure peace to the southwestern frontier. Mr Hammond, a minister plenipotentiary from his British Majesty, has had an audience, and has been announced by the President of the United States.

By the latest accounts from France, the new Constitution of Government has been ratified by the King, and will probably secure to the people of that nation the peaceful enjoyment of civil and religious liberty; which may probably have a good effect on the other nations of Europe, and strengthen the alliance between France and these States.

The public papers here contain but little news. I have enclosed a morning and an evening paper of this day. I am Sir with much respect and esteem,

Your Excellency's obedient humble servant,

ROGER SHERMAN.

On the last day of this session, Mr. Sherman, in the following letter, gave Gov. Huntington an account of the work of the session.

PHILADELPHIA, May 8th, 1792.

SIR, — The Congress will close their session this day. It has been about six weeks longer than I at first expected. Many bills have been passed of a public nature, and considerable time has been spent on private applications. Measures have been taken to lessen that branch of business in future, by enabling the executive departments to give relief. The first bill that passed the two Houses for fixing the number of Representatives at one hundred and twenty was disapproved by the President; that is the only instance in which he has exercised his power of negative. The last act fixes the number at one hundred and five, allowing the State of Connecticut to choose seven. The Indian war has made it necessary to increase the imposts on some articles, part of which is limited to two years. Measures will be taken by the Ex- · ecutive to obtain a conference with the hostile tribes of Indians in order to settle a permanent peace.

The enclosed paper contains a copy of the law for regulating the Militia of the several States. Another act is passed for calling them into service on necessary occasions, which I have not a copy of, but all the laws will soon be transmitted to your Excellency officially by the Secretary of State. Mr Thomas Pinckney who is appointed Minister to the Court of Great Britain is now in this city. He says he expects to embark for London within about six weeks. I don't learn that much progress has been made in any negotiations with the British Minister here.   If we could get possession of the Western Posts, I believe it would be a favorable circumstance for obtaining and preserving peace with the Indians.   I am Sir with the most perfect respect,

Your Excellency's obedient humble servant,

ROGER SHERMAN.

•

CHAPTER XII.

RELIGIOUS OPINIONS.

ON the 14th of March, 1742, a few weeks before completing his twenty-first year, Roger Sherman united with the Congregational Church in Stoughton. His father had died the year previous, and the care of his mother and four younger brothers and sisters devolved upon him. So that his religious life began with the performance of these filial and fraternal duties. This was the type of his religious character throughout his life. He was neither a mystic nor an ascetic. The faithful performance of duty, in the family, in the church, in the State, was the constant rule of his life.

As soon as he was settled in New Milford, he transferred his church relations from Stoughton to that place. In the church in New Milford, we find him performing the duties of clerk, of treasurer, and of deacon. He was equally active in church work when he removed to New Haven. His contribution to the College Chapel, the first year of his residence in New Haven, illustrates his readiness, according to his means, to help every good work. The Rev. Jonathan Edwards, the younger, who was his pastor during the last twenty-four years of his life, says of him, — " He was ready to bear his part of the expense of those designs, public and private, which he esteemed useful; and he was given to hospitality."

Mr. Sherman's interest in the church in New Haven, and his attachment to Dr. Edwards, is shown in the following letter to his son-in-law, Simeon Baldwin.

NEW YORK, Feb. 4th, 1790.

DEAR SIR, — I this day received a letter from my son John dated Jan. 14th, enclosing one for his wife which I have forwarded to you.

He writes that he has recovered his health, that Issac is there and their prospects are good. You wrote me some time ago that you were notified to attend a meeting of some members of our society. I wish to be informed whether there is any new difficulty arisen, and how the members stand affected to Dr. Edwards. . . . I esteem him one of the best of preachers that I am acquainted with, sound in faith, and pious and diligent in his studies and attention to the duties of his office. I should be very sorry to have anything done to grieve him or weaken his hands in the great and important work committed to his charge. If he should leave the Society I should expect they would be divided and broken up. I hope all the well wishers to pure religion will use their influence to preserve peace, and avoid calling Society meetings unnecessarily, as I think it would only promote dissention. Our Savior says "Wo to the world because of offences; but wo to that man by whom the offence cometh." I am willing that anything I have written should be

made known if it will do any good, not only to the
friendly but to the disaffected if there be any such
— I feel well affected to all the members, and wish
to have cordial harmony restored.   Perhaps there
is nothing more pleasing to the adversary of mankind than discord among Christian brethren. — I
shall enclose to you next Saturday's paper, which
will contain the news.

The joining with the first Society in Lectures
has been urged by some, but a majority of the
church did not think it expedient.   I believe it has
never been moved for on the part of Dr Dana nor
do I think he would wish to have it take place.   It
is a matter of no great importance, if there were
no diversity of sentiment between the two pastors,
but as there really is, and as some members of our
church would be dissatisfied with it, I think it
would be highly criminal to insist upon it, so as to
break the unity of the church.   Let each preach
his own lecture, and every one may attend either,
or both, at pleasure.   As to Dr Beardsley's affair,
I understand he is pretty well fixed in his mind
not to return to our Society, but to join the first,
in which I think it is best he should be indulged.
I think that Deacon Austin could do as much to
reconcile matters as any member of the Society,
and that it is the duty of every one to use their influence to that end, and to strengthen the hands
and encourage the heart of Dr. Edwards in his
ministerial work.

I am very respectfully yours,

ROGER SHERMAN.

SIMEON BALDWIN, Esqr.

While tolerant of differences of opinion on religious matters, he disliked and distrusted irreligious men, who made a boast of their impiety. On this ground he opposed the confirmation of Gouverneur Morris as minister to France.

He admitted Mr. Morris's ability, but urged in objection to him his practice of speaking irreverently of the Christian religion, and said that in his experience he had not found men who were lacking in religious sentiment trustworthy in ordinary affairs; and that for this reason he had never put confidence in General Arnold or recommended him for promotion in the public service.

Although Mr. Sherman's religion was of a decidedly practical character, he was very fond of the metaphysics of theology. The only writings of his on this subject which have been preserved, are confined to the last four years of his life, while he was a member of Congress. They display the same acuteness and good sense which characterize his political writings and speeches. They also show great familiarity with the Bible, of which he was a constant student. It was his custom to purchase a Bible at the commencement of every session of Congress, to peruse it daily, and to present it to one of his children on his return home.

During Mr. Sherman's connection with the White Haven Church, its creed was twice changed, once in 1776, and again in 1788. Each time it became briefer, simpler, and more like the creeds of Congregational Churches of the present day. The following confession of faith, in the handwriting of Mr. Sherman, was doubtless prepared by

him at the time of the formation of the creed of
1788; and seems to have been used by the person
or committee who drew up that creed.

CONFESSION OF FAITH.

I believe that there is one only living and true
God, existing in three persons, the Father, the
Son, and the Holy Ghost, the same in substance
equal in power and glory.   That the scriptures of
the old and new testaments are a revelation from
God, and a complete rule to direct us how we may
glorify and enjoy him.   That God has foreordained
whatsoever comes to pass, so as thereby he is not
the author or approver of sin.   That he creates all
things, and preserves and governs all creatures and
all their actions, in a manner perfectly consistent
with the freedom of will in moral agents, and the
usefulness of means.   That he made man at first
perfectly holy, that the first man sinned, and as he
was the public head of his posterity, they all became sinners in consequence of his first transgres-
sion, are wholly indisposed to that which is good
and inclined to evil, and on account of sin are
liable to all the miseries of this life, to death, and
to the pains of hell forever.   I believe that God
having elécted some of mankind to eternal life, did
send his own son to become man, die in the room
and stead of sinners, and thus to lay a foundation
for the offer of pardon and salvation to all mankind, so as all may be saved who are willing to
accept the gospel offer: Also by his special grace
and spirit, to regenerate, sanctify and enable to

persevere in holiness, all who shall be saved; and
to procure in consequence of their repentance and
faith in himself their justification by virtue of his
atonement as the only meritorious cause. I believe a visible church to be a congregation of those
who make a credible profession of their faith in
Christ, and obedience to him, joined by the bond
of the covenant.

That a church of Christ hath power to choose
its own officers, to admit members, and to administer discipline upon offenders according to the
rules of Christ, either by admonition or excommu-
nication. I believe that the sacraments of the new
testament are baptism and the Lord's supper, that
baptism is a sign and seal of engrafting into Christ,
of a participation of his benefits, and of the obligation of the subject to be the Lord's. That in the
Lord's supper the worthy receivers are by faith
made partakers of all the benefits of Christ, to
their growth in grace. I believe that the souls of
believers are at their death made perfectly holy,
and immediately taken to glory: that at the end of
this world there will be a resurrection of the dead,
and a final judgment of all mankind, when the
righteous shall be publickly acquitted by Christ the
Judge and admitted to everlasting life and glory, and
the wicked be sentenced to everlasting punishment.

In the early part of 1790, a correspondence took
place between Roger Sherman and Rev. Justus
Mitchell, who married a daughter of Mr. Sherman's brother Josiah, on the question of moral
and natural inability. In Mr. Sherman's letter

18

occurs the following passage on moral good and evil, which gives a clearer statement as to his belief on these matters than is contained in his Confession of Faith.

"I suppose that moral good or evil consists not in dormant principles, but voluntary exercises, that regeneration simply considered is not a moral virtue, but the holy exercises that flow from it are — and on the other hand no propensities in animal nature are in themselves sinful, if not indulged contrary to law, that moral good consists in right exercises of the natural powers and principles of the soul, in settling the affections on right objects &c. and moral evil in placing the affections on wrong objects. And mankind having the power of free agency are justly accountable for the exercise of their natural powers, and that any indisposition to do what they know to be their duty can be no excuse for not doing it."

In 1789, Mr. Sherman published in New Haven a sermon written by himself, entitled "A short sermon on the duty of self-examination preparatory to receiving the Lord's Supper, with an Appendix containing extracts from Richard Baxter's works." A copy of this sermon is in the library of Yale College. President Stiles in his Diary speaks of it as "A well and judiciously written sermon." In a letter to Dr. H. Williams, December 17, 1791, Mr. Sherman states his reasons for publishing that sermon, and gives his views on the extracts from Richard Baxter, relating to infant baptism, contained in the Appendix to that sermon. His conclusion is that none can be entitled to spiritual or saving blessings on account of their infant baptism, or their relation to believing parents, unless when they arrive at the age of discretion they exercise personal faith and holiness; and that they cannot be entitled to adult membership in the church without a credible profession of these virtues.

In the year 1790, Mr. Sherman had a correspondence with Dr. Samuel Hopkins on the theory of " disinterested submission," or " the duty of man to be willing to give up his eternal interest for the glory of God, and the general good." Dr. Hopkins adduces, in support of the affirmative of this proposition, two arguments.

First. If it is the duty of man, as is conceded, to give up his temporal interest for the glory of God, it must be his duty to give up his eternal interest for the same cause.

To this Mr. Sherman replies that God does not command us to give up our eternal interest for his glory, but, on the contrary, urges us to endure the ills of this life in view of the rewards of the life to come.

He might have added that the sufferings of the righteous in this life are entirely different in kind from the sufferings in the future life of the finally impenitent. The former are independent of the sufferer's will; they come upon him from without and do not affect his spiritual nature. The latter are the natural outcome of a sinful nature, — the fruits of the sufferer's voluntary wrong-doing.

Second. Dr. Hopkins' second argument is to this effect. It is for the glory of God and the

general good, that some men should sin and suffer
endless punishment. If it be as necessary that we
should sin and suffer, in order to answer the same
end, we must be willing that this should take place,
if we love God with all our hearts, and our neighbor as ourselves.

To this Mr. Sherman replies that this doctrine
involves in it this absurdity, that a person ought
to be willing to be fixed in a state of eternal enmity
to God, from a principle of supreme love to him.

In reference to the glory of God, Mr. Sherman
says: " His goodness is his glory, and that is displayed or manifested in his doing good."   In illustration of this truth he cites the striking passage
from Exod. xxxiii. 18, 19, where Moses in the
mount asks for a revelation of God's glory, and
the Lord replies, " I will make my goodness pass
before thee."

Dr. Hopkins cites, in support of his view, the
language of Paul, Rom. ix. 3, where he says he
could wish himself accursed from Christ for his
brethren.   To which Mr. Sherman replies that
this evidently is not to be understood literally,'
but was only a strong way of stating his love for
his brethren.   Besides, he adds, every wish of a
good man is not a good wish.   Moses, in a like
expression, Exod. xxxii. 32, seems not fully to
have met with the divine approbation, as appears
by the answer, verse 33 : "And the Lord said unto
Moses, Whosoever hath sinned against me, him
will I blot out of my book."

These letters were published in 1889 by the
American Antiquarian Society, with an introduction

on Hopkinsianism by Rev. Andrew P. Peabody. Mr. Sherman's good sense contrasts most favorably with the scholastic subtleties, in which the theologian loses himself. In a letter, dated May 7, 1895, from Dr. Edwards A. Park, the peculiar views of Dr. Hopkins on this subject are thus referred to.

" I have always heard that Sherman agreed with the elder President Edwards in theological doctrine, but disapproved of Hopkins' theory concerning 'disinterested submission.' The majority of the Edwardeans disapproved of Hopkins' theory on the subject. He was very injudicious in his style of treating the topic. Still, Dr. William E. Channing, who was the grandson of Mr. Ellery, always spoke with the highest respect of Mr. Hopkins, and in particular of Hopkins' views on 'disinterested submission.' Professor Frederic Hedge spoke in the same manner, for the views of Hopkins were those of the old Quietists. It is a singular fact that Thomas Hooker of Hartford, whose statue adorns the Connecticut Capitol, was more Hopkinsian than Hopkins himself."

The following correspondence between Roger Sherman and Dr. Witherspoon may properly find a place here, as the argument employed is of a biblical character.

NEW HAVEN, July 10th, 1788.

SIR, — I herewith send you Mr. Trumbull's appeal to the public respecting divorce. Upon reading of which you will see that he supposes divorce is not lawful in any case except for incontinency.

The law of this State admits of divorce, for fraudulent contract, adultery, or three years wilful desertion and total neglect of duty.

Herein it agrees with the Westminster confession of Faith article 24th. The late President Edwards was also of the same opinion, as appears by the enclosed note extracted from his writings. As the subject is important and interesting to the public as well as to individuals, I should esteem it a favor to know your opinion respecting it.

It is evident that those who admit wilful desertion as a sufficient ground for divorce, found their opinion on 1 Cor. 7: 15, which they suppose contains an apostolic direction in a case not mentioned by our Lord in the Evangelists, and perfectly consistent with what he has said on the subject. They suppose that what is contained in the Evangelists, and referred to in Cor. 7: 10, 11 as said by the Lord, imports no more than that no separation or voluntary departing or putting away except for incontinency, is lawful, or if the wife should accept a bill of divorce from the husband, and thereupon voluntarily leave him, it would not dissolve the bond of matrimony, and either party that should marry another in consequence of such a separation would be guilty of adultery. But in case there should be a wilful desertion of one party, either by going away and leaving the other, or by cruelty and abuse compelling the other to go away, this conduct obstinately persisted in, so as totally to deprive the other of all the benefits and comforts of the marriage state; the innocent party, after using all proper means to reclaim the other, and waiting a reasonable time, and there appearing no prospect of a reconciliation, may, upon application to public authority be lawfully declared free from the bond of marriage, and be at liberty to marry another. This distinction they suppose is evident from what the apostle says in the 12th verse, " To the rest speak I, not the Lord." This was therefore a new case on the same subject, about which our Lord had not given any direction. As Mr Trumbull has fully stated the arguments in support of one side of the question, I thought it might be proper to give these few hints of what has been said in support of the other side, and submit the whole to your consideration. I am Sir with great respect and esteem,

Your humble servant,

ROGER SHERMAN.

PRINCETON, July 25, 1788.

DEAR SIR, — I received a few days ago your favor of the 10th inst. with copy of Mr Trumbull's Discourse relating to Divorce. I have read it over with attention and am fully of opinion with Dr Edwards that the declaration of our Saviour against frivolous divorces ought not to be so interpreted that it should be impossible to liberate an innocent party any other way. As all contracts are mutual and this of marriage in a particular manner, an obstinate and perpetual refusal of performance on one side seems in the nature of things to liberate the other. Therefore the Protestant Churches in general and ours in particular have always admitted wilful or obstinate desertion as a cause of divorce, and have supposed the passage of the Apostle Paul to be a confirmation of this by a particular instance. This ought not to be considered as any contradiction to our Saviour's declaration; on the contrary it may be considered as falling under it for in the law of obstinate desertion adultery may be very justly questioned in law, as the person cannot be supposed to desert in order to live the life of a monk or nun, but from alienated affection, especially as in most cases of this kind they withdraw themselves out of the reach of observation or proof.

I think Mr. Trumbull has not proved his theoretical point, but if he has given a just account of facts it would appear that either your laws are lax upon the subject or the Courts have been lax in the execution of them, but this must depend upon the fairness and fulness of his representation, which I cannot judge of with certainty in my situation. Remember me to your neighbor, Dr Stiles. I have the honor to be, Sir,

Your most humble and obedient servant,

JNO. WITHERSPOON.

Dr. Edwards, in speaking of Mr. Sherman as a theologian, remarked that, in the general course of a long and intimate acquaintance, he was materially instructed by his observations on the principal subjects of doctrinal and practical divinity.

CHAPTER XIII.

LAST DAYS.

IN the 4th volume of the "American Literary Magazine," June, 1849, is an article on Roger Sherman, by Professor Denison Olmsted, of Yale College, in which the following account of his death is given:

"On the 23rd day of July, 1793, he finished his eventful career, at his own quiet residence in New Haven, where, most of all, he was beloved and honored. He was cheered and sustained in the last conflict by the power of that religion which he had early embraced, and whose precepts and duties he had uniformly illustrated by a long life of virtue and usefulness. He had enjoyed almost uninterrupted health through life, and at the age of seventy was able to mount his horse with the agility of youth, and to ride thirty or forty miles without fatigue. But, as a mound which has long withstood the pressure of the floods unmoved and seemingly immovable, yields at last to the silent influences that have been insensibly infusing into its structure the elements of decay and weakness, and is all at once borne away; so his constitution that seemed equal to the severest labors, suddenly failed, and he sunk into the arms of death. His last effort was in attempting to lead the family devotions: but the accents of prayer died away on his lips, before the service was completed. Still his mind was serene, and when asked by his daughter if he was ready to die, he looked up with that sweet expression which many have seen and felt in the 'dying smile,' and replied, 'Father, not my will, but thine be done.'"

The following letters from Josiah Stebbins to Roger Minot Sherman give further particulars of the last sickness of Roger Sherman and an account of the funeral.

NEW HAVEN, Sunday Evening.

DEAR SIR; I know not that I can tell you anything of note except with regard to the good Squire Sherman. The account you heard of him was perfectly just. No disease seems to be upon him but a biliousness to which I understand he has been subject, but he is debilitated to such a degree that as I was this evening told in the family, he is unable to turn himself in bed — as is — in his case, he is unusually drowsy, sleeps almost the whole day and night — and in a word is by all looked on as a man beyond a possibility of recovering. I have not seen him but shall not be surprised if he bid the world adieu in a few days. . . . Respects to Mr and Mrs Strong and

Yours as usual,

JOSIAH STEBBINS.

[On back.] Monday morning Esq. Sherman declines, is weaker, no other alteration.

In haste   J. S.

JULY 21, 1793.

NEW HAVEN, Monday Morning, 5 Aug.

DEAR SIR: You desired me to write in case of the good Squire's death. I neglected it supposing that you would doubtless hear it as soon as I could convey you a letter. The funeral was attended on Thursday with the tokens of respect which the object of them merited. The city officers attended as mourners. Pres. Stiles (if I did not misunderstand) prayed at the house. The procession then moved to Doct. Edwards meeting house where a sermon with the usual prayers was delivered by Doct. Edwards, and to do the Doct. Justice he preached better than I expected to hear him, and seemed to keep almost free from *moral obligation, cause* and *effect* &c. The procession then moved to the grave, four bells tolling in alternate strokes. The collection was the largest I ever knew on such an occasion — unavoidable haste prevents my adding another word but that

I am yours,

JOSIAH STEBBINS.

The following extract from the Diary of Ezra Stiles, President of Yale College, gives an account of the death and funeral of Mr. Sherman, and an estimate of his character.

" 1793, July 23, at about seven o'clock, or about sunsetting, a bright luminary set in New Haven: the Hon. Roger Sherman Esq. died at seven o'clock. . . . He was formed for thinking and acting, but law and politics were peculiarly adapted to his genius. He was an admirer of

Vattell's Laws of Nature and Nations. He was for many years Treasurer of Y. C. and a friend to its interests and to its being and continuing in the hands of the Clergy, whom he judged the most proper to have the superintending of a religious as well as a scientific college. . . . He was exemplary for piety and serious religion, was a good Divine, once printed a well and judiciously written sermon of his own composition, though never preached. He was far from all enthusiasm. He was calm, sedate, and very discerning and judicious. He went though all the grades of public life and grew in them all and filled every office with propriety, ability and though not with showy brilliancy, yet with that dignity which arises from doing every thing perfectly right. In no part of his employment has he displayed his intrinsic merit and acquired that glory so much as in Congress. He then became almost oracular for the deep sagacity, wisdom, and weight of his counsels. Though of no elocution he was respected and listened to with attention; and was successful in carrying the points he labored. He was an extraordinary man, a venerable uncorrupted patriot.

"July 25. The funeral of the Mayor was attended. The Students and Tutors of the University formed the head of the procession, then the two city sheriffs preceded the city officers, the common council, four aldermen, two justices, two members of Congress, and a Judge of the Superior Court, the clergy, eight ministers, the bearers and corpse (no pall bearers), mourners and citizens, male and female, a large concourse. Repairing to Dr. Edwards' meeting house a sermon was preached by Dr. Edwards from Ps. 46: 1. Then the procession moved from the meeting house to the grave. Dr. Dana spoke at the grave, as I had prayed at the house before the funeral. Every part was conducted with respectful decency and solemnity."

The following obituary notice was published in the " Connecticut Journal," July 31, 1793.

" New Haven, July 31. On the 23 instant died at his house in this city the Honorable Roger Sherman Esqr. . . . [account of his life]. It is worthy to remark that though he sustained so many offices in the civil government both of the State and of the United States, to all which he was promoted by the free suffrages of his fellow citizens, and in the most of which he could not without a new election continue longer than a year, and in the rest not longer than two, three or four years; and although for all these offices there were as there always are in popular governments many competitors at every election, yet Mr. Sherman was never removed from any one of them, but by promotion, or rendering the offices incompatible with each other. Nor with the restriction just mentioned did he ever lose his election to any office to which he had once been elected, except his election as a Representative of the town in the General Assembly; which office we all know is almost constantly shifting. This shows to how great a degree and how invariably he possessed the confidence of his fellow citizens.

They found by long experience that both his abilities and his integrity merited their confidence. To have been constantly employed in the public service for forty-eight years, to have sustained so many and so important public offices, and to have sustained them all with honor and reputation; to have maintained an amiable character in every private relation; to have been from early youth an ornament to Christianity, and to have died in a good old age in the full possession of all his honors, and of his powers both of body and mind, is a rare attainment, and as to him at least an happy juncture of circumstances."

The following inscription is recorded upon the tablet which covers his tomb.

" IN MEMORY OF

THE HON. ROGER SHERMAN, Esq.

MAYOR OF THE CITY OF NEW HAVEN,

AND SENATOR OF THE UNITED STATES.

HE WAS BORN AT NEWTOWN, IN MASSACHUSETTS,

APRIL 19TH, 1721.

AND DIED IN NEW HAVEN, JULY 23RD, A. D. 1793,

AGED LXXII.

Possessed of a strong, clear, penetrating mind,
and singular perseverance,
He became the self-taught scholar,
eminent for jurisprudence and policy.
He was nineteen years an assistant,
and twenty-three years a judge, of the superior court,
in high reputation.
He was a delegate in the first congress,
Signed the glorious act of Independence,
and many years displayed superior talents and ability
in the national legislature.

He was a member of the general convention,
approved the federal constitution,
and served his country, with fidelity and honor,
in the House of Representatives,
and in the Senate of the United States.
He was a man of approved integrity ;
a cool, discerning Judge ;
a prudent, sagacious politician ;
a true, faithful, and firm, patriot.
He ever adorned
the profession of Christianity
which he made in youth ;
and, distinguished through life
for public usefulness,
died in the prospect
of a blessed immortality."

CHAPTER XIV.

CONCLUSION.

IN reviewing the life of Roger Sherman we are impressed, not merely with the length and variety of his public services, but with the number of important offices which he held at the same time. From 1755, when he was chosen to represent the town of New Milford in the Colonial Assembly of Connecticut, to his death in 1793, a period of thirty-eight years, he was, with the exception of two intervals of two or three years each, continually in the public service. At first, he was, for a few years, a member of the Court of Common Pleas, and then, for twenty-three years in succession, he was a Judge of the Superior Court. After a few years' service in the lower House of the Connecticut Assembly, he was chosen a member of the upper House, where he was kept, by annual election, for nineteen successive years. He was for eight years a member of the Continental Congress, and during two years of this period he was a member of the Connecticut Council of Safety. He was a member of the Constitutional Convention of 1787, and from the formation of the national government in 1789 to his death in 1793, he was a member of Congress, — for the first two years a Representative, and for the last two a Senator. From 1784 to his death, he was Mayor of the City of New Haven.

Many of these offices he held at the same time.
During the nineteen years that he was a member
of the upper House of the Connecticut Assembly,
he was also a judge of the Superior Court; during
eight of these years he was a delegate in the Continental Congress; and for two years that he was
a delegate in Congress, he was a member of the
Council of Safety, and the last year that he was a
delegate in Congress he was Mayor of the City of
New Haven.

To have held so many, and so important offices,
for so long a time, shows the high regard which the
people of Connecticut had for his abilities and integrity. But it was not merely by the citizens of
his own State that he was held in high esteem. In
the Continental Congress, he took rank at once
with the ablest men from all parts of the country,
and was placed on the most important committees.
He formed intimate friendships with the great revolutionary leaders of the north and the south, —
with John Adams, and Samuel Adams, and Richard
Henry Lee. He took an active and influential
part in the debates of the various deliberative assemblies with which he was connected. And yet
he was utterly destitute of oratorical graces. Indeed, it was something more than that. His manner seems to have been the personification of
awkwardness. John Adams, an enthusiastic admirer of Mr. Sherman, in his Diary, under date of
September 15, 1775, thus describes his style of
speaking: —

"Sherman's air is the reverse of grace; there
cannot be a more striking contrast to beautiful

19

action than the motion of his hands; generally he stands upright, with his hands before him, the fingers of his left hand clenched into a fist, and the wrist of it grasped with his right.   But he has a clear head and sound judgment; but when he moves a hand in anything like action, Hogarth's genius could not have invented a motion more opposite to grace; it is stiffness and awkwardness itself, rigid as starched linen or buckram; awkward as a junior bachelor or a sophomore."

It was a common saying in New Haven, that when Mr. Sherman was interested in speaking, his gesture was like that of a shoemaker drawing a thread.

And yet singularly enough, the greatest admirers of this awkward man, were the foremost orators of their day.   In Henry Howe's Historical Collections of Virginia, he says, in speaking of Patrick Henry that, — "When a member of the Continental Congress, he said the first men in that body were Washington, Richard Henry Lee, and Roger Sherman: and, later in life, Roger Sherman and George Mason [were] the greatest statesmen he ever knew."

John Adams in a letter to his wife, dated March 16, 1777, speaks of Sherman as "that old puritan, as honest as an angel, and as firm in the cause of American Independence as Mt. Atlas."   In his old age, Mr. Adams wrote the following letter concerning Roger Sherman to the editor of Sanderson's Biographies: —

QUINCY, November 19th, 1822.

DEAR SIR: I have received your obliging favor of the 15th instant. It relates to a subject dear to my memory and my heart. The honorable Roger Sherman was one of the most cordial friends which I ever had in my life. Destitute of all literary and scientific education, but such as he acquired by his own exertions, he was one of the most sensible men in the world. The clearest head and steadiest heart. It is praise enough to say, that the late Chief Justice Ellsworth told me he had made Mr Sherman his model in his youth. Indeed I never knew two men more alike, except that the Chief Justice had the advantage of a liberal education, and somewhat more extensive reading.

Mr Sherman was born in the State of Massachusetts, and was one of the soundest and strongest pillars of the revolution. I am, sir,

Your most obedient and humble servant,

JOHN ADAMS.

Fisher Ames the leader of the Federal party in the House of Representatives during the administration of Washington and the most accomplished orator in that body, was accustomed to say, — " That if he happened to be out of his seat when a subject was discussed, and came in when the question was about to be taken, he always felt safe in voting as Mr. Sherman did; for he always voted right."

Similar tributes were paid to Mr. Sherman by other eminent men. On one occasion Mr. Jeffer-

son accompanied Dr. Spring of Newburyport to
the halls of Congress, and pointing out Mr. Sherman, said, — " That is Mr. Sherman of Connecticut,
a man who never said a foolish thing in his life."
Nathaniel Macon, of North Carolina, who himself
had a great reputation for wisdom, once remarked
to Mr. Reed of Marblehead, that " Roger Sherman
had more common sense than any man he ever
knew." Jonathan Edwards the younger, one of
the most eminent divines which this country has
produced, was accustomed to speak of Roger
Sherman as " my great and good friend, Senator Sherman." Dr. Dwight, when instructing the
senior class at Yale College, observed that Mr.
Sherman was remarkable for not speaking in debate without suggesting something new and important, which frequently gave a different character
to the discussion. Thomas Jefferson wrote the
following letter concerning Mr. Sherman to Roger
S. Baldwin.

MONTICELLO, March 9th, 1822.

SIR, I have duly received your letter of February 22nd, and am sorry it is in my power to furnish
no other materials for the biography of your very
respectable grandfather, than such as are very generally known. I served with him in the old congress in the years 1775 and 1776: He was a very
able and logical debater in that body, steady in
the principles of the revolution, always at the post
of duty, much employed in the business of committees, and particularly, was of the committee of
Doctor Franklin, Mr J. Adams, Mr Livingston,

ar d myself, for preparing the Declaration of Independence. Being much my senior in years, our intercourse was chiefly in the line of our duties. I had a very great respect for him, and now learn, with pleasure, that the public are likely to be put into possession of the particulars of his useful life.

I pray you accept the assurance of my great respect.

THOMAS JEFFERSON.[1]

The Connecticut Academy of Arts and Sciences published in 1811, vol. 1, No. 1, " A statistical account of the City of New Haven," by Timothy Dwight, President of Yale College, which contains the following estimate of Roger Sherman.

" Mr. Sherman possessed a powerful mind: and habits of industry which no difficulties could discourage, and no toil impair. In early life he began to apply himself with inextinguishable zeal to the acquisition of knowledge. In this pursuit, although he was always actively engaged in business,

---

[1] Mr. E. P. Whipple, in his essay on " Daniel Webster as a Master of English Style," introductory to his collection of the " Great Speeches and Orations of Daniel Webster," says: —

" There is no word which the novelists, satirists, philanthropic reformers, and Bohemians of our days have done so much to discredit and make disrespectable to the heart and the imagination, as the word 'respectable.' Webster always uses it as a term of eulogy." In illustration of this statement, Mr. Whipple quotes the following passage from Mr. Webster's oration on the completion of the Bunker Hill Monument. " I would cheerfully put the question to day to the intelligence of Europe and the world, what character of the century, upon the whole, stands out in the relief of history most pure, most respectable, most sublime; and I doubt not that by a suffrage approaching to unanimity, the answer would be, Washington."

he spent more hours than most of those who are professedly students. In his progress he became extensively acquainted with mathematical science, with natural philosophy, with moral and metaphysical philosophy, with history, logic and theology. As a lawyer and a statesman he was eminent. The late Judge Ingersoll, who has been already mentioned, once observed to me, that, in his opinion, the views which Mr. Sherman formed of political subjects, were more profound, just, and comprehensive, than those of almost any other man with whom he had been acquainted on this continent. His mind was remarkably clear and penetrating and more than that of almost any other man, looked from the beginning of a subject to the end. Nothing satisfied him but proof; or where that was impossible, the predominant probability which equally controls the conduct of a wise man. He had no fashionable opinions, and could never be persuaded to swim with the tide. Independent of everything but argument, he judged for himself: and rarely failed to convince others that he judged right.

" As a man, as a patriot, and as a citizen, Mr. Sherman left behind him an unspotted name. Profoundly versed in theology, he held firmly the doctrines of the Reformation. Few men understood them so well: and few were equally able to defend them. What he believed he practiced."

The following memorandum prepared by Hon. Wm. M. Evarts, August 30, 1893, contains two very interesting estimates of Mr. Sherman.

"Among my acquaintances at the Union Club

was Isaac Bell who lived to a great age dying in 1860, ninety-three years old. Two of his sons, Isaac Bell, Jr. and Edward R. Bell were quite intimate friends of mine and members of the same club. Isaac Bell, Sr. retained his faculties of memory and intelligence through this advanced age, and from my intimate relations with his sons I became acquainted with their father. One day when talking with him about events in the early history of our government, it occurred to me that as he was some twenty-two or twenty-three years of age at the time of Washington's inauguration in New York, he might probably have seen my grandfather, Roger Sherman, who as a member of the new government was conspicuous among the attendance at that ceremony. If this should be so, as Mr. Bell's memory was accurate and retentive, I thought I might learn something of the impression made upon a casual observer of the inauguration. Mr. Bell replied that he did not see the proceedings of the inauguration as he was then absent from New York and, as I now think, in China. He then recurred to the subject by saying 'Was Roger Sherman your grandfather?' and on my replying he said, 'I never saw Roger Sherman but I can tell you something that Theodore Sedgwick said to me about him. Mr. Sedgwick said, " Roger Sherman was the man of the selectest wisdom that I ever knew. No law or part of law that Mr. Sherman favored failed to be enacted."' I was struck with the peculiar epithet of 'selectest' and it impressed me that Mr. Sedgwick's words had been remembered and repeated by Mr. Bell.

" In the latter part of General Scott's life, though quite before the outbreak of the civil war, I was thrown very agreeably in company with the general and occasionally with one or two other friends, as well as at larger dinners, I listened to very interesting narratives and comments from him about the men and events of our Revolutionary and following periods. On one occasion when two or three of us were dining together with General Scott at the Union Club, he made the following reference to Roger Sherman in relation to the actors in the Revolution and the formation of the new government. He said, ' I think Roger Sherman is entitled to be considered as the fourth man in these transactions embracing the whole revolutionary period and the formation of the new government. The only three that can be placed before him are Washington, John Adams, and ' — the third whose name I cannot completely recall as to whether it was Patrick Henry or Madison. He added, ' I leave aside the name of Jefferson as his participation in these events made so famous by his authorship of the Declaration of Independence, did not show as large and continuous connection with the whole period to which I am referring as these four men whom I have named.' General Scott showed very thorough acquaintance with all the important events in the whole series, and his comments upon the different actors in them showed that he had given these matters much reflection."

The estimate of Mr. Sherman by President Stiles has been given in the chapter next preceding this.

As Mr. Sherman was destitute of those shining

qualities which are essential to the success of the orator, the enquiry naturally arises, wherein did his strength consist? The opinions of his contemporaries which we have just cited show that the quality which most impressed them was his good sense. Ordinarily we think of this as a valuable quality in the practical affairs of life, but not as one which elevates a man to the highest rank. But in Roger Sherman the quality of good sense was so highly developed that it resembled genius. He had a clearer perception than most men of the rights and duties of men in civil society, and of the best means of securing the one, and enforcing the other. He had a remarkable sagacity in judging, not only what measures were best for a community, but what the people were willing to bear. His influence over men was greatly strengthened by his strong sense of justice; and his remarkable success in so often securing the adoption of the measures he advocated was owing to the fact that he was believed to be, not only a wise man, but a wise man striving to do right.

Another source of his power, was a self-control, and evenness of temper, and catholicity of spirit, which enabled him to keep on good terms with those from whom he differed, even on theological questions.

These qualities were seen in their highest manifestation, and in their most beneficent effects, in the Constitutional Convention of 1787. By his firm but conciliatory spirit he carried through that great compromise in reference to representation in the two Houses of Congress, without which no constitution would have been formed, or, if formed, would have been adopted.

Mr. Sherman remarked to his family that, before he had attained the age of twenty-one, he learned to control and govern his passions; and this important achievement he ascribed, in a considerable degree, to the perusal of Dr. Watts's excellent treatise on the subject. His passions were naturally strong, but he obtained such a mastery over them, that he was habitually calm, sedate, and self-governed.

Many anecdotes are related of his self-control. At family prayers, he boxed the ears of one of the children who was making a disturbance. Thereupon his mother, whose mind had become enfeebled by age, walked across the room, and boxed his ears, saying, "You strike your child, and I strike mine." The worship went on as if nothing had happened.

A farmer called at the house one day to sell some cider. Mr. Sherman having made some enquiry about the quality of the cider, the farmer stormed and swore at a furious rate. Finding Mr. Sherman perfectly unmoved at his tirade, he looked up at him in astonishment, exclaiming, "The Devil himself could n't provoke you."

His house was opposite the college grounds, and he was accustomed to sit at his desk, by the front window. One day a roguish student, on the college grounds, with a piece of looking-glass flashed the sunlight in the old gentleman's eyes. Mr. Sherman quietly rose, closed the blind, and resumed his work.

An heirloom silver tankard had been lost or stolen when he was absent, and the family hardly dared to tell him of it. When they gravely imparted the news, he replied, " How much anxiety and trouble is saved. We shall have no more trouble putting it away so carefully every night."

Mr. Sherman had none of that foolish pride which makes a man ashamed of having been engaged in a lowly occupation in early life, or of that other pride, equally foolish, which leads a prosperous man who has risen from obscurity, to boast of the contrast between his early and his later career. On one occasion, as a member of a committee in the Continental Congress for investigating frauds in army contracts, he showed so much practical knowledge about the manufacture of shoes that he was asked how he acquired it. He replied, " I was formerly a shoe-maker myself." His pastor and friend, during the last twenty-four years of his life, Dr. Edwards, said of him, " With all his elevation, and all his honors, he was not at all lifted up, but was perfectly unmoved." He was profoundly grateful to his fellow-citizens for the honors they conferred upon him, but he seemed to value them chiefly for the enlarged opportunities they afforded him of serving the public.

Dr. Edwards, in the sermon which he preached at Mr. Sherman's funeral, thus speaks of his political services: " For usefulness and excellence in this line, he was qualified, not only by his acute discernment and sound judgment but especially by his knowledge of human nature. He had a

happy talent of judging what was feasible and
what was not feasible, or what men would bear
and what they would not bear in government.
And he had a rare talent of prudence, or of timing
and adapting his measures to the attainment of his
end. By this talent, by his perseverance and his
indefatigable application, together with his general
good sense and known integrity, he seldom failed
in carrying every point in government which he
undertook, and which he esteemed important to
the public good."

One of the most interesting things about Mr.
Sherman is that fairness and openness of mind
which kept him fresh and vigorous to the end.
With each re-perusal of the debates in the Constitutional Convention of 1787, I have been more and
more impressed with the progress he made in the
course of those debates. He entered the Convention as a strong confederate: he left it as a firm
nationalist. Although sixty-eight years of age
when he entered the House of Representatives,
the speeches he made on the tariff and the public credit were the best he ever made, and were
not surpassed by those of any of his fellow-
members.

John C. Hamilton, in his " History of the Republic," after speaking of the objections to the assumption of the State debts made by certain members
of Congress, thus refers to Mr. Sherman's speech
in reply: "These objections were replied to in a
very able speech by Roger Sherman. The early
position held by Sherman in the public estimation
is shown by the fact that he was appointed one of

the committee of five members to draw the Declaration of Independence. In the several Congresses elected during the Revolutionary War, he is seen to have filled a conspicuous place; and when that body, sinking in importance, confided its duties to a committee of the States, he was selected of that committee. Chosen a member of the Federal Convention, his course in that body shows the workings of a mind alive to the necessity of an enlargement of the powers of the government, but restrained as to its organization by the opinions and prejudices of the State he represented. In the compromises which were adopted between State influence and popular rights, his mind advanced with the advancing opinions of the convention towards a National Government; and though the shackels of State opinions were not entirely thrown off, yet in all questions touching the great powers of national defence, commerce, revenue, public justice, his views were broad and explicit. As to the debts incurred by the States for the general cause, he would have provided, in the Constitution, a large and equal rule."

In the "Life and Writings" of Jared Sparks (Vol. I, page 523) is an extract from Mr. Sparks's Journal, dated October 5, 1826, in which, giving an account of a visit to Ebenezer Baldwin, of Albany, he says: " Mr. Baldwin showed me the correspondence between John Adams and Roger Sherman on a point in the Constitution of the United States, particularly that relating to the President's negative. It is a rencounter of deep, keen minds, and I shall take a copy. Mr. Baldwin has the originals, being the grandson of Sherman. The argument is well sustained on both sides, and in a manner particularly characteristic of the two men. Adams had the wrong side, and experience has shown his objections to be imaginary." In another passage in the same Journal, Mr. Sparks says, "Sherman was a self-taught man, but has rarely been excelled in native good sense, soundness of judgment, singleness of heart, and uprightness of character."

George Bancroft, in his History of the Constitution of the United States (Vol. II. pp. 48–50), speaking of the members of the Constitutional Convention of 1787, says: "Roger Sherman was a unique man. No one in the convention had so large an experience in legislating for the United States. . . . There was in him kindheartedness and industry, penetration and close reasoning, an unclouded intellect, superiority to passion, intrepid patriotism, solid judgment, and a directness which went straight to its end. . . . In the convention he never made long speeches, but would intuitively seize on the turning point of a question, and present it in terse language, which showed his own opinion and the strength on which it rested."

In his "Plea for the Constitution," Mr. Bancroft speaks of those "Master-builders of the Constitution, Roger Sherman, George Washington, Charles Cotesworth Pinckney, James Madison, and Alexander Hamilton."

No great man was ever more perfectly self-educated than Mr. Sherman; but this did not lead him to undervalue an academic education.   It made him prize it the more highly, for he was sensible of the difficulties and embarrassments which hindered his own progress. He assisted his brothers to obtain a collegiate education, and four of his own sons were graduated at Yale. Late in life, he said that if he were to educate his sons again for either of the three professions, he should have them give at least one year's study to each of the other two.

Some of the sayings of Mr. Sherman which have been preserved illustrate not only his wisdom, but a certain dry humor, not found in his speeches or his letters. One we have already mentioned, — his proposal to present the tardy messenger who brought the news to Congress of Burgoyne's surrender, with a pair of spurs. When Rhode Island was complaining of the encroachments of her neighbors, Mr. Sherman observed that Rhode Island might annex Connecticut if she wished. The Continental Congress voted to build a monument at Yorktown, a purpose never accomplished until 1881. Somebody in the first Congress complained of the delay. Mr. Sherman said, "The vote is the monument." Mr. Sherman used to say that he never liked to decide a doubtful or perplexing question without submitting it for the opinion of some intelligent woman. In his last sickness, the friends, having decided to have a consultation of physicians, asked him if he would object. He replied, with a smile, "No, I don't object; only I have noticed that in such cases the patient generally dies." When invited to make a speech at the opening of a new bridge,

— after inspecting it and walking across it he re-
maked, "I don't see but it stands steady."

When a young man, just entering upon a legislative career, called upon him for advice, Mr.
Sherman said, "When you are in a minority, talk;
when you are in a majority, vote."

One anecdote about Mr. Sherman has had a
good deal of currency, but has no foundation in
fact. It is this, — that John Randolph, provoked
at something Mr. Sherman said in debate, asked
him what had become of his leather apron. To
which Mr. Sherman replied, "Cut it up into moc-
casins for the descendants of Pocahontas." As
John Randolph was only twenty years old when
Mr. Sherman died, and did not enter Congress till
six years after that event, we shall have to give up
this anecdote, and we can do so without any sense
of loss.

John Randolph did, however, allude to Mr.
Sherman, in a speech in the House of Representatives, on February 1, 1828, which showed his
high regard for him. Speaking of the superiority
in public affairs of men of practical sense over men
of mere book learning, Mr. Randolph said, "Sir,
who would make the better leader, in a period of
great public emergency, — old Roger Sherman, or
a certain very learned gentleman from New York,
whom we once had here, who knew everything
in the world for which man has no occasion,
and nothing in the world for which man has
occasion?"

Dr. Edwards says of Mr. Sherman, "His person was tall, unusually erect and well proportioned,

and his countenance agreeable and manly." His portrait shows him to have had a fair complexion, blue eyes, and brown hair.

In private life, though he was naturally reserved and of few words, yet in conversation on matters of importance he was free and communicative. Judge Jeremiah Smith said of him that " it was a great treat to hear him converse." He was naturally modest; and this disposition, increased perhaps by the deficiencies of his early education, often wore the appearance of bashfulness. In large companies, it is said, he appeared obviously embarrassed, and his speech was often slow and hesitating. It was this reserve and bashfulness, joined perhaps at times to a certain absent-mindedness, which led some persons not well acquainted with him to think him aristocràtic.

The liveliest picture that has been preserved of Mr. Sherman's habits and manners is the following from the Autobiography of Jeremiah Mason, who was a law student in the office of Judge Simeon Baldwin, at New Haven, about 1789 : —

" I soon went to New Haven, entered Mr. Baldwin's office, and lived in his family. Then, as at the present time, very little instruction in the course of study was given in a private office. I spent a year in Mr. Baldwin's office reading pretty diligently. My time passed pleasantly; I had access to very good society. He married a daughter of the celebrated Roger Sherman and lived near him. He had a family of children, some near my age. I was often at the house, and very frequently saw Mr. Sherman. His reputation was then at the zenith. His manners, without apparent arrogance, were excessively reserved and aristocratic. His habit was, in his own house, when tea was served to company, to walk down from his study into the room, take a seat and sip his tea, of which he seemed very fond, and then rise and walk out without speaking a word or taking any manner of notice of any individual. In the street he saw nobody, but wore his broad beaver pointing steadily to the horizon, and giving no idle nods. Still, I fancy Roger Sherman was capable of the most adroit address when his occasion required it. Several years after this, being in New Haven, I met Mr. Sherman in the street, expecting to pass by him unseen, as usual: I was surprised by his stopping and kindly greeting me, requesting me to call at his house before I left the city. When I called, he received me most courteously, and in a flattering manner congratulated me on my success in my profession, of which he said he had been informed. He then told me that being a member of the old Congress of the Confederation during the time Vermont (in which State he erroneously supposed I was settled) was asserting against New York its claim to independence, believing the claim just, he had been an earnest advocate for it; that during the pendency of the claim, the agents of Vermont often urged him to accept grants of land from that State, which he refused, lest it should lessen his power to serve them. Now, as their claim was established, and the State admitted into the Union, if the people of Vermont continued to feel disposed to make him a grant of some of their ungranted lands, as his family was large and his property small he had no objection to accepting it. I was sorry to be obliged to tell him that I belonged to New Hampshire and not to Vermont, but that living on the borders of that State, and being much acquainted with many of the inhabitants, I would do what I could to have his wishes complied with. This I afterwards did by stating the circumstances to several influential men of Vermont. They readily recognized the merit of Mr. Sherman's services, and said he ought to have a liberal grant. But I never heard that anything was done in the matter, and presume his case made another item in the history of the ingratitude of republics. The time the Vermonters needed his services was passed."

George Sherman, the son of Roger Sherman, Jr., in a letter already referred to, thus speaks of his grandfather: " He was so devoted to public business that relatives were seldom afforded more than a minute or two. That, he said, was enough for our affairs." And yet no man ever had kindlier feelings for his relatives, or was more ready to assist them. In the same letter, it is stated, " Father said that in grandfather's time and long after, all had kindly social feelings and regard for each other." His affection for his brothers and sisters was extended to their children, who were often members of his family.

In the last mentioned letter, it is stated of Roger Sherman that " he disliked pretension, especially in a seat or pew in church, preferring a back seat." He had no ear for music, and disliked to have the last line in a hymn sung over twice. He thought once was enough.

For many years Mr. Sherman was engaged in mercantile pursuits, first at New Milford, and afterwards at New Haven. The same qualities which made him a wise legislator, and an able judge, made him a prosperous business man. Had he continued in business, instead of devoting himself to public affairs, he would undoubtedly have been a rich man. As it was, he acquired sufficient property to live comfortably, and was able to indulge in acts of beneficence and hospitality.

Senator Hoar, in a recent letter to me, relates the following interesting incident illustrating Mr. Sherman's kindness of heart. "I remember one of my mother's stories of her father. He came into the house one day, when she was a little girl, and told her mother that he had bought a piece of property which belonged to a very poor neighbor, and was utterly worthless to him or to anybody. He had given a very large price for it. My grandmother exclaimed, 'Why Mr. Sherman, how could you give so much for that? You don't want it in the least.' To which grandfather answered that he did not want it, but that Mr. So-and-So was very poor, and needed a new coat. He thought it would hurt his feelings if he offered to give him one, so he had taken that way of supplying his needs."

It is not strange that such a man received from the people so many honors. It would be strange if posterity did not keep his memory green. Rising from the humblest rank to the highest by

his own unaided efforts; in every upward step
keeping his head clear and his heart pure; wear-
ing his honors meekly, and using them only for the
public good; with a mind ever receptive of the
truth; loving justice, and resolute in maintaining
it; overthrowing error with a remorseless logic, yet
ever tolerant of weakness and error in others; —
he rendered to his country the highest service in its
most perilous hour, and left to his countrymen a
shining example of that priceless truth that

" The path of duty is the way to glory."

APPENDIX.

CORRESPONDENCE BETWEEN JOHN ADAMS AND ROGER SHERMAN ON THE CONSTITUTION.

John Adams to Roger Sherman.

RICHMOND HILL, (NEW YORK,) 17 July, 1789.

DEAR SIR, — I read over, with pleasure, your observations on the new federal constitution, and am glad to find an opportunity to communicate to you my opinion of some parts of them. It is by a free and amicable intercourse of sentiments, that the friends of our country may hope for such a unanimity of opinion and such a concert 'of exertions, as may sooner or later produce the blessings of good government.

You say, " It is by some objected that the executive is blended with the legislature, and that those powers ought to be entirely distinct and unconnected. But is not that a gross error in politics? The united wisdom and various interests of a nation should be combined in framing the laws by which all are to be governed and protected, though it should not be convenient to have them executed by the whole legislature. The supreme executive in Great Britain is one branch of the legislature, and has a negative on all the laws; perhaps that is an extreme not to be imitated by a republic; but the negative vested in

the president by the new constitution on the acts of congress, and the consequent revision, may be very useful to
prevent laws being passed without mature deliberation,
and to preserve stability in the administration of government ; and the concurrence of the senate in the appointment to office will strengthen the hands of the executive,
and secure the confidence of the people much better
than a select council, and will be less expensive."

Is it, then, " an extreme not to be imitated by a republic," to make the supreme executive a branch of the
legislature, and give it a negative on all the laws? If you
please, we will examine this position, and see whether it
is well founded. In the first place, what is your definition of a republic? Mine is this : *A government whose
sovereignty is vested in more than one person.* Governments are divided into *despotisms, monarchies* and *republics.* A despotism is a government in which the three
divisions of power, the legislative, executive and judicial,
are all vested in one man. A monarchy is a government
where the legislative and executive are vested in one man,
but the judicial in other men. In all governments the
sovereignty is vested in that man or body of men who
have the legislative power. In despotisms and monarchies, therefore, the legislative authority being in one
man, the sovereignty is in one man. In republics, as the
sovereignty, that is, the legislative, is always vested in
more than one, it may be vested in as many more as
you please. In the United States it might be vested in
two persons, or in three millions, or in any other inter-
mediate number ; and in every such supposable case the
government would be a republic. In conforming to these
ideas, republics have been divided into three species,
monarchical, aristocratical, and democratical republics.
England is a republic, a monarchical republic it is true,
but a republic still ; because the sovereignty, which is the

legislative power, is vested in more than one man ; it is
equally divided, indeed, between the one, the few, and
the many, or in other words, between the natural division
of mankind in society, — the monarchical, the aristocratical, and democratical. It is essential to a monarchical
republic, that the supreme executive should be a branch
of the legislature, and have a negative on all the laws. I
say essential, because if monarchy were not an essential
part of the sovereignty, the government would not be a
monarchical republic. Your position is therefore clearly
and certainly an error, because the practice of Great
Britain in making the supreme executive a branch of the
legislature, and giving it a negative on all the laws, must
be imitated by every monarchical republic.

I will pause here, if you please ; but if you will give
me leave, I will write another letter or two upon this subject. Meantime I am, with unalterable friendship,

Yours,

JOHN ADAMS.

DEAR SIR, — In my letter of yesterday I think it was
demonstrated that the English government is a republic,
and that the regal negative upon the laws is essential
to that republic. Because, without it, that government
would not be what it is, a monarchical republic ; and,
consequently, could not preserve the balance of power
between the executive and legislative powers, nor that
other balance which is in the legislature, — between the
one, the few, and the many ; in which two balances the
excellence of that form of government must consist.

Let us now inquire, whether the new constitution of
the United States is or is not a monarchical republic, like
that of Great Britain. The monarchical and the aristocratical power in our constitution, it is true, are not
hereditary ; but this makes no difference in the natnre

of the power, in the nature of the balance, or in the name of the species of government. It would make no difference in the power of a judge or justice, or general or admiral, whether his commission were for life or years. His authority during the time it lasted, would be the same whether it were for one year or twenty, or for life, or descendible to his eldest son. The people, the nation, in whom all power resides originally, may delegate their power for one year or for ten years; for years, or for life; or may delegate it in fee simple or fee tail, if I may so express myself; or during good behavior, or at will, or till further orders.

A nation might unanimously create a dictator or a despot, for one year or more, or for life, or for perpetuity with hereditary descent. In such a case, the dictator for one year would as really be a dictator for the time his power lasted, as the other would be whose power was perpetual and descendible. A nation in the same manner might create a simple monarchy for years, life, or perpetuity, and in either case the creature would be equally a simple monarch during the continuance of his power. So the people of England might create king, lords, and commons, for a year, or for several years, or for life, and in any of these cases, their government would be a monarchical republic, or, if you will, a limited monarchy, during its continuance, as much as it is now, when the king and nobles are hereditary. They might make their house of commons hereditary too. What the consequence of this would be it is easy to foresee; but it would not in the first moment make any change in the legal power, nor in the name of the government.

Let us now consider what our constitution is, and see whether any other name can with propriety be given it, than that of a monarchical republic, or if you will, a limited monarchy. The duration of our president is neither perpetual nor for life; it is only for four years; but his power during those years is much greater than that of an avoyer, a consul, a podesta, a doge, a stadtholder; nay, than a king of Poland; nay, than a king of Sparta. I know of no first magistrate in any republican government excepting England and Neuchatel, who possesses a constitutional dignity, authority, and power comparable to his. The power of sending and receiving ambassadors, of raising and commanding armies and navies, of nominating and appointing and commissioning all officers, of managing the treasures, the internal and external affairs of the nation; nay, the whole executive power, coextensive with the legislative power, is vested in him, and he has the right, and his is the duty, to take care that the laws be faithfully executed. These rights and duties, these prerogatives and dignities, are so transcendent that they must naturally and necessarily excite in the nation all the jealousy, envy, fears, apprehensions, and opposition, that are so constantly observed in England against the crown.

That these powers are necessary, I readily admit. That the laws cannot be executed without them; that the lives, liberties, properties and characters of the citizens cannot be secure without their protection, is most clear. But it is equally certain, I think, that they ought to have been still greater, or much less. The limitations upon them in the cases of war, treaties, and appointments to office, and especially the limitation on the president's independence as a branch of the legislative, will be the destruction of this constitution, and involve us in anarchy, if not amended. I shall pass over all particulars for the present, except the last; because that is now the point in dispute between you and me. Longitude and the philosopher's stone, have not been sought with more earnestness by philosophers than a guardian of the laws has been studied by legislators from Plato to Montesquieu ; but every project has been found to be no better than committing the lamb to the custody of the wolf, except that one which is called a balance of power. A simple sovereignty in one, a few, or many, has no balance, and therefore no laws. A divided sovereignty without a balance, or in other words, where the division is unequal, is always at war, and consequently has no laws. In our constitution the sovereignty, — that is, the legislative power, — is divided into three branches. The house and senate are equal, but the third branch, though essential, is not equal. The president must pass judgment upon every law ; but in some cases his judgment may be overruled. These cases will be such as attack his constitutional power ; it is therefore, certain he has not equal power to defend himself, or the constitution, or the judicial power, as the senate and house have.

Power naturally grows. Why? Because human passions are insatiable. But that power alone can grow which already is too great; that which is unchecked; that which has no equal power to control it. The legislative power, in our constitution, is greater than the executive ; it will, therefore, encroach, because both aristocratical and democratical passions are insatiable. The legislative power will increase, the executive will diminish. In the legislature, the monarchical power is not equal either to the aristocratical or democratical; it will, therefore, decrease, while the other will increase. Indeed, I think aristocratical power is greater than either the monarchical or democratical. That will, therefore, swallow up the other two.

In my letter of yesterday, I think it was proved, that a republic might make the supreme executive an integral part of the legislature. In this, it is equally demonstrated, as I think, that our constitution ought to be amended by a decisive adoption of that expedient. If you do not forbid me, I shall write to you again.

DEAR SIR, — There is a sense and degree in which the executive, in our constitution, is blended with the legislature. The president has the power of suspending a law ; of giving the two houses an opportunity to pause, to think, to collect themselves, to reconsider a rash step of a majority. He has a right to urge all his reasons against it, by speech or message ; which, becoming public, is an appeal to the nation. But the rational objection here is not that the executive is blended with the legislature, but that it is not enough blended ; that it is not incorporated with it, and made an essential part of it. If it were an integral part of it, it might negative a law without much noise, speculation, or confusion among the people. But as it now stands, I beg you to consider it is almost impossible, that a president should ever have the courage to make use of his partial negative. What a situation would a president be in to maintain a controversy against a majority of both houses before a tribunal of the public ! To put a stop to a law that more than half the senate and house, and consequently, we may suppose more than half the nation, have set their hearts upon ! It is, moreover, possible, that more than two thirds of the nation, the senate, and house may, in times of calamity, distress, misfortune, and ill success of the measures of government, from the momentary passion and enthusiasm, demand a law which will wholly subvert the constitution. The constitution of Athens was overturned in such a manner by Aristides himself. The constitution should guard against a possibility of its subversion ; but we may take stronger ground, and assert that it is probable such cases will happen, and that the constitution will, in fact, be subverted in this way. Nay, I go further, and say, that from the

constitution of human nature, and the constant course of
human affairs, it is certain that our constitution will be
subverted, if not amended, and that in a very short time,
merely for want of a decisive negative in the executive.

There is another sense and another degree in which
the executive is blended with the legislature, which is
liable to great and just objection; which excites alarms,
jealousies, and apprehensions, in a very great degree. I
mean, 1st, the negative of the senate upon appointment
to office; 2nd, the negative of the senate upon treaties;
and 3rd, the negative of the two houses upon war. I
shall confine myself at present, to the first. The negative
of the senate upon appointments is liable to the following
objections: —

1. It takes away, or, at least, it lessens the responsibility
of the executive. Our constitution obliges me to say,
that it lessens the responsibility of the president. The
blame of an injudicious, weak, or wicked appointment, is
shared so much between him and the senate, that his part
of it will be too small. Who can censure him, without
censuring the senate, and the legislatures who appoint
them? All their friends will be interested to vindicate the
president, in order to screen them from censure. Besides, if an impeachment against an officer is brought
before them, are they not interested to acquit him, lest
some part of the odium of his guilt should fall upon
them, who advised to his appointment?

2. It turns the minds and attention of the people to
the senate, a branch of the legislature, in executive matters. It interests another branch of the legislature in the
management of the executive. It divides the people between the executive and the senate; whereas all the
people ought to be united to watch the executive, to
oppose its encroachments, and resist its ambition. Senators and representatives, and their constituents, in short,

the aristocratical and democratical divisions of society
ought to be united on all occasions to oppose the executive or the monarchical branch when it attempts to
overleap its limits. But how can this union be effected,
when the aristocratical branch has pledged its reputation
to the executive, by consenting to an appointment?

3. It has a natural tendency to excite ambition in the
senate. An active, ardent spirit, who is rich and able,
and has a great reputation and influence, will be solicited
by candidates for office. Not to introduce the idea of
bribery, because, though it certainly would force itself in,
in other countries, and will probably here, when we grow
populous and rich, it is not yet to be dreaded, I hope,
ambition must come in already. A senator of great influence will be naturally ambitious and desirous of increasing his influence. Will he not be under a temptation to
use his influence with the president as well as his brother
senators, to appoint persons to office in the several states,
who will exert themselves in elections, to get out his enemies, or opposers both in senate and house of represen-
atives, and to get in his friends, perhaps his instruments?
Suppose a senator to aim at the treasury office for himself, his brother, father, or son. Suppose him to aim at
the president's chair, or vice-president's, at the next election, or at the office of war, foreign, or domestic affairs.
Will he not naturally be tempted to make use of his whole
patronage, his whole influence, in advising to appointments, both with president and senators, to get such
persons nominated as will exert themselves in elections
of president, vice-president, senators, and house of representatives, to increase his interest and promote his views?
In this point of view, I am very apprehensive that this
defect in our constitution will have an unhappy tendency
to introduce corruption of the grossest kinds, both of
ambition and avarice, into all our elections, and this will

be the worst of poisons to our government. It will not
only destroy the present form of government, but render
it almost impossible to substitute in its place any free
government, even a better limited-monarchy, or any other
than a despotism or a simple monarchy.

4. To avoid the evil under the last head, it will be in
danger of dividing the continent into two or three nations,
a case that presents no prospect but of perpetual war.

5. This negative on appointments is in danger of involving the senate in reproach, censure, obloquy, and
suspicion, without doing any good. Will the senate use
their negative, or not? If not, why should they have it?
Many will censure them for not using it; many will ridi-
cule them, and call them servile, &c. If they do use
it, the very first instance of it will expose the senators to
the resentment of not only the disappointed candidate
and all his friends, but of the president and all his friends,
and these will be most of the officers of government,
through the nation.

6. We shall very soon have parties formed; a court
and country party, and these parties will have names given
them. One party in the house of representatives will
support the president and his measures and ministers;
the other will oppose them. A similar party will be in
the senate; these parties will study with all their arts,
perhaps with intrigue, perhaps with corruption, at every
election to increase their own friends and diminish their
opposers. Suppose such parties formed in the senate,
and then consider what factious divisions we shall have
there upon every nomination.

7. The senate have not time. The convention and
Indian treaties.

You are of opinion "that the concurrence of the
senate in the appointments to office, will strengthen
the hands of the executive, and secure confidence of

the people, much better than a select council, and will be less expensive."

But in every one of these ideas, I have the misfortune to differ from you.

It will weaken the hands of the executive, by lessening the obligation, gratitude, and attachment of the candidate to the president, by dividing his attachment between the executive and legislative, which are natural enemies. Officers of government, instead of having a single eye and undivided attachment to the executive branch, as they ought to have, consistent with the law and the constitution, will be constantly tempted to be factious with their factious patrons in the senate. The president's own officers, in a thousand instances, will oppose his just and constitutional exertions, and screen themselves under the wings of their patrons and party in the legislature. Nor will it secure the confidence of the people. The people will have more confidence in the executive, in executive matters, than in the senate. The people will be constantly jealous of factious schemes in the senators to unduly influence the executive, to serve each other's private views. The people will also be jealous that the influence of the senate will be employed to conceal, connive at, and defend guilt in executive officers, instead of being a guard and watch upon them, and a terror to them. A council, selected by the president himself, at his pleasure, from among the senators, representatives, and nation at large, would be purely responsible. In that case, the senate would be a terror to privy counsellors; its honor would never be pledged to support any measure or instrument of the executive beyond justice, law, and the constitution. Nor would a privy council be more expensive. The whole senate must now deliberate on every appointment, and if they ever find time for it, you will find that a great deal of time will be required and consumed in this service. Then, the president might have a constant executive council; now, he has none.

I said, under the seventh head, that the senate would not have time. You will find that the whole business of this government will be infinitely delayed by this negative of the senate on treaties and appointments. Indian treaties and consular conventions have been already waiting for months and the senate have not been able to find a moment of time to attend to them; and this evil must constantly increase. So that the senate must be constantly sitting, and must be paid as long as they sit. . . . But I have tried your patience. Is there any truth in these broken hints and crude surmises, or not? To me they appear well founded and very important.

I am, with usual affection, yours,

JOHN ADAMS.

NEW YORK, 20 July, 1789.

SIR, — I was honored with your letters of the seventeenth and eighteenth instant, and am much obliged to you for the observations they contain.

The subject of government is an important one, necessary to be well understood by the citizens, and especially by the legislators of these states. I shall be happy to receive further light on the subject, and to have any errors that I may have entertained corrected.

I find that writers on government differ in their definition of a *republic*. Entick's Dictionary defines it, " A *commonwealth without a king.*" I find you do not agree to the negative part of his definition. What I meant by it was, a government under the authority of the people, consisting of legislative, executive, and judiciary powers; the legislative powers vested in an assembly, consisting of one or more branches who, together with the executive, are appointed by the people, and dependent on them for continuance, by periodical elections, agreeably to an established constitution; and that what especially denominates it a *republic* is its dependence on the *public* or *people at large*, without any hereditary powers. But it is not of so much importance by what appellation the government is distinguished, as to have it well constituted to secure the rights, and advance the happiness of the community.

I fully agree with you, sir, that it is optional with the people of a state to establish any form of government they please; to vest the powers in *one*, a *few*, or *many*, and for a limited or unlimited time; and the individuals of the state will be bound to yield obedience to such government while it continues; but I am also of opinion, that they may alter their frame of government when they please, any former act of theirs, however explicit, to the contrary notwithstanding.

But what I principally have in view, is to submit to your consideration the reasons that have inclined me to think that the qualified negative given to the executive by our constitution is better than an absolute negative. In Great Britain, where there are the rights of the nobility as well as the rights of the common people to support, it may be necessary that the crown should have a complete negative to preserve the balance; — but in a republic like ours, wherein is no higher rank than that of common citizens, unless distinguished by appointment to office, what occasion can there be for such a balance? It is true that some men in every society have natural and acquired abilities superior to others, and greater wealth. Yet these give them no legal claim to offices in preference to others, but will doubtless give them some degree of influence, and justly, when they are men of integrity; and may procure them appointments to places of trust in the government. Yet, they having only the same common

rights with the other citizens, what competition of interests can there be to require a balance? Besides, while
the real estates are divisible among all the children, or
other kindred in equal degree, and entails are not admitted, it will operate as an agrarian law, and the influence arising from great estates in a few hands or families
will not exist to such a degree of extent or duration as to
form a system, or have any great effect.

In order to trace moral effects to their causes, and
vice versa, it is necessary to attend to principles as they
operate on men's minds. Can it be expected that a chief
magistrate of a free and enlightened people, on whom he
depends for his election and continuance in office,
would give his negative to a law passed by the other two
branches of the legislature, if he had power? But the
qualified negative given to the executive by our constitution, which is only to produce a revision, will probably be
exercised on proper occasions; and the legislature have
the benefit of the president's reasons in their further deliberations on the subject, and if a sufficient number of
the members of either house should be convinced by them
to put a negative upon the bill, it would add weight to
the president's opinion, and render it more satisfactory to
the people. But if two thirds of the members of each
house, after considering the reasons offered by the president, should adhere to their former opinion, will not that
be the most safe foundation to rest the decision upon?
On the whole, it appears to me that the power of a complete negative, if given, would be a dormant and useless one,
and that the provision in the constitution is calculated to
operate with proper weight, and will produce beneficial
effects.

The negative vested in the crown of Great Britain has
never been exercised since the Revolution, and the great
influence of the crown in the legislature of that nation is

derived from another source, that of appointment to all offices of honor and profit, which has rendered the power of the crown nearly absolute ; so that the nation is in fact governed by the cabinet council, who are the creatures of the crown. The consent of parliament is necessary to give sanction to their measures, and this they easily obtain by the influence aforesaid. If they should carry their point so far as directly to affect personal liberty or private property, the people would be alarmed and oppose their progress ; but this forms no part of their system, the principal object of which is revenue, which they have carried to an enormous height. Wherever the chief magistrate may appoint to offices without control, his government may become absolute, or at least aggressive ; therefore the concurrence of the senate is made requisite by our constitution.

I have not time or room to add or apologize.

II.

I RECEIVED your letter of the twentieth instant. I had in mine, of the same date, communicated to you my ideas on that part of the constitution, limiting the president's power of negativing acts of the legislature ; and just hinted some thoughts on the propriety of the provision made for the appointment to office, which I esteem to be a power nearly as important as legislation.

If that was vested in the president alone, he might, were it not for his periodical election by the people, render himself despotic. It was a saying of one of the kings of England, that while the king could appoint the bishops and judges, he might have what religion and law he pleased.

It appears to me the senate is the most important branch in the government, for aiding and supporting the executive, securing the rights of the individual states, the government of the United States, and the liberties of the people. The executive magistrate is to execute the laws. The senate, being a branch of the legislature, will naturally incline to have them duly executed, and, therefore, will advise to such appointments as will best attain that end. From the knowledge of the people in the several states, they can give the best information as to who are qualified for office; and though they will, as you justly observe, in some degree lessen his responsibility, yet their advice may enable him to make such judicious appointments as to render responsibility less necessary. The senators being eligible by the legislatures of the several states, and dependent on them for re-election, will be vigilant in supporting their rights against infringement by the legislature or executive of the United States; and the government of the Union being federal, and instituted by the several states for the advancement of their interests, they may be considered as so many pillars to support it, and, by the exercise of the state governments, peace and good order may be preserved in places most remote from the seat of the federal government, as well as at the centre. And the municipal and federal rights of the people at large will be regarded by the senate, they being elected by the immediate representatives of the people, and their rights will be best secured by a due execution of the laws. What temptation can the senate be under to partiality in the trial of officers of whom they had a voice in the appointment? Can they be disposed to favor a person who has violated his trust and their confidence?

The other evils you mention, that may result from this power, appear to me but barely possible. The senators will doubtless be in general some of the most respectable citizens in the states for wisdom and probity, superior to mean and unworthy conduct, and instead of undue influence, to procure appointments for themselves or their friends, they will consider that a fair and upright conduct will have the best tendency to preserve the confidence of the people and of the states. They will be disposed to be diffident in recommending their friends and kindred, lest they should be suspected of partiality and the other members will feel the same kind of reluctance, lest they should be thought unduly to favor a person, because related to a member of their body; so that their friends and relations would not stand so good a chance for appointment to offices, according to their merit, as others.

The senate is a convenient body to advise the president, from the smallness of its numbers. And I think the laws would be better framed and more duly administered, if the executive and judiciary officers were in general members of the legislature, in case there should be no interference as to the time of attending to their several duties. This I have learned by experience in the government in which I live, and by observation of others differently constituted. I see no principles in our constitution that have any tendency to aristocracy, which, if I understand the term, is a government by nobles, independent of the people, which cannot take place, in either respect, without a total subversion of the constitution. As both branches of Congress are eligible from the citizens at large, and wealth is not a requisite qualification, both will commonly be composed of members of similar circumstances in life. And I see no reason why the several branches of the government should not maintain the most perfect harmony, their powers being all directed to one end, the advancement of the public good.

If the president alone was vested with the power of appointing all officers, and was left to select a council for himself, he would be liable to be deceived by flatterers and pretenders to patriotism, who would have no motive but their own emolument. They would wish to extend the powers of the executive to increase their own importance ; and, however upright he might be in his intentions, there would be great danger of his being misled, even to the subversion of the constitution, or, at least, to introduce such evils as to interrupt the harmony of the government, and deprive him of the confidence of the people.

But I have said enough upon these speculative points, which nothing but experience can reduce to a certainty. I am, with great respect,

> Your obliged humble servant,
>
> ROGER SHERMAN.

III.

GEORGE BANCROFT'S LETTER ON THE ·FOREGOING CORRESPONDENCE.

NEW YORK, 14 April, 1851.

MY DEAR SIR : Let me not delay for a single day my hearty acknowledgment of your prompt and liberal courtesy in favoring me with copies of the interesting and most instructive correspondence between J. Adams and Sherman. The part which Sherman took in the convention for framing our constitution, where no one excelled him in logical consistency, prepared me for the good clear sense and patriotism and political foresight which distinguish his letters. His calm confidence in the perpetuity of the great constitution which he assisted to form, does him enduring honor. If there were any of the politicians of that day who did not comprehend what they had achieved, he was not of the number.

A somewhat similar correspondence took place between

John and Samuel Adams; in which John yet more decidedly avows his peculiar views of a desirable republic; and is thoroughly and calmly set right by the plain wisdom of his kinsman.

The letters you have been so good as to send illustrate the same opinions: but in my judgment derive their greatest interest from the unshaken confidence of Roger Sherman in the durability of the Union, at the very moment of its inauguration. I remain, my dear Sir,

Very truly your obliged

GEORGE BANCROFT.

HON. R. S. BALDWIN.

IV.

ROGER SHERMAN ON HALF PAY OF ARMY OFFICERS.

ANNAPOLIS, March, 1784.

SIR, — Congress have received your letter of Nov., 1st, 1783, enclosing an address from the House of Representatives of the State of Connecticut setting forth, that in the statement of the public debt accompanying the recommendations and address of Congress of the 18th of April last they observe a charge of five millions of dollars as due to the officers of the army granted them by Congress in exchange for half pay for life.

That they are not satisfied that half pay for life, or five years full pay in lieu thereof, are warranted by the Articles of Confederation, or that the power to make such grant was ever delegated to Congress.

That it is considered as an unnecessary exercise, if not an unwarrantable stretch of power; and that they cannot reconcile it to principles of justice, more especially as it respects the officers of that State.

That on account of the above considerations, it seems impracticable to execute any means for raising its quota of the public debt as stated ; though they are not disposed to pass a negative on the requisition of Congress on the ground of its being unsupported by the Articles of Confederation as to the mode of collection.

That they most earnestly request the serious attention of Congress to this important subject and that they will take measures consistent with public faith and the principles of justice to remove all causes of jealousy and complaint.

From the above observations the following questions are suggested.

First. Whether the Congress that passed the resolution of the 21st of October 1780 were authorized and empowered to make the grant of half pay for life contained therein?

Second. If they were vested with power to make such a grant, whether it was necessary or expedient?

With respect to the first question, it cannot be expected that the present Congress should define the powers under which the delegates from the several States acted previously to the Confederation. The States themselves have not done it — they all gave general powers to carry on the war and to oppose the then enemy effectually.

The resolution of Congress referred to, appears by the yeas and nays to have been passed according to the then established rules of that body in transacting the business of the United States. The resolution itself had public notoriety and does not appear to have been formally objected against by the Legislature of any State till after the Confederation was completely adopted ; and by the 12th article of the Confederation all debts contracted by or under the authority of Congress, before the assembling of the United States in pursuance of the present Confederation shall be deemed and considered as a charge against the United States for the payment of which the faith of the United States is solemnly pledged.

The question is not whether Congress are vested by the Confederation with a power to grant half pay for life. This need not be enquired into. It is whether by the 12th article of the Confederation they can do otherwise than to acknowledge that a debt was created by the resolution of the 21st of October 1780 which resolution was agreed to by persons having plenipotentiary powers from their respective States, to do whatever appeared to them necessary and expedient for opposing the then enemy effectually.

With respect to the expediency or necessity of the measure, we can only observe that if we were clearly empowered we have great reason to distrust our own competency to judge in this matter, none of the delegates present having been in Congress at that particular time. That a proper degree of respect to the States obliges us to suppose that they appointed persons most worthy of the trust and confidence placed in them.

That tenderness to the character of those who constituted that Congress, who acted from an immediate view of the most cogent reasons that operated in favour of it, which we cannot now be fully impressed with, demands liberality of sentiment in this respect.

The alteration of the mode of payment cannot be material in the question unless it can be proved that the exchange is less favourable to the United States, than the half pay for life.

We have omitted to remark on several other matters contained in the address ; and have confined ourselves to that which seems to have been the occasion thereof. We have only to request a candid examination of the question, by the House of Representatives of the State of Connecticut, and we can not but flatter ourselves that the Union will have in this as in all other federal matters their firm support, that they will always exercise that candor and liberality of sentiment toward the opinions of others, without which it will be impossible to provide for the general interests of the United States.

ROGER SHERMAN.

MR OSGOOD ⎫
MR LEE   ⎬ *Committee.*
MR ELLERY ⎭

That the paymaster general be and he hereby is directed to govern himself in settling the accounts of the army since the year 1779, by the payment made by the respective States to their lines, so that where the pay has been secured by any State the same shall not be again secured by the United States.

V.

ROGER SHERMAN TO JOSIAH BARTLETT ON THE VERMONT CONTROVERSY.

PHILADELPHIA, July 31, 1781.

SIR, — Enclosed is a copy of an act of the general court of the State of Massachusetts, respecting the State of Vermont. The matter has been debated for several days past in Congress on a report of a committee to whom was referred a letter from the President of your State. The committee reported as their opinion that copies of the act of Massachusetts be sent to the States of New Hampshire and New York, and that the expediency of passing similar acts be referred to them, and in case they relinquish their claim of jurisdiction over the grants on the west side of Connecticut river, bounded east by P. river, north by latitude forty-five degrees, west by Lake Champlain and the west lines of several townships granted by the governor of New Hampshire to the northwest corner of Massachusetts, and south by the north line of Massachusetts, Congress will guaranty the lands and jurisdiction belonging to the said States respectively without the said limits against all claims and encroachments of the people within those limits. What will ultimately be done in Congress is uncertain; some gentlemen are for declaring Vermont an independent State ; others for explicitly recommending to the States aforesaid to relinquish their claims of jurisdiction ; others only for referring it to their consideration as reported by the committee, and some few against doing anything that will tend to make a new State.

I am of opinion that a speedy and amicable settlement of the controversy would conduce very much to the peace and welfare of the United States, and that it will be difficult if not impracticable to reduce the people on the east side of the river to obedience to the government of New Hampshire until the other dispute is settled, that the longer it remains unsettled the more difficult it will be to remedy the evils — but if the States of New Hampshire and New York would follow the example of Massachusetts respecting the grants on the west of Connecticut river the whole controversy would be quieted very much to the advantage and satisfaction of the United States, and that the inhabitants of New Hampshire and New York living without the disputed territory would return to their allegiance.

The British Ministry esteem it an object of great importance to them, to engage the people of Vermont in their interest and have accordingly instructed Gen. Clinton and Gen. Haldiman to use their best endeavors for that end, and though I don't think the people have any inclination to come under the British yoke or to do anything injurious to this country, yet if left in the present situation, they may be led to take steps very prejudicial to the United States.

I think it very unlikely that Congress can attend to the settlement of the dispute by a judicial decision during the war. For though the parties were heard last fall respecting their claims, yet it cannot now be determined upon the right without a new hearing, because there are many new members that were not then present. I am credibly informed that a great majority of the members of the Legislature of the State of New York at their last winter session were willing to relinquish their claim of jurisdiction over that district, and that they should be admitted to be a separate State, but the governor for some reasons prevented an act passing at that time.

We have no news remarkable here. Paper currency is very much at an end. The new bills are negotiated some, rather as a merchandize than money, but silver and gold is the only currency. The prices of commodities are much fallen, many articles are as low as before the war.

I send you two of the last News Papers. I am with great esteem and regard

Your humble servant,

ROGER SHERMAN.

HONORABLE JOSIAH BARTLETT.

VI.

REPORT ON ROBERT MORRIS'S ACCOUNTS.

IN view of some severe criticisms of Robert Morris, this tribute to the value of his public services written by Roger Sherman, seems worth preserving.

The committee appointed upon the memorial of Robert Morris, late Superintendent of the Finance of the United States, to inquire into the receipts and expenditures of public monies during his adminstration in said office, Report

That they conceived it unnecessary to examine in detail the public accounts under the administration of the late superintendent of finance, they having been examined and passed in the House, and the views of the memorialist would be best complied with by obtaining from the register the statements of the receipts and expenditures with the other extracts from the public records herewith submitted together with a more particular statement of the accounts made out and published in the year 1784, in such a number of printed copies of each as will furnish to each member of Congress the best practicable means of appreciating the services of the memorialist and the utility of his administration, under which in the opinions of your committee the United States derived signal advantages.

That from these documents it appears that the monies received into the Treasury of the United States during the said administration amounted to 8,177,431.1–2 dols. And the expenditures amounted to 8,155,445. Leaving in the Treasury at the close of the administration a balance of 21,986.1–2 dols.

The acts of the late Congress respecting said office, and reports and letters of the superintendent in the course of his administration, which are on file in the public offices are referred to in the close of the document first mentioned.

All which is humbly submitted.

VII.

ROGER SHERMAN'S CLAIMS AGAINST CONNECTICUT.

NEW HAVEN, Oct. 17th, 1789.

SIR, The Honorable the General Assembly in January last ordered that one hundred and fifty pounds should be advanced to each of the members of Congress from this state for their expenses to be paid over to the United States on account of the specie requisitions made on this state when they should receive a compensation for their services and expenses. But on consideration of the great expenses incurred by this state in the course of the late war, and advancements of money to the United States, and for supporting invalids since the peace, the members of Congress for this state thought it might be advisable for the state to retain the monies in their own hands, until there should be a final liquidation of their accounts. The sum advanced to me I am willing to repay in such manner as the Honorable Assembly shall direct; but on this occasion I would take the liberty humbly to represent that there is now due to me from the state the sum of 775 pounds and 13 shillings being the balance due for my services and expenses as a member of Congress for their state between the 10th day of May 1775 and sometime in October 1780 as pr account liquidated by the committee of pay table, which was then due and payable out of the civil list funds, but there not being money in the Treasury to pay it at that time I took a note for it payable in hard money by a special order of the General Assembly which note is dated Nov. 29th 1780 which I expected would be paid at any time when I should have occasion for it after the close of the war, but not being under necessity for it until now, I did not request payment.

But I have lately been at considerable expense, by advancements by way of settlement to several of my children, and do really stand in need of some part of it. It would greatly oblige me if the whole of the 150 pounds advanced to me as aforesaid might be offset toward said note, but if only 100 pounds of it shall be advanced to be retained by me for that purpose, or any lesser sum it would afford me some relief.

I loaned some hundred pounds in money to the state for which I have Treasurer's note now due, but that sum that was due for my services and expenses I always considered payable in hard money out of the civil list funds or some other as good. I would humbly request your Excellency to lay this letter before the Honorable the General Assembly that they may take such order thereon as in their wisdom and justice shall seem meet. I am with great respect your Excellency's

Humble servant

ROGER SHERMAN.

His Excellency GOVERNOR HUNTINGTON.

VIII.

ISAAC SHERMAN.

GEN. WASHINGTON TO GOV. TRUMBULL, RECOMMENDING
ISAAC SHERMAN FOR PROMOTION.

October 9th, 1776.

Am. Archives, 5th Series, vol. 2, p. 58.

" I WOULD also recommend Major Sherman, son of Mr. Sherman, of Congress, a young gentleman who appears to me, and who is generally esteemed an active and valuable officer, whom the General Officers have omitted to set

down in their lists, expecting, I suppose, (if they thought
of him at all) that he would be provided for in the Massachusetts regiment, because he is [in] one at this time.
But as it is probable promotions in that State will be confined to their own people, I should apprehend that he
should be properly noticed in your appointments, lest we
should lose an officer who, so far as I can judge, promises
good service to his country."

STONY POINT.

ON the 17th of July, 1779, the day after the capture of
Stony Point, General Wayne, while suffering from the
wound received on that occasion, sent a report to General
Washington, in which he failed to mention several officers
who distinguished themselves in the assault.   In a letter
to the President of Congress, on the 10th of August,
1779, acknowledging a note of thanks, he rectified this
mistake as follows : —

" I feel much hurt that I did not, in my letter to him
(Gen. Washington) of the 17th of July, mention (among
other brave and worthy officers) the names of Lieut.
Col. Sherman, Majors Hull, Murphy, and Posey whose
good conduct and intrepidity justly entitled them to that
attention.   Permit me therefore, thro' your Excellency,
to do them that justice now, which the state of my
wound diverted me from in the first instance."

IX.

WYOMING.

DYER, SHERMAN AND DEANE TO Z. BUTLER AND OTHERS.

PHILADELPHIA, August 2nd, 1775.

GENTM. — It has been represented to the Continental Congress that there is great danger of discord and contention if not hostility and bloodshed between the people settling under Connecticut claim and those under Pennsylvania which would be attended with the most unhappy consequences at this time of general calamity and when we want our whole united strength against our common enemy. We are therefore desired to write to you and press upon you the necessity of peace and good order not only among yourselves, but by no means to give the least disturbance or molestation to the persons, property or possessions of those settled under the proprietaries of Pennsylvania and especially to the family, property or possessions of those who are gone as riflers into the service of their country and to join the army near Boston. The delegates from the province of Pennsylvania are desired to write to their people or the heads of them to urge upon them the same peaceable disposition towards the settlers under Connecticut and that they make no attempts upon the possessions of each other but both sides to remain in peace and quiet and to be cautious and not to interfere in jurisdictions in the exercise of government but that they all live together in peace and good order and unite in the greatest harmony in the common defence if there should be occasion. You are desired to make no settlement by force nor use any threats for that pur-

pose.   We are desired by the Congress to write to you to
the purpose above and as they may have further to do in
this affair, we hope your conduct will be such as to give
no offence to that respectable body.

We are your friends and honorable Servants,

ELIPHT DYER
ROGER SHERMAN
SILAS DEANE.

To COL. BUTLER
ESQ. DENNISON
ESQ. JUDD
ESQ. SHERMAN, etc., etc.

ROGER SHERMAN TO ZEBULUN BUTLER.

PHILADELPHIA, Sept. 13th, 1787.

SIR, — I am informed by Col. Denison that the commissioners appointed by the State of Pennsylvania are
proceeding in examining the claims of the people settled
under the claim of Connecticut and that they appear
disposed to do justice to the claimants so far as they are
enabled by the law.   I hope it will be a happy means of
quieting the inhabitants in their posssessions — I hear
that some of the claimants are opposed to the measure
but it appears to me it will be for the interest of all of
them to get a confirmation of their title to as much land
as they can under that law, though they may not get so
much as they may think themselves entitled to ; whatever
they get confirmed they may enjoy peaceably or dispose
of as they please — the many and great calamities that
the people of the settlement have undergone have given
me great concern — their future peace and prosperity
would give me much pleasure.

ZEBULUN BUTLER, Esq., Wyoming.

Roger Sherman to Zebulun Butler.

Philadelphia, February 14th, 1791.

Sir, — I received your letter of the 3rd instant pr. Capt. Baldwin. I am sorry to find that the old controversy respecting your lands is likely to be revived after having been quieted by a solemn act of the Legislature ; it appears to me that the repeal of that act was a very improvident measure. As to the writs you mentioned, I am not enough acquainted with the laws and mode of process in this State to give an opinion in the case, but I suppose that Captain Baldwin has consulted counsel learned in the law on the subject and obtained the necessary information. If the claimants under the proprietors of Pennsylvania will prosecute their claims in a course of law, the claimants under Connecticut will have right to a fair and impartial trial in the courts of the United States ; where they may avail themselves of their titles derived under Connecticut as fully as if the decision at Trenton had not been made, because (as) they were not parties to that suit their claims cannot be affected by it.

How far they may avail themselves of the quieting act of Pennsylvania, in law, or by a suit in equity in the Supreme Court of the United States for a specific performance of the terms therein stipulated, notwithstanding the repeal, I have not at present formed an opinion. I hope the controversy will be terminated in a just and peaceable manner.

I am with due regards your humble servant,

ROGER SHERMAN.

ZEBULUN BUTLER TO ROGER SHERMAN.

WILKESBARRE, Nov. 6th, 1791.

DEAR SIR, By the bearer Capt. P. Schotts I favor this desiring your opinion on the following subject. The State of Connecticut in —73 (at which time we were subjects of said State) entered into resolves that the inhabitants suffering material losses by the depredations of the enemy should be compensated therefor — in a manner pointed out by the same law — This county — then named Westmoreland under her jurisdiction — was cut off — and each inhabitant more or less very sensibly injured. I recollect — agreeably to the alluded to resolve soon after we resettled the country — Persons for that purpose appointed under solemn oath — took from each of us an estimate of our several losses — but before anything further was done — a change of jurisdiction took place and we annexed to the State of Pennsylvania. Of course we have been entirely neglected. But query — as we at the period in which we were distressed — were subject of Connecticut — and all along paid to them our proportion of the country taxes — shall the change of jurisdiction which took place long after our sufferings deprive us of the benefit of that law? If so — is there no provision made by the present or former Congress? Your advice in the premises will much oblige one who is with the truest esteem your friend and

Humble servt.

ZEBU. BUTLER.

ROGER SHERMAN, Esquire.

X.

GEN. DAVID WOOSTER.

GEN. WOOSTER TO ROGER SHERMAN.

MONTREAL, Feb. 11th, 1776.

DEAR SIR, I am much obliged to you for your favor of the 20th ult. I was happy to hear that the Congress had made provision for our speedy reinforcement in this Province. Yet I fear it will not be sufficient if, as many conjecture, the ministry should send a large army here early in the Spring. Mr. Walker and Mr. Price, two gentlemen zealously attached to our cause, I have requested to go to Congress. They are the best acquainted with this province and with the tempers and dispositions of the Canadians, of perhaps any men in it. They will inform you much better than I can, of every thing concerning them.

I have sent to Congress copies of several letters which have passed between General Schuyler and me. By which, and my letter upon the subject you will see that we are not upon the most friendly terms. Which of us has occasioned the coolness the Congress will judge upon examining the letters. I think it a great unhappiness that we cannot agree among ourselves. I am conscious however of no fault or neglect of mine to occasion it. I can write freely to you. As you have lately been in Connecticut you must have heard the general dissatisfaction (among the troops of that Colony who were employed in this department) at the treatment they met with from General Schuyler. It was as much as I could do to keep them easy and in the service, and had it not been for their expectation of my arrival among them the consequences might have been fatal to our operations in this country. You will not think that this proceeds from vanity or private pique, be assured, Sir, it is from a real concern for our country. The uneasiness in the army was and is now by no means confined to the Connecticut troops, but is universal among all who have served under him. And should he come into this country to take the command many of the best officers in the army would immediately throw up their commissions provided it can be done without risking every thing. I wish he had as much consideration.

It is not from ambitious views of keeping the command myself that I make these observations, though my services and experience might possibly entitle me to it. I should have been happy to have served under General Montgomery. He once, from some trouble he met with from some of his officers determined to leave the service and actually resigned the command to me, but apprehending unhappy consequences might follow from it, I persuaded him, though with great difficulty to reassume it. You will readily perceive the terrible consequences that may follow from a want of confidence in the commanding officer. I greatly fear in the first place that it will be difficult to raise the men, and when they are raised they will soon catch the opinions of those now in the army. I hope the evils apprehended will prove less than our fears.

Col. Hazen and Col. Antill both inform me that the Congress have appointed me Maj. General. As General Schuyler has not informed me of it and as there is nothing of it in the extracts of the Resolves of Congress sent to me by him, I shall be obliged to you for information. You will be pleased to remember me respectfully to Messrs. Huntington and Woolcot and believe me with the greatest truth and sincerity your real friend and most obedient

Very humble servant,
DAVID WOOSTER.

Mr Hare is in this town and shall be used with every civility and furnished with a proper passport and assistance.

HON. ROGER SHERMAN, Esq.

WILLIAM S. JOHNSON TO ROGER SHERMAN.

NEW YORK, April 20th, 1785.

DEAR SIR, I am sorry to hear by General Woolcot that you are not coming to N. York, as Capt. Wooster gave me to expect you would, about this time. I extremely want your opinion and advice relative to the pursuing Mrs. Wooster's petition before Congress. The difficulty is this. Congress have very lately upon the petition of Gen. Thomas' widow of Massachusetts, fully explained the doubt there was, whether he was entitled to brigadier's or Colonel's pay deciding it in favor of the former. Thus, one of the grounds of Mrs Wooster's petition is effectually removed. What remains, is only that the State of Connecticut will not pay it, though the requisition of Congress is as full as they can make it, if they should take up the subject again. And is it to be presumed that Congress will take it up themselves, merely because Connecticut will not do what she ought? Nay will the finances of the United States admit of such a measure? Yet more, can they do it when the other States have actually taken upon themselves, and are now in the payment of similar demands, as N. York of Mrs Montgomery, N. Jersey of Mrs Barber, &c, &c? Would

not this derange everything? Will not the matter now
stand solely upon the ground, and appear in the light, of
a complaint against the State? If so, can I advocate
it? Will not everything of the nature come with a very
ill grace from a delegate of the State? Finally, for I dare
not presume to ask any more questions, is it not most
advisable, since Congress have explained the only doubt
there was in the case, and that the session of the General
Assembly is so near, for Mrs Wooster to apply once more
to the Assembly before she pursues the matter further
here.   Your sentiments upon this subject would give
great relief to, and extremely oblige, Dear Sir,

Your most obedient humble servant,

WM. SAML. JOHNSON.

Gen. Woolcot will tell you our situation here, since the
blow we have received from N. York.   I am loath to revive the idea of so severe and fatal a defeat.

After I had written the within, I had the honor to
receive your favor of the 12th inst.   That I had nothing
agreeable to acquaint you with, must be my apology for
not writing, and I presume you had long since heard that
N. York had, in Senate, finally rejected the 5 per cent
impost.   It will not be resumed again this year.   Georgia
too has neglected to grant it.   In consequence whereof
a most respectable grand jury of the State, have, before
their Supreme Court, indicted the whole legislature of a
high handed misdemeanor.   This however will produce
no immediate benefit to the United States, and their
credit must for the present languish.   Our only actual resource is the Western Territory, (for I consider requisitions as extremely precarious) ; this we have been diligently
at work upon for some time, and I hope shall now soon
complete.   I think I may assure you, it will be settled to

sell in townships, of about 7 miles square, to be divided for purpose of sale to the several States, to be disposed of at auction, fixing however a price say 6/ per acre, below which it shall not go. The army also to take in townships. I could wish the plan you propose with respect to the impost could take place, but it is so bold and decided a measure that I fear we are not at present sufficiently in spirits to adopt it. The cession of Connecticut has been long depending before a committee of 5, most of whom attend with reluctance, but when they meet contest it with vigor. It will nevertheless be pushed, if possible, to a decision. The Massachusetts cession has been just now accepted which is no unfavorable circumstance. The wish is that we would cede the whole of our right, or at least as far as New York and Massachusetts have done, viz, to a line twenty miles west of the strait of Niagara. But I am of opinion that if Connecticut proceeds in the affair with firmness and prudence, she may yet retain the boundary she has proposed, but something must be determined upon soon, for the reserved territory will be included in the sale proposed by Congress, except that part of it reserved by the Indians. The running the Western line of Pennsylvania, which is to be done this Spring, will give us clearer and more determinate ideas of that country. The case of Vermont has not been brought before Congress, owing to its having been depending all winter before the Legislature of this State, under a general expectation, which had taken place, that they would declare them independent and request Congress to receive them into the Union. It appears now, within a few days, that it will not be done this session, and why Vermont is not here to pursue the matter in Congress I know not.

We have pretty certain intelligence that the western inhabitants of Virginia, and of North Carolina, are erecting themselves into separate and independent States. This renders it extremely necessary that the United States should take immediate care of their Western Territory. Seven hundred men are recommended to be raised for this and other purposes. I wish this number may be sufficient. Mr Kirkland has just now been with me. He appears to be a worthy and well informed man, and I sincerely wish he could be re-established among the Indians. I shall certainly do all in my power to give facility and effect to his application to Congress. But the feeble finances of the United States give a check to every liberal and enlarged idea. They damp the ardor of the generous, and are an effectual screen for the illiberal and contracted. I do not despair, however, that something may be done. Col Cook leaves us to-morrow. I beg your influence to send on some other gentleman in the delegation, as well to supply his place, as to relieve me, that I may, about the middle of May, attend the General Assembly, where I have business of importance, for a few days; after which, if it be thought expedient, I will without hesitation return here again, and am with the sincerest esteem and respect, Dear Sir,

Your most obedient humble servant,

WM. SAML. JOHNSON.

Superscribed HON. ROGER SHERMAN, New Haven.

XI.

DESCENDANTS OF ROGER SHERMAN.

I HAD expected at one time, to be able to give a list of Roger Sherman's descendants as far as the third generation. To have made this list complete would have delayed too long the publication of the Memoir. In its place I can only offer this hurried sketch of a few of those descendants written by Senator Hoar just before he left for Europe.

The three sons of Roger Sherman by his first wife, John, and William and Isaac, were, as we have seen, officers in the Revolutionary Army. Isaac died unmarried. William left one daughter, who married and was the ancestor of many descendants. John, the oldest son, died at Canton, Mass., August 8, 1802. He was the father of Rev. John Sherman, who was the owner of Trenton Falls, a very accomplished person in his day, of whom there is a charming sketch by N. P. Willis, in a little book called Trenton Falls, which also contains an interesting paper by Mr. Sherman himself.

Chloe, the only daughter of the first marriage who grew up, married Dr. John Skinner, a physician in New Haven, the grandfather of the Hon. Roger Sherman Skinner, an eminent mayor of New Haven, and of Mrs President Dwight.

Roger Sherman, Jr., the oldest son of the second marriage, graduated at Yale in 1787. He preserved his health and activity to a great age. He spent his life and died in the house that his father built. He was a merchant in New Haven, highly esteemed for integrity and benevolence. He made Washington a visit of a fortnight at Mt. Vernon shortly after the war of which he wrote an interesting account.

Oliver, the second son by the same marriage, was graduated at Yale in 1795. After graduating he entered into mercantile business in Boston and died of yellow fever at the West Indies in 1820.

Five of the daughters of Roger Sherman and Rebecca Prescott lived to maturity. It is a proof of the quality which must have been inherited by them from their parents that each of them became the wife of a person strongly resembling their father in integrity, public spirit, earnest religious faith, sound judgment and large mental capacity. Martha married Jeremiah Day, D.D., thirty years President of Yale College. Rebecca married Judge Simeon Baldwin of New Haven, a highly venerated citizen, a member of Congress from Connecticut and Judge of the Supreme Court of that State. She died leaving three children, Ebenezer, the historian of Yale College, Roger Sherman, Governor of Connecticut, and Senator in Congress, who made the famous argument in the Amistad case before the Supreme Court of the United States, and was a member of the Peace Congress of 1861. She also left a daughter, Rebecca.

After her sister's death Judge Baldwin was married to Elizabeth Sherman and left by her one son, Simeon, a merchant in New York. Judge Simeon Baldwin enjoyed the confidence and esteem of Mr. Sherman as much as any human being toward the close of his life. There can be little doubt that the following passage in an address from an oration delivered by Simeon Baldwin, July 4, 1788, the year of the adoption of the Constitution of the United States, expresses the opinion of his father-in-law: "The labours of the patriot and the friend of humanity are not yet completed. It is their task to remove those blemishes which have hitherto sullied the glory of these States. We may feed our vanity with the pompous recital of noble achievements — we may pride ourselves in the excellency of our government — we may boast of the anticipated glories of the western continent. — But virtue will mourn that injustice and ingratitude have, in too many instances, had the countenance of the law. — Humanity will mourn that an odious slavery cruel in itself, degrading to the dignity of man, and shocking to human nature, is tolerated, and in many instances practised with cruelty. — Yes, even in this land of boasted freedom, this asylum for the oppressed, that inhuman practice has lost its horrors by the sanction of custom.

"To remedy this evil will be a work of time. God be thanked it is already begun. Most of the southern and middle states have made salutary provision by law for the future emancipation of this unfortunate race of men, and it does honor to the candor and philanthropy of the southern States, that they consented to that liberal clause in our new constitution evidently calculated to abolish a slavery upon which they calculated their riches."

It is well known that Mr. Sherman's intimate friend and pastor, Jonathan Edwards, was one of the leaders in the abolition of slavery in Connecticut.

Mehetabel Sherman became the wife of Jeremiah Evarts and mother of William M. Evarts of New York, Senator, Secretary of State, and Attorney-General of the United States, the famous advocate who argued and won three of the greatest causes ever decided by the forms of a judicial trial, — the trial of a President of the United States on impeachment, — the trial before the Electoral Commission of the title to the office of President, — and the case of the United States against England before the Arbitration Tribunal at Geneva. Mr. Evarts was also counsel for Henry Ward Beecher, the celebrated pulpit orator, in the famous case of Tilton against Beecher. The father, Jeremiah Evarts, was one of the founders, and was the chief organizer and first treasurer, and afterwards secretary of the American Board of Commissioners for Foreign Missions. He was one of the twelve men who met in Samuel Dexter's office in Boston in 1812, and initiated the great temperance reform. He died May 10, 1831, while engaged in the vain effort to prevent the outrage of the removal of the Cherokees from Georgia.[1]

[1] The first husband of Mehetabel Sherman was Daniel Barnes, a West India merchant, by whom she had one son, Daniel Barnes of New York.

The youngest daughter Sarah was the wife of Samuel
Hoar of Concord, Mass., an eminent advocate, highly
esteemed for his integrity and ability.   His mission to
South Carolina for the purpose of arguing the constitutionality of the laws of that State under which colored
seamen were imprisoned, and his expulsion from that
city in 1844, were among the causes which led to the
state of public feeling which resulted in the Rebellion
and the overthrow of slavery in the United States.   Ralph
Waldo Emerson has drawn his portrait, faithful and noble
as a picture by Van Dyke.   He was a member of the
Convention of 1820 for revising the Massachusetts Constitution.   When he first rose to speak in that body, John
Adams said, " That young man reminds me of my old
friend Roger Sherman."

INDEX.

23

LaVergne, TN USA
09 November 2009
163518LV00001B/115/A